The Clinical Study of Social Behavior

THE CENTURY PSYCHOLOGY SERIES

Richard M. Elliott, Gardner Lindzey, and
Kenneth MacCorquodale

Editors

DONALD R. PETERSON
University of Illinois

The Clinical Study of
Social Behavior

New York

APPLETON-CENTURY-CROFTS
Division of Meredith Corporation

PRINTED IN THE UNITED STATES OF AMERICA
E70625

Preface

About five years ago, I became more profoundly depressed than usual by the state of affairs in clinical psychology. Psychotherapy had become a questionable enterprise. Psychodiagnosis had fallen into doubtful repute. A clinician, it seemed, could only practice anyway and learn to endure his own hypocrisy, or turn to research. I had mainly done the latter in my career up to that point, but in the year 1959–1960 I took sabbatical leave from my usual engagements, and began to look at my own work and that of others from a more distant and possibly clearer perspective. I was concerned, as I have been concerned all my professional life, with clinical assessment, and most of the research in the field seemed to be either trivial, slovenly, or unrelated to the problems which matter to us all as clinicians. At one time, I had thought that adequate answers to nearly all important problems in psychology lay in Lots of Good Research, but as I considered the problems of clinical assessment more thoughtfully I saw that the difficulties lay less with the quantity and quality of research in the field than with the basic conceptual and methodological structures on which available assessment systems were based.

So I decided not to do any more research until I had taken the time either to resolve some of these issues or at least to consider them more carefully than I had before. As my colleagues in the academic establishment know, a decision to eschew active research, however temporary, can create some problems of its own, but I managed to sustain a survival quantum of output during the period, and spent the rest of my available time reading, thinking, walking about the campus, drinking coffee and other beverages, until my ideas on diagnostic work in the study of disordered behavior had become sufficiently elaborate and stable to merit discussion with somebody else.

In the fall of 1965 I offered a seminar on the clinical study of social behavior, and it was as an accompaniment to the seminar that this book took its literal shape. The seminar was initially planned for one semester. Naturally we were not done by the end of that time, and our discussions were continued for another term. When that was done, we still were not finished—problems of this kind are inherently interminable—but certain topics had been considered, we had left those and moved on to others, and a condition of reasonable stability had been attained in my own conceptualization of major issues. I wrote as the seminar proceeded, and the first draft of the book was essentially completed by the end of the year.

I then sent copies of the draft to a number of people whose opinions I value, in an effort to obtain suggestions for useful change from people representing some variety of professional background and ideological position. Perry London, Lewis V. Kurke, Sidney Bijou, Wesley Becker, Herman Eisen, Leonard Ullman, J. McV. Hunt, Theodore Sarbin, Kenneth MacCorquodale, Marjorie McQueen, Catherine Crocker, Titus McInnis, and Richard Hagen all offered comments which influenced the revised version in some way, and I am grateful for the time and thought they gave to the task. In the second semester of 1966–67, the manuscript was used in still another clinical laboratory-seminar. During that term, arrangements for publication were made and the final copy was prepared.

Now that the book is done, there are still parts which should be changed, but I have chosen not to do that, for everything you will see has been changed a number of times already, in my thoughts if not in writing, and the process of revision is truly endless. My goal in any case is not to offer a definitive and final statement on clinical assessment. I have tried to formulate some problems in the clinical study of social behavior more powerfully than they have been formulated before, and to suggest some resolutions which might be more helpful than those which are otherwise available. I hope the book will be read by psychologists, social workers, psychiatrists, and any others who are interested in the clinical study of social behavior. I naturally hope it will have some influence on clinical practice and research in the field. But if the book leads to still clearer definition and more effective resolution of the issues all clinicians face, my basic aim will be fulfilled.

D. R. P.

Contents

Preface   v

1. The Need for New Approaches to Clinical Assessment   1

   Implications of some recent developments in treatment pro-
      cedure for the clinical study of social behavior
   Some theoretical considerations and their meaning for the assess-
      ment of behavior
   Procedural considerations

2. The Person and the Environment   15

   The influence of person and setting on the social behavior of
      children in a residential treatment center
   Studies of examiner influence in projective test behavior
   The generality of verbal personality factors
   Task and temperament in leadership research
   The prediction of antisocial behavior
   Direct comparisons of situation, response, and person variance
      in test behavior

3. Behavior Change and Behavior Assessment   32

   Changing individual behavior.
   Changing social transactions
   Changing social systems
   Unity and diversity in behavior modification
   Behavior change and behavior assessment

4. Behavior Theory and Behavior Assessment   59

   Faults in previous attempts at theory construction
   The analysis of action
   The study of interaction
   The study of social organization
   Unity and diversity in behavior theory

5. Methods for Studying Social Behavior   102

    Procedures for gathering clinical data
    Observation
    Interview procedures
    The experimental analysis of behavior
    The use of tests in studying social behavior

6. Three Cases: A Person, a Group, and a Social System   142

    Walter Lilly: the study of a person
    The Carleton Browns: the study of a family
    Elba State Hospital: the study of a social system

7. Scientific, Professional, and Ethical Issues   221

    Assessment and research
    Assessment and practice
    Assessment and ethics
    Clinical assessment in retrospect and prospect

References   239

Index   249

The Clinical Study of
Social Behavior

I

The Need for New Approaches
to Clinical Assessment

The clinical assessment of psychological problems has traditionally gone somewhat as follows. The social worker conducts an intake interview in which an attempt is made toward problem definition, a quick study of the individual, and a description of the social environment in which·the individual is situated. A full social history may or may not be taken at this point, but in anything like a complete clinical evaluation, the facts of the applicant's life experience are covered in some detail.

The psychiatrist then conducts a psychiatric examination. This is also an interview of one kind or another. Depending on the past training and current proclivities of the psychiatrist, interview procedures may range from a completely unstructured free-associative narration by the patient to a rather tightly defined mental status outline. If medical problems are apparent or in question, appropriate physical examinations are also made though many psychiatrists prefer to send their patients to "real doctors" for study of this kind.

The psychologist performs a psychological evaluation. This may involve a brief interview but consists mainly of a battery of tests. Intelligence is usually assessed and any other functions thought to be important are evaluated by whatever methods the psychologist has learned to use. "Personality" is studied, ordinarily

1

by means of the Rorschach, TAT, and other projective devices, and/or by means of structured tests like the MMPI.

Everybody writes a report. The reports are shared and typically the case is discussed in a staff conference where segmental information from the various specialists is synthesized. The product of this conference and the return from all the effort which has been invested in previous study is a diagnosis.

Let us be generous about what this can mean. It may consist only of a Kraepelinian APA-style disease name such as "Schizophrenic reaction, paranoid type, with obsessive features, in a passive-aggressive personality," or "Personality pattern disturbance, cyclothymic type." This is a *typological* outcome. Or it may be composed of individual scores on a number of continua—a profile of traits. This is a *dimensional* outcome. Frequently the diagnosis is designed not merely to describe but to explain the disorder. The alleged explanation is ordinarily accomplished by reference to the underlying motives, conflicts, defenses and other dispositions of the patient, and is usually stated in psychoanalytic language. This is a *dynamic* outcome. Treatment recommendations, if any, are presumably based on the diagnostic summary.

But it is growing more and more apparent that there are serious flaws in the traditional approach to psychodiagnosis and that the means by which clinicians have studied personality need to be complemented and possibly replaced by improved procedures. For several decades evidence has been accumulating on the validity and utility of clinical personality measures. Over all, the results are discouraging. Kelly and Fiske (1951) found little predictive use in the usual kinds of clinical procedures. Little and Schneidman (1959) found recognized experts in use of the best known personality tests to disagree radically in the inferences they made from the tests. Meehl has reported that 83 percent of a sample of psychotherapists did not think the usual kinds of clinical diagnostic information were of much help in psychotherapy (Meehl, 1960). The pertinent chapters in the *Annual Reviews of Psychology* all look the same. So do those in Buros' *Mental Measurements Yearbook*. Each critic's list of studies is a little different from everyone else's but the general evaluations come out much alike. Personality tests are not doing as well as most people hoped they would. There were some technical limitations in literally all the studies done so far on clinical assessment by means of tests. But the cumulative negative evidence is quite compelling and strong positive evidence for validity and utility is nowhere to be seen. A clinical psychologist who seeks to develop his professional identity as a diagnostician using psychological tests as the basic data source is taking a perilous risk. Use of tests for restricted purposes seems justified but there is no doubt at all any more about the need for major innovation in assessment procedures. It does not appear that further refinement of present devices will offer the precision or even the kinds of data needed. More and more, it looks as if entirely new approaches to the clinical study of behavior will have to be developed.

Psychiatry and social work have done no better than clinical psychology in the area of behavior study, and possibly not as well. Psychiatric diagnosis seems to be conducted in one of two extreme and equally questionable ways; either by following a mental status outline somewhat rigidly and arriving at a Kraepelinian diagnosis, or by encouraging free narration on the part of the patient and arriving at some kind of dynamic formulation of his inner mental condition. The promising and sometimes exciting innovations which have taken place under the name of social psychiatry have not been accompanied by any systematic attempt to develop revised improved diagnostic procedures, however piously each new grant request emphasizes the importance of program evaluation. Social work, which ought to have been doing the kinds of things proposed here, has been so concerned with professional status that needs for more effective procedures have gone unattended. Having subordinated themselves to psychiatrists, social workers fell into the trap of adopting the basic theories and viewpoints, mainly psychoanalytic, of their psychiatric leaders and began to engage in the professional activities, mainly psychotherapeutic, which were most prestigious in the eyes of their superiors. Social work is presently campaigning to upgrade standards and that is commendable, but at the very time when social workers should have been moving out into the community, honoring their traditions by developing better ways of dealing with man in society, many have been retreating comfortably into private offices, talking to individuals, calling it casework so nobody will punish them for treating the sick.

Clinical psychologists have reacted to the failure of their procedures and hence to the repudiation of a basic function and a loss of professional identity in three general ways. Some have turned to research. Others have devoted more and more of their time to treatment, particularly psychotherapy. Still others have continued to try to do diagnostic work, employing the same procedures their studies said had failed, and evidently reducing the consequent dissonance either by devaluating the research they had examined in graduate school or by developing a fairly bitter cynicism about the dilemma they and their profession have gotten themselves into. The negative findings about diagnostic techniques have had no material influence on the actual everyday practices of clinical psychologists. Sundberg's (1961) report on the diagnostic habits of clinicians suggests that the Rorschach and TAT are still going as strong as ever. Reports of the activities of VA psychologists have shown no particular shift over the past several years. The psychologists still say they spend most of their time in conventional diagnostics. A survey by McCulley (1965) of internship supervisors in approved agencies across the United States shows that they still employ projective techniques as much as ever, still demand that trainees learn to use the tests, and still insist that universities are obliged to teach them. One of the few changes in recent years is that trainees are doing *less research* than they formerly did on projective methods.

It is not plausible that the clinicians who have continued to do diagnostic work despite the limitations of available procedures have persisted in their ways wholly out of ignorance, self-deception, or temperamental perversity. It seems much more likely that they have continued to do diagnostic work because clinical decisions still have to be made, somehow, by someone, whether the methods in stock are effective or not. Clinicians have continued to use the familiar but fallible procedures because no better methods have appeared to supplement or supplant the old ones.

This failure, however, is more than a technological matter. It is increasingly clear that the flaws in clinical assessment are not only procedural but conceptual. Not only have we been using faulty methods, we have been trying to get the wrong kinds of data, in the framework of misleading conceptions of disordered behavior.

The main difficulty with the typological, disease-oriented approach to the study of human problems is simply that we are not dealing with disease types in the assessment and modification of disordered behavior. A child who strangles kittens or spits at his mother does not have a disease. He *does* something somebody defines as a problem, and this is so even when the behavior is covert and the judgment of the problem is subjective. The therapeutic need is to get the client to change his behavior, not to cure his illness, and the vital diagnostic need is for information contributory to the behavior changing enterprise.

The usefulness of a typology depends on three conditions. The first is *homogeneity within classes*. Members of each class must resemble one another closely in regard to the characteristics on which the typology is based. In traditional nosologies of psychiatric illness this requirement has only been imposed, much less met, for peripheral symptoms, but most psychiatric classification systems are also based on the assumption that homogeneity can ultimately be found at the level of central psychopathology, in lawful relationship with distal symptom clusters. The second requirement for a useful typology is *independence among classes*. If the types are not only cohesive within themselves, but distinct one from another, efficiency is gained in the structure of the descriptive system and clarity is gained in its application. The third requirement of a typology, or of any other clinically useful descriptive scheme for that matter, is *pertinence to treatment*. If membership in a disease class is to mean anything to the patients, differential treatment procedures must be available for the various forms of illness, and choice among these must be implied by the particular disorders patients are found to have. For syphilis, penicillin; for each mental disease, a proper mental treatment.

Unfortunately, clear-cut types of behavior disorders do not seem to occur in nature. None of the conditions stated above is met in fact by any present typology. This is fairly clear now both from clinical experience and from research. Efforts to employ Q-factor analysis as a means of identifying unitary, independent classes of behavior disorders have been conspicuously unprofitable. In one series of studies, for example, type-R factor analyses yielding three dimensions of delinquent behavior, namely psychopathy, neuroticism, and subcultural deviation (Peterson, Quay, & Tiffany, 1961) were accompanied by two attempts to reproduce the behavioral dimensions as classificatory types. In both studies, nearly random distributions of subjects were found (Bowen, 1960; Tiffany,

Peterson, & Quay, 1961). The dimensional traits could be identified
with great dependability, but people did not fall into discrete
classes as an effective typology requires. The more general literature on psychiatric typology is less conclusive, but a generalization
about it can be ventured. The statement is in an extreme form to
allow clear refutation if that is what the data eventually show:
no Q-factor analysis to date, using even reasonably adequate procedures and tolerably unbiased samples of any general psychiatric
population, has generated a nonrandom distribution of subjects
in any psychiatrically meaningful descriptive hyperspace.

The failures which are slowly becoming apparent through the
accumulation of negative research findings on psychiatric classification have been reflected for a long time in the day-to-day behavior of clinicians. Practitioners who have tried to use traditional
nosologies as a basis for clinical description have had to add so
many qualifiers to the basic disease labels they attach that they
might as well forget entirely about the original classification system. Diagnosticians who try to describe the people they see in a
conscientiously accurate and complete way have not been content
to call people schizophrenic, manic-depressive or any other single
thing and let it go at that. They have spoken instead of "schizo-
affective reactions with paranoid features," or of "sociopathic personality disturbance, antisocial reaction, with schizoid features and
occasional hysteroid manifestations." Violations of artificial class
boundaries have been forced by the facts of clinical reality.

Dimensional formulations would appear to offer certain advantages over typology. In good psychometric tradition, we have
assumed that anything which exists exists in some amount and can
be measured. Objective tests can be developed for quantifying
personality characteristics, and then the position of any subject
can be established for whatever dimensions the investigator has
chosen to define. Given continuous scales and an indefinite number
of scales in the construct system, the individuality of any person
can be taken into account and numerically expressed in his personality profile.

The most serious problem with presently available dimensional schemes appears to be that the traits involved are insuffi-
ciently general over method and situation to have much predictive
utility (see Chapter 2 for some documentation of this claim).

Teacher ratings, for example, have little to do with self-ratings on dimensions which seem to represent the same dispositional tendency. The unitary traits we have so far defined seem to be determined more by the perceptual tendencies of observers than by the behavioral tendencies of the people under observation. And even if situation and method generality could be attained it is not immediately clear what the descriptions have to do with treatment. That is what we are up to, after all. No dimensional system available today is very useful in providing the kinds of information needed to help the people we labor so hard to describe.

Dynamic formulations of personality are designed to "penetrate the symptom facade" and reveal the (largely unconscious) psychic bases for the disorders people display. For the most part, these are based operationally on depth interviews, ordinarily of a free associative nature and on various projective tests, where unstructured stimuli are presented to elicit the latent personality tendencies of the individual. The data from tests and talks are usually interpreted in the framework of one version or another of psychoanalytic theory, and verbally fluent diagnosticians are capable of writing very compelling accounts of the inner mental life of the patients they see.

One needs to be skeptical, however, about the basic validity of such accounts, to say nothing of the reliability and generality of the methods used to generate the accounts. On all these scores, projective techniques have done very badly. Depth interviews have not been validated at all, nor can they be in their present amorphous state.

At best dynamic accounts are useful for planning certain kinds of individual psychotherapy. If we are going to invest most of our treatment capital in some other enterprise, elaborate dynamic accounts would probably be a waste. And even for individual psychotherapy, the utility can be questioned. Consider again the survey of therapists' opinions in which over 80 percent said the usual kinds of clinical diagnostic information were of little use in psychotherapy (Meehl, 1960). If Rorschach output is useless in planning psychotherapy, it may be worse than useless in planning a shift in the social reinforcement system or in other nonevocative forms of treatment.

Dissatisfaction with present methods does not immediately suggest a direction for new and better procedures. This demands a more fundamental logical analysis and a definition of the criteria an effective assessment system should meet.

IMPLICATIONS OF SOME RECENT DEVELOPMENTS IN TREATMENT PROCEDURE FOR THE CLINICAL STUDY OF BEHAVIOR

A clinically useful assessment system must above all yield information relevant to treatment. One way or another, the inquiry must generate decisions which will be helpful to the client. But the kinds of treatment which appear most promising today are different from those in widest use a few years ago, and assessment methods must take these innovations into account. Three very important changes have occurred in clinical treatment in the past several years. These were not unheralded by earlier efforts, but the major advances are quite recent. One is the development of social psychiatry, including principally the various milieu programs in mental health facilities as well as more general sociological shifts in community psychology. Another is the development of group procedures for treatment, particularly those approaches which employ natural primary groups, such as families and work crews, as the units in which treatment is done. The third is the development of behavioral approaches to the modification of disordered behavior; the effort to base treatment operations and procedural innovations on general behavior theory, notably on learning principles, rather than a separate theory of psychopathology.

The developments within social psychiatry which seem clinically most useful and most clearly accessible to systematic research are the social milieu programs which have been introduced at various mental hospitals. In institutions, the positions and roles and hence the socially influential behavior of personnel and residents apparently can be changed to the benefit of patients and staff alike. Custodial institutions have been transformed into active treatment agencies. When this is well done the effects are appreciable and appear to last.

In the field of group therapy, outcome research has been slow to appear, but some of the innovations in family treatment—family group and conjoint family therapy—and the quasi-therapeutic functioning of work groups, appear quite promising.

The major implications for clinical assessment are clear. If one of the most effective things we can do for a disturbed or disturbing person is to alter his social environment, then we need to study the social environment systematically as an integral part of the assessment enterprise. In work with groups, there is an obvious need to study interpersonal transactions and relationships as well as individual behavior. In the study of milieu programs, we need to be concerned not only with the discrete interpersonal relationships between significant others and a person whose behavior is disordered, but with the organizational characteristics of the social systems in which the individual participates.

The many developments which have taken place under the name of behavior therapy have equally strong implications for changing assessment procedure. We are no longer just talking to people, trying to get them to understand themselves. Now we are trying to modify behavior explicitly and predictably by application of the principles of behavior which make up psychology itself. If learning is defined broadly enough (as any change whatever in covert or overt behavior) behavior therapy amounts exactly to the modification of behavior by the application of learning principles. This makes therapy a psychoeducational task. And it demands of assessment far more than a study of the individual, however profound or correct that study might be. The competent practice of behavior therapy requires knowledge of the conditions (external as well as internal) which arouse maladaptive responses, of the reinforcing consequences which sustain the maladaptive behavior, and of stimulus changes which might elicit and sustain a more acceptable pattern of activity. Designations of disease are useless. No profile of traits will do. No knowledge of dynamics is sufficient. One needs to accomplish a functional analysis of the problem behavior itself, i.e., a detailed study of problem behavior in relation to antecedents and consequences, by means of experimental, observational, and interrogative procedures.

SOME THEORETICAL CONSIDERATIONS AND THEIR MEANING FOR THE ASSESSMENT OF BEHAVIOR

The second basic condition for an effective assessment rationale is its pertinence to a general conception of behavior. Theoretical pertinence does not mean that each and every operation in the assessment system must relate to a definite proposition derived hypothetico-deductively from a comprehensive, fully articulated theory of human behavior. It means only that assessment efforts guided by some specified framework of behavioral concepts are likely to be more coherent and better defined, and hence may contribute more to knowledge about human behavior than a battery of operations assembled without regard to theory. We are concerned not only with the clinical utility of diagnostic information but with promoting some general gain in knowledge about the human condition.

The conception we employ need not be very definite as to substance. We do not need to decide here and now what the hypothetical relationships might be among the variables we examine although some manner of relationship is assumed if the characteristics are to be studied at all. We do not need to know, for instance, precisely how patterns of parental reinforcement are related to antisocial behavior on the part of children. That is what we are trying to find out. At this juncture all we need to know is that parental reinforcement patterns probably have some relationship to child behavior and hence are important to examine if we are interested in changing the antisocial activity. The level of theoretical specificity appropriate to our task is one which is sufficiently definite to tell us what variables to observe, but neutral regarding the exact relationships among variables.

The problem of defining a useful conception is not one of invention but of choice and synthesis—the supply of available theories is rich and plentiful. If we wish to integrate assessment with treatment, and treatment with theory, however, we can dispense with perhaps 90 percent of the formulations out of hand. For the reasons outlined above, I propose that we reject all typological-disease models, all dimensional-trait models, and all dynamic-intrapsychic models as the central bases for assessment, treatment, and research.

But what is left? What theory can offer the scope, the coherence, and the power needed for an effective clinical technology? There is only one answer. The conception we need must be as large as behavioral science itself. Parallel with developments in social psychiatry, treatment in natural primary groups, and the behavioral treatment of individuals, theoretical formulations concerning the organization of social systems, interpersonal transactions in groups, and individual action must be included. Concepts which have traditionally fallen within the scope of sociology, social psychology, and individual psychology are all required and some attempt at synthesis must be made.

The phenomena in all three classes require behavioral specification. A sociological concept of *communication system*, for example, must ultimately be defined by stipulating who-says-what-to-whom-under-what-conditions-to-what-effect. A social psychological concept like *relationship* must be stated in terms of recurrent transactions. Sooner or later, if one is to be clear about the nature of the relationship, he has to tell who does what to whom. Behavior theory thus lies at the core of the general conceptual system, and insofar as clinicians are concerned with treatment, the central concepts are those of learning. If concepts relating to individual action, group transaction, and social organization can all be given behavioral definition, then a basis for defining useful clinical assessment procedures may be provided, a system for continual self-correction may be established, and by the union between science and practice which this may accomplish, the enrichment and clarification of both may be achieved.

In developing improved conceptions of human behavior and in extending these to a technology for clinical assessment, it is important to take environmental factors as well as intrapersonal factors into systematic account. If one fact has become more painfully clear than others from recent research on personality, it is that we have been committing a very serious *organism error* in the study of personality. All along, we have known that behavior was a function of the person *and* the environment in which he was situated, but in clinical diagnostic procedures and in research instrumentation alike we have continued to study the person alone. It is obviously necessary to begin taking the environment into orderly purview in procedures of clinical inquiry. The object of clinical study is not the individual alone nor his environment alone, but the individual-in-his-environment, as both aspects may be viewed in the context of general behavioral science and as both may be changed for the benefit of man and society alike.

PROCEDURAL CONSIDERATIONS

All assessment procedures need to be addressed to the same central issues, namely description of the problem and the conditions which affect it. The study of individual behavior is procedurally fundamental to the study of sociological and social problems, as well as purely psychological problems. Diverse approaches, however, may be taken to the study of human behavior. If we abandon hope of developing global personality tests which will tell us all we need to know about a person, we are forced back to a rather primitive epistemology. If we are going to find out about a person's reactions to effective stimuli, we have to study his reactions to effective stimuli as directly as we can. Three general methods can be employed, namely observation, interview, and experimental manipulation.

Observations

We need to watch individuals behaving in situations that matter. We need to observe people interacting in groups and to obtain the most direct knowledge we can of organizational functions as expressed in the behavior of the people involved. The ideal observational method, of course, is a complete totally objective around-the-clock recording of every action subjects make in all the situations they enter. Clinicians are naturally unable to manage this, partly in principle (because some of the crucial observations would have to be made in the past, and because Heisenberg's ideas about indeterminacy apply with much greater force to psychological than to physical phenomena) and partly because of obvious limitations on practical feasibility.

The most that seems practicable in the usual clinical situation is a limited observation of the disturbed person in interaction with some significant others in his social world. Employment of parents, teachers, nurses, aides, or other informants as systematic observers offers considerable promise, but may present serious practical problems in many cases. Placement of a staff observer in crucial real-life situations frequently alters the event under observation, and is a difficult and expensive procedure even if no such effect occurs. We need to extend direct observational methods, but in practice this is hard to do.

Interviews

The methodological difficulties in direct observation require use of other procedures. Guided interviews offer some promise. As a general strategy, interviews may be conducted not only with the person under study but with others in the social systems of major importance to him. All these interviews should focus on the problem behavior under study, and on the social stimulus properties, as models, instigators, and reinforcers, of the significant others who are interviewed or about whom information is gained. The interview protocol must not be regarded as the "truth" about the individual and his environment, but as another form of data whose reliability, validity, and decisional utility must be subjected to the same kinds of scrutiny required for other modes of data collection.

Experimental Procedures

Given information from observations and interviews, some planned manipulative changes may be exercised in the person's stimulus situation, and changes in his behavior may be recorded. The stimulus changes can be general or specific, multiple or single, brief or extended—this will depend on the case—but only in an experimental way can some of the most important hypotheses concerning behavior disorders be examined. Thus if a mother's solicitous behavior appears to be sustaining tantrums on the part of a child, let us try to get the mother to change her way of treating the child and observe any shift in child behavior which may result. The resulting data are in the nature of *functional relationships* between disordered behavior and the conditions which influence it. Knowledge of such relationships is of obvious and direct relevance to treatment, and is therefore a more useful kind of information than any sort of typological, dimensional, or dynamic account whatever. In an analogous way, changes in group transactions and interpersonal relations may be deliberately and planfully altered, and a social system may be reorganized to improve functional effectiveness.

In a very basic sense, all forms of treatment, psychological, social, or sociological, are experimental procedures. This does not imply a loss of compassion or a lack of interest in human well-being. It does imply that the treatment be planned as carefully as available knowledge permits, that the treatment activity be specified as clearly as possible, that any changes which come about be faithfully recorded, that the information about functional relationships thus gained be employed in a reformulated appraisal of the problem, and that revised treatment measures then proceed in an indefinite cycle of diagnostic information and therapeutic action.

2

The Person and the Environment

In beginning psychology courses all students learn a classic formulation which asserts that behavior is a function of the organism and the situation in which behavior is observed—$B = f(O,S)$; $B = f(P,E)$, or however it may be phrased. The formulation is, of course, silent regarding the exact nature of the function and it does not entail specification of equal determinative power for person and environment, but both elements are clearly included.

How remarkable, then, is the contrast between most psychological experimentation, where almost exclusive emphasis is placed on variations in stimuli, and clinical diagnosis, where attention is turned almost entirely toward the person. With few exceptions, laboratory science in psychology has neglected the study of variance contributed by organisms. And with equally few exceptions, clinical assessment practices ignore situational determinants of behavior.

The latter statement is most obviously true when diagnostic procedures are employed to permit classification of the "disease" a patient may possess. The patient is examined. His symptoms are described. His illness is then diagnosed; he is classified as to form of disorder and an appropriate label is attached. In the examination, to be sure, some attention may be paid to the social history of the person, and informants in present situations are frequently interviewed. But these data are usually collected to confirm or disconfirm the diagnostic impression formed principally by inference from examination of the person's present functioning. The diagnostician may seek to determine whether his patient has had the kinds of experience he thinks are related to the forms of mental illness under consideration, or he may wish to enrich and clarify impressions gained directly from the patient by gathering information from other sources. Data concerning social history or contemporary situations are not assigned high importance in their own right. The objective, in traditional psychiatric diagnosis, is to specify a disease, and the disease is presumed to reside within the individual.

A similar imbalance characterizes those assessment practices designed to generate dimensional descriptions. A profile of traits, however carefully defined and however "configurally" derived or interpreted, is still a description only of the individual. Nothing is told of the circumstances in which behavior is elicited or evoked. A pattern of internal dispositions is described and that is all. Conceptions and statistical models have been developed to accommodate situational parameters (Cattell, 1963; Tucker, 1964), but these do not provide a systematic means for introducing data about situations into the descriptive lattice. Cattell's specification equation, for instance, can take situational variance into account. Such variance can be given weight to equal or exceed that contributed by individuals. But the contrast between the amount of attention which has been devoted to methods for examining individuals and that which has been devoted to methods for studying situations is very severe.

Study of situations has also been neglected in most efforts to arrive at dynamic formulations of personality. The psychodiagnostician pursuing this goal is ultimately concerned with stipulation of the motives, conflicts, anxieties, defenses and other internal determinants of behavior. As in pure typing of disease, information about social history is ordinarily collected and present circumstances are considered. In dynamic analyses, however, environmental history is studied primarily to foster understanding of the present psychological state of the individual. One seeks to determine "how the patient got that way." And a glance is taken toward contemporary life circumstances mainly to allow adjustments in diagnostic inference. Reports may be differentially interpreted depending on the employment status or the home situation of the patient, for

example, as well as the immediate circumstances in which information is gathered. But concern about, and systematic study of environmental conditions for their own sake, as essential elements in
the matrix of behavior determinants has been neglected in most
dynamic psychodiagnostic procedures.

Results from several kinds of research are now converging to
show how serious an error the exclusion of situational behavior
determinants has been. Findings from six lines of inquiry will be
considered: (a) the influence of setting and individual personality
on the social behavior of children in residential treatment, (b)
examiner influence on projective test behavior, (c) the situational
generality of personality factors as inferred from questionnaires and
ratings, (d) trait and task determinants of effectiveness in leadership, (e) the prediction of antisocial behavior, and (f) analyses
of situation and person variance in reported anxiety reactions.
These will show how serious our neglect has been of situational
elements in behavior determination and how important it is to
incorporate such determinants in psychological methods for the
study of behavior.

THE INFLUENCE OF PERSON AND SETTING ON
THE SOCIAL BEHAVIOR OF CHILDREN IN A
RESIDENTIAL TREATMENT CENTER

Some very provocative work was done by Harold Raush and
his colleagues at the Child Research Branch of the National Institute of Mental Health (Raush, Dittmann, & Taylor, 1959). They
dealt with the behavior of six hyperaggressive preadolescent boys
whose disorders seemed to be "born of insufficient ego controls"
rather than the group mores of the delinquent gang. The children
were engaged in a general treatment program whose rationale has
been described in fine clinical detail elsewhere (Redl & Wineman,
1957), but which was based on a form of ego psychology designed
to promote the formation of controls by individual psychotherapy
and a variety of presumably therapeutic group activities. The children were observed systematically in six settings, sampled from
the much larger universe of available situations on theoretical
grounds. The children were observed at breakfast, leaving a period

of sleep which had often been filled with night terrors and other disturbances, and entering the world of real social interaction again. They were observed at other meals, which theoretically lacked the major ambivalent qualities of awakening but which assumed significance mainly because of the close association which appeared to exist on the part of many of the children between eating and emotional-interpersonal security. They were seen in structured game activities, where issues of cooperation and controlled competition, success and failure, were inherently involved, and in unstructured group activities, where roles were more loosely defined but the issue of getting along with others was still of paramount importance. They were observed during arts and crafts sessions—a task-oriented situation involving primary transactions with adults—which was examined as something of a surrogate for the school setting because one set of observations happened to be made during the summer months, when school was not in session. Finally, the children were observed at snack time before going to bed—an unstructured situation where some of the ambivalences of morning were probably appearing again.

All observations lasted for about ten minutes. The observers dictated their reports immediately, recording as fully as possible all they had seen. The resulting typescript protocols were coded in the 16 categories of the Circle of Interpersonal Mechanisms developed by Freedman, Leary, et al. (1951), which orders behavior in reference to two major polar coordinates: hostility vs. friendliness, and dominance vs. submission. The coded interactions of each subject were treated separately for behavior toward adults and toward peers, and the entire observational operation was performed twice with a span of approximately 18 months between the two phases of the inquiry.

Data were treated by a method of multivariate information transmission (McGill, 1954) designed to evaluate significant associations among nominally scaled values by means of distribution-free tests. Statistical significance can be evaluated by converting rates of information transmission to chi-square values in this scheme, and methods are provided for studying situational influences independent of personal determinants, personal influences with situations partialled out, and the interactions between situational and individual as related to interpersonal behavior.

Results showed that predictive uncertainty was reduced more by considering situational factors alone than by considering individual factors alone, but the difference between these values was not examined for statistical significance and the authors wisely refrained from concluding that the situation was more important than individual personality in determining behavior. By far the most dramatic finding was that the *interaction* between situation and person reduced predictive uncertainty far more than situation alone, individual factors alone, or the sum of the individual-difference and setting influences.

Which is more important for behavior, the person or the situation? Raush and his colleagues agree that this is a meaningless question—like heredity and environment, the two cannot be uncoupled. But the method they have employed and the results from its application vividly show the advantage to be gained from studying situations as well as persons and from examining interactions between these in the effort to comprehend and predict human behavior.

STUDIES OF EXAMINER INFLUENCE ON
PROJECTIVE TEST BEHAVIOR

Research on situational and interpersonal determinants of projective test behavior has been reviewed by Masling (1960) and descriptions of some illustrative studies from that survey follow. In one of the first investigations of this kind, Lord (1950) found style of administration to have a strong effect on Rorschach responses. When examiners behaved in a friendly, personable, charming way toward subjects, the Ss produced more responses, more evidence of creative imagination, less stereotyped thinking, and increased evidence of greater ease in interpersonal relationships. When the examiners acted coldly by showing little friendly concern for the subjects, the number of imaginative creative responses decreased, responses generally taken to indicate withdrawal from emotional stimuli increased, and there was a rise in self-critical verbalization.

A similar experimental variation was employed by Luft (1953), who studied preferences for inkblots under warm-friendly and cold-brusque examiner conditions. Warmly treated Ss liked, on the average, 7.6 of the ten inkblots. Those who were treated coldly liked an average of 3.1 inkblots.

Masling's review is longer and more comprehensive in scope than these comments can indicate. The findings are highly consistent and very persuasive. They all show that situational and interpersonal conditions have systematic and substantial effects on projective test behavior. This really should not be surprising. Rosenthal and his colleagues (Rosenthal, 1963; Rosenthal & Fode, 1963) have shown that the biased beliefs of investigators can influence the behavior of albino rats significantly and sometimes dramatically in experimental learning tasks. Orne (1962) has shown how powerful the demand characteristics of experimental situations can be in determining behavioral outcomes of psychological research. The shock of Masling's review is experienced only by people who believe that projective test performance is determined entirely or almost entirely by the internal personality characteristics of the subjects examined—exactly the belief most clinicians have harbored in the recent past of our profession. The presence of an examiner effect obviously does not negate the possible operation of subject effects. But in the face of generally negative findings on the validity of projective test inferences, the presence of definite, orderly situation-response covariation is worthy of remark.

THE GENERALITY OF VERBAL PERSONALITY FACTORS

My own interest in this issue began with some discoveries I made about the lack of trans-instrumental and trans-situational generality of personality factors inferred from questionnaires and ratings. For nearly ten years I had been working with what I considered to be reasonable ingenuity and rather meticulous care to define measurable parameters of personality and problem behavior in children. The work had several facets and a number of colleagues and students became involved in it. By the time a considerable number of replicated investigations had been performed, we thought we had fairly successfully defined an adjustment factor and an intraversion-extraversion factor in general personality (Peterson, 1960), conduct problem and personality problem factors in children's behavior disorders (Peterson, 1961), and psychopathy, neuroticism, and subcultural deviation factors in the questionnaire responses of delinquent boys (Peterson, Quay, & Tiffany, 1961). The factors were remarkably stable from one study to the next. Internal consistencies were quite high. Inter-judge agreements, where these could be estimated, were fairly respectable. Like most other trait theorists, we presumed that the covarying clusters of responses and ratings had mainly to do with the behavior of subjects and that they represented personality traits within the people under study.

But then we began to examine the validity of our indicants, or more precisely, the generality of scores over situations, instruments, and judges, and this is where the weaknesses in the system began to show. The first sign that something was wrong appeared in a study of parent-child relationships (Peterson, Becker, et al., 1961). We examined, as dependent variables, the problems children displayed and we used parent and teacher ratings as the bases for evaluation. Teachers, representing roughly similar viewpoints to each other, observing the same children in the same situations over the same time periods, agreed rather well in describing the conduct and personality problems of their pupils. Correlations of .82 and .62, respectively, were found for the two factors. The two parents, who had seen their children in many of the same situations and who represented somewhat overlapping viewpoints, still showed some accord in evaluating the problems their children displayed, though they did not agree as closely as the teachers. Correlations of .48 and .52 were found. But the teachers and the parents, who may represent rather different viewpoints and who had seen the children in different situations, agreed less closely. Correlations between pooled teacher ratings and pooled parent ratings were .41 and .24 for conduct problems and personality problems, respectively.

How high a correlation of this kind has to be to justify assertion of a personality trait, or how low it can get before one has to stop talking about a general trait, is a matter of discretion. It is reasonable to assume generality and then proceed to pool ratings, correlate with other variables, and so on, with coefficients of .80, or even .70. But for most of the clinical purposes for which these relationships might matter, it becomes disturbing when the numbers get down around .30, for then assumptions of trait generality begin to look very questionable. And that is where most of the convergent validities for personality traits appear to stand. If teachers say that a child is displaying a personality problem and his parents say that he is not—the low correlations show that this sort of descriptive phenomenon is the rule rather than the exception—who is to say whether he *has* a personality problem or not? One can, of course, concern himself with the veridical qualities of the reports, and begin to explore the possibilities of distortion on the part of defensive parents and various forms of bias on the part of teachers. Naturally such distortions do occur, and it is a naive researcher or clinician who is not alert to them. But maybe more than this is involved. Perhaps the teachers, within their limitations as behavior reporters, are telling the truth, and a child they have observed really is displaying personality problems in the school. Perhaps the parents, with their own human frailties as judges, are also telling the truth, and the same boy does not show personality problems at home. If this is so, we are led to examine the changes in behavior from one situation to the other, and we are led to examine the specific conditions in each situation which give rise to the behavior under consideration.

The study mentioned above was followed by a number of others with equally disturbing findings. We tried, for example, to relate the conduct problem and personality problem factors derived from ratings to the psychopathy and neuroticism factors derived from questionnaire responses. They certainly looked alike on paper. But the correlations were close to zero. We did not publish the results because we were not sure at the time what was going on. It was clear enough, however, that something was wrong with our methods, basic conceptions of personality, or both.

In 1960, Becker published a review of Cattell's work in which he examined the extent to which criteria of convergent and discriminant validity were met in the multifactor multimethod assessment system Cattell had developed. In one of the studies whose results were most favorable to propositions asserting trait generality (Meeland, 1952), the average correlation between "matched" behavior rating and questionnaire factors was .37, and the average for "nonmatching" factors was .32. Other results were still less convincing and Becker concluded that the available evidence did not support claims of correspondence between rating and questionnaire measures of alleged personality traits.

My own research and that of some students who worked with me (McDonald, 1964; Wetzel, 1965) led to analogous but extended conclusions. What we found was that the most significant share of the common factor variance in verbal descriptions of the "personality sphere" could be expressed in two factors, namely perceived adjustment and extroversion-introversion; that the covariation which gave rise to these factors could be determined as much by the meaning systems and perceptual tendencies of observers as by the behavioral characteristics of the people under observation; that the factors could be measured as well by two simple ratings as by the much more cumbersome rating schedules and questionnaires our grinding technology had taken so long to produce; but that the generality of these measures over method and situation was still not high enough to justify perpetuating the traditional conceptions of personality (Peterson, 1965). The findings required abandonment of a line of research to which I had devoted ten years of my life as a psychologist. The results also required a change in beliefs about the nature of personality. This research, per se, did not say which way the conceptual shift should go, but it suggested very strongly that traditional conceptions of personality as internal behavior dispositions were inadequate and insufficient.

TASK AND TEMPERAMENT IN LEADERSHIP RESEARCH

Fiedler and his colleagues at the University of Illinois have been concerned for many years with the social psychology of leadership. Some of their early work was addressed to the measurement of leadership ability conceived more or less as a personality trait, and led to the development of a number of devices for measuring such a trait. The procedure which they have employed in much of their recent work requires a subject to describe the one person, among all those he has ever known, with whom he has had the greatest difficulty working. The descriptions are made on a scale containing 20 items, such as friendly or unfriendly, and cooperative or uncooperative. Each item is scored from 1 to 8, with high scores indicating a favorable description (e.g., friendly) and low scores an unfavorable description (e.g., unfriendly). From these, a score known in the Fiedler literature as LPC (Least Preferred Co-worker) is obtained. A high score indicates that the subject has described his least preferred co-worker in relatively favorable accepting terms, while low scores show that the subject has described his least preferred co-worker in unfavorable rejecting terms.

As a number of studies have shown, LPC scores are systematically related to leadership style, in that high LPC leaders tend to be rather democratic, permissive, and considerate, while low LPC leaders behave more directively and autocratically.

When research was extended to leadership effectiveness, however, some puzzling results began to emerge. Sometimes LPC scores would correlate with effectiveness and sometimes they would not. Sometimes high LPC scores were related to effectiveness and sometimes low scores went with effectiveness. At this point, Fiedler and his colleagues had an enormous mass of data, believed that there was sense in it somewhere, but were considerably confused about the kind of order which might emerge.

The facts did not begin to fall into place until Fiedler began to examine some rather complicated interactions between leadership style as a personality trait, and the situations in which leadership was required. He has recently developed a three-dimensional contingency model (Fiedler, 1965a) that seems to put the facts in place better than any previously available system, and whose most significant aspect, for the present argument, is that the model was constructed to define group-task *situations*. Only when these are taken into account can leadership be adequately understood.

The dimensions of concern are task structure (the degree to which the task is defined), leader-membership relations (the degree to which the leader is esteemed by the group), and position power (the degree of power inherent in the leadership role).

In examining the interactions between these situational variables and leadership style, Fiedler and his colleagues have shown that directive managing leaders are usually most effective in situations which are either very favorable or very unfavorable for them. Permissive accepting leaders are best suited to intermediate situations. The correlations between leader LPC scores and group performance scores in structured situations, where leaders are esteemed by the group and the leader position power is strong, are negative (around −.50), which seems to mean that autocracy works best in these situations. Likewise, when leader-member relations are poor, the task is unstructured, and position power is weak, low LPC scores are associated with high group performance (rs range around −.50). But when leaders are liked by the group, the task is unstructured, and position power is weak, the correlation between LPC scores and group performance is positive and about the same magnitude (.50) as those rs just mentioned. This means that in these situations, and in certain others which Fiedler has defined, a permissive leader functions most effectively.

It is also known by now that leadership attitudes are very hard to change and that neither intensive training programs nor lengthy experience seem to have any visible effect on leader effectiveness. This suggests that the best way to solve the leadership problem is not to train leaders better, nor even to select them better, but to engineer the task to fit the leader (Fiedler, 1965a). Regardless of the ultimate outcome of these attempts, the need for systematic definition of the situation as well as the person is dramatically clear in Fiedler's research on leadership. Only when both are examined does order begin to appear.

THE PREDICTION OF ANTISOCIAL BEHAVIOR

Consider next the literature on prediction of juvenile delinquency, in particular the research by Sheldon and Eleanor Glueck on the identification of conditions related to antisocial behavior and the use of this knowledge in predicting legally delinquent activity. From their early work in *Unravelling Juvenile Delinquency* the Gluecks (1950) developed several sets of items which distinguished between the delinquents and nondelinquents in their sample. Some of these were personality or character traits defined by Rorschach output and behavior during psychiatric interviews. Others were social factors based on observations of the home and interviews with parents. The five social factors were (1) discipline of boy by father, (2) supervision of boy by mother, (3) affection of father for boy, (4) affection of mother for boy, and (5) cohesiveness of the family. The prediction studies done since that time have concentrated on the social factors rather than personality traits and have led to the development and use of the well-known Glueck Social Prediction Table.

The most recent report of this work is based on an abbreviated form of the Table containing only ratings of family cohesiveness, supervision by mother, and discipline by mother. Elimination of other variables was necessitated by difficulties in getting reliability in judgments of affection, and in getting any information at all about fathers in the predominantly matriarchal families so common in the high-delinquency areas where the Gluecks did their research. The three-item scale correlates .96 with the five-item scale, so the same basic information is involved.

Some data are now available on the actual prediction of delinquency, rather than retrospective classification of delinquents and nondelinquents. In 1952, the New York City Youth Board selected two schools in very high-delinquency areas and applied the Glueck Table to all the boys in the entering grades. A follow-up inquiry was conducted when the boys were around 15 years of age for an effective sample of 223 cases. Of 186 boys for whom nondelinquency was predicted, 176, or about 95 percent, were still in fact nondelinquent. Of 37 boys for whom delinquency was predicted, 13 were already adjudicated delinquents and four more were "unofficial offenders," for a total of 46 percent accurate predictions. If the unofficial offenders are excluded, predictions of delinquency still were right in 35 percent of the cases, and naturally there is a chance that some of the boys for whom an "error" was made actually had committed undetected delinquent acts or would become visibly delinquent later on.

There are serious problems in evaluating the utility of scales of this kind. For one thing, the base rate of delinquency, even in the zones of highest risk, is so low that statistically superior results can be obtained simply by calling everybody nondelinquent (cf. Voss, 1963). And there are very serious ethical problems which attend calling children predelinquent and letting people know about it, as one must if preventive measures are to be taken. Such designations may become self-fulfilling prophecies and actually intensify the problems they were designed to ameliorate (cf. Kahn, 1965). But aside from these practical and ethical difficulties, it is scientifically interesting that the Gluecks were correct in predicting delinquency-nondelinquency in approximately 85 percent of the cases, using a scale that does not contain any information about personality at all. The Glueck Social Prediction Table, in all its forms, is exclusively composed of *situational* variables, specifically those having to do with cohesiveness and control in the home, and these variables alone permit surprisingly accurate prediction of a long term behavioral outcome of considerable consequence.

DIRECT COMPARISONS OF SITUATION, RESPONSE, AND PERSON VARIANCE IN TEST BEHAVIOR

Finally, consider some research of quite direct pertinence to the issue at hand. The work began with some logical analyses by J. McV. Hunt of the meaning of trait ratings (Hunt, 1959). As a kind of methodological cliché, Hunt noted that such ratings have to be based on two kinds of observables, namely the responses of the persons observed, and the situations in which the responses occur. But in actual ratings, both situations and responses are rarely if ever sampled in any systematic way. Judges leap immediately to complex inferences about the O between S and R, without taking care to see what kinds of stimuli may be operating or what kinds of responses may actually be occurring.

This line of thought suggested a new format for trait inventories and led to the development of an "S-R Inventory of Anxiousness" which Endler, Hunt, and Rosenstein (1962) have used in their investigations. Anxiety was chosen as a likely trait to study, mainly because of its assumed importance in human behavior. Eleven situations were then defined in which anxiety might arise. Some of these involved a physical threat of some kind, such as being in a sailboat on a rough sea or being on a ledge, high on a mountainside. Others involved social threats of one sort or another, such as giving a speech before a large group or undergoing an interview for an important job. Fourteen modes of response were specified, some physiological (e.g., heart beats faster, mouth gets dry), some having to do with the subjective experience of anxiety (e.g., getting an uneasy feeling) and others designating motor actions related to the anxious state (e.g., wanting to avoid situation, becoming immobilized). Subjects were asked to describe their own reactions on five-point scales for each response made in each situation.

The inventory was administered to two groups of college students, 67 from the University of Illinois and 169 from Pennsylvania State University, and the results were analyzed in several ways. The method of greatest interest here was a three-way analysis of variance which allowed assessment of the relative contributions of subjects, situations, and modes of response to variance in degree of reported reaction.

The results were very surprising to the authors, and their conclusions emphasize what they found.

A three-way analysis of the variance in the responses to the inventory showed that modes of response contributed most to the overall variance, with situations next, and individual differences among Ss a poor third. In the Penn State sample, the situations contributed over 11 times as much of the variance as did the individual differences among Ss. In fact, the variance contributed by individual differences is only approximately equal to that contributed by the interaction between modes of response and situations. By the customary statistical tests, all these contributions to the variance were highly significant, as were also the interaction between modes of response and Ss and the interaction between situations and Ss. The predominance of situational variance over S variance clearly supports the contention of social psychologists that knowing the situation is more important for predicting behavior than knowing personal idiosyncrasies. (Endler, *et al.*, 1962, p. 29)

In the Illinois sample, situation variance was four times as great as person variance, in spite of the fact that the sample had been deliberately selected from a larger group to exaggerate the range of anxiety. The Illinois sample consisted of Ss in the top 15 percent and the bottom 15 percent on the Mandler-Sarason Test Anxiety Questionnaire (Mandler & Sarason, 1952). Inclusion of the intermediate subjects would probably have reduced the person effect still further relative to the much stronger variance contribution of situations.

These studies, of course, deal only with reports of behavior in hypothetical situations. Whether, for instance, telemetrically monitored physiological responses and immediately recorded accounts of subjective experience in actual situations would yield the same results can only be determined by the appropriate experiments. But Endler and Hunt are taking steps to find out the answers to questions of this kind.

The apparent dominance of situational influences over personal ones is not completely convincing in the findings so far. One could swing that balance either way by judicious selection of subjects and situations. In fact, a data reanalysis by Endler and Hunt (1966) led to a much greater emphasis on the interactions among subjects, situations, and modes of response than had appeared in the report just cited. The significance of the research may ultimately be seen to lie in the model within which person-situation-response relationships are conceived and examined. But the model, the logic supporting the model, and the findings to date are equally strong in their demand for inclusion of situational parameters in the study of personality.

Perhaps these data will suffice. They are not intended as an exhaustive survey of empirical literature on stimulus determinants of behavior. The very notion of an exhaustive review is meaningless in a time of exploding knowledge. The available facts, however, do support the contention that situational influences may very profitably be introduced in psychological research and conceptualization generally, and that this is a direction which should be pursued in efforts to improve procedures for clinical assessment. Of course the idea of getting situational influence into theory and research in psychology is not new. Claude Bernard spoke of the *milieu externe* along with *milieu interne*. To George Herbert Mead, man was essentially a social being, vitally influenced by others in his social environment, though not a passive creature of that environment. Egon Brunswick was particularly concerned with this matter in its implications for psychological research. His concept of representative design (Brunswick, 1947), which implies application of sampling principles to situations as well as subjects, is both more general (in regard to substantive scope) and more specific (in entailing particular strategies for defining populations and samples) than the present argument. But in the simple raw concern about the ecology of behavior, Brunswick's message and this one are just the same.

Hammond (1954) has been particularly active in stressing concepts of representative design in clinical psychology, and has revealed a strange discord in the logic and method of most research in clinical psychology. Psychologists customarily study large samples of subjects, place them all in one or a very limited number of situations, and then exercise close restraint in generalizing to the larger subject population, while they make irresponsibly loose generalizations to a larger universe of situations with perfect serenity.

The need to study the environment is not new to psychologists, and of course to sociologists this whole chapter will appear superfluous. They have known all along that the impact of society on the individual is far stronger than the impact of the individual on society. It is obvious to them that individual behavior must be understood in its cultural context, and they must find it quaint that anyone should ever have thought otherwise.

Although bringing environmental influences into clinical assessment systems is an urgent concern, it is important to avoid excesses. There is no virtue in becoming a situationist (cf. Allport, 1966). Persons must still be studied. The proper subject for psychological study is not man alone, not situation alone, it is man-in-his-environment. But the direction of imbalance at the present time is very clear—situational factors are badly neglected—and this imbalance should be righted with all possible speed.

If one is to begin taking the situation into account, however, it is necessary to specify the situational influences which need to be considered. It is not very helpful to know that the environment matters, unless one also can say what it is about the environment that matters in what way to whom. Sells (1963) has proposed a taxonomy of basic aspects of stimulus situations which he hopes will be useful to emerging psychological science, and he has made an effort to get everything that might matter into the system. He lists gravity, humidity, and the nature of the terrain as aspects of the human environment. Of course they are. If a man is going to be spun off into space, the influence of gravity will be very important to him, and so it must be included in any comprehensive description of human ecology. But any useful list of situational parameters for the clinical study of behavior must narrow the scope of concern. For most of the problems faced by clinicians, gravity can fairly comfortably be ignored.

What are the bases for defining parameters of special concern for the clinical study of behavior? There were two suggestions in the previous chapter: (a) relevance to treatment and (b) pertinence to theory. If these criteria are to be applied, however, one must specify the kind of treatment for which assessment is performed and outline the theoretical framework within which the related operations of assessment and treatment are to be performed. In the next chapter, a general paradigm will be suggested for the modification of behavior in social situations.

3

Behavior Change and
Behavior Assessment

Like any other behavior, the activity of clinicians in "psycho-diagnosis" is largely determined by situational demands. The demands, furthermore, are often of a spurious kind. The real reason many clinicians conduct psychological examinations is that someone expects it of them. All too frequently, they administer and interpret Rorschachs, code MMPI's, and prepare reports for no clear reason beyond the scheduled expectation of a staff conference, the knowledge that they are going to be asked what "the psychologicals look like," and prescience of an embarrassed silence if they have nothing to say. The diagnosis has to be written into the record, and since someone in charge may ask for an opinion, the diagnostician feels obliged to have one ready, with some kind of test data to support it. Many clinical psychologists have been caught in an irrational system which requires useless answers to meaningless questions, and once entrapped they have rarely been able to do anything but yield to the demand.

But the only legitimate reason for spending time in clinical assessment is to generate propositions which are useful in forming decisions of benefit to the persons under study. Diagnostic knowledge should help other people somehow, not just make clinicians feel secure. Cronbach and Gleser (1957) have made the basic point very clearly in their analysis of the use of tests in personnel management. Tests are to be evaluated mainly by their utility in making decisions, not by the glow of confidence they engender in the tester, nor even by their validity in any traditional psychometric sense. Hathaway (1959) has stated the same principle in particular reference to the use of tests in clinical psychology. "The chief contribution of psychology to clinical efficiency is the use of psychometric devices to more quickly and accurately effect clinical decisions" (Hathaway, 1959, p. 192).

While Hathaway's proposition is generally appropriate, it can be extended in one respect and limited in another to arrive at a more widely applicable and still more useful statement of the basic purpose of clinical assessment. Hathaway suggests that the major procedural contribution of clinical psychologists lies in their use of psychometric devices. That definition should be broadened to include a wider range of psychological methods, such as guided interviews, systematic observations, and experimental procedures which may be applied by qualified professional clinicians of several traditions. And Hathaway's statement about the use of information to effect clinical decisions can be more precisely specified. The clinical decisions which matter most are those related to behavior change. Whatever the clinician may personally want to know about a patient, the facts which matter to the client are those which pertain to treatment. A revised functional definition of psychodiagnostic study might therefore read as follows: *Effective clinical diagnosis can be accomplished by the use of psychological assessment procedures to gain information which contributes to decisions about desired changes in behavior.*

If this definition is adopted and the essential subordination of diagnosis to treatment is assumed, however, one must specify the kind of treatment for which decisions are required. Psychotherapy addressed to the unfolding of authenticity in *I-Thou* relationships (*v.* Chapter 5) will require different knowledge from that needed in shaping the verbal behavior of an autistic child. One need not decide about the full and final worth of the treatment methods over all conditions and for all time to come. This decision is impossible to reach. But one must affirm some apparent value for the treatment measures to be employed, and anyone who sets out to develop an effective assessment technology must believe that the treatment methods to which the appraisal procedures are related have a fairly substantial degree of cultural durability—that they are here to stay, at least in their basic features, for a good long time to come. Fads must be identified and avoided, and so must any traditional procedures which persist in the face of documented futility. One must predict the future of the treatment system about which assessment strategies are constructed as well as possible, on the basis of limited and imperfect data, fallible reason, and an appalling sense of the historical collapse of nearly every system man has ever devised for dealing with disordered behavior. That is the existential reality one faces in an enterprise of this kind. The major source of the courage needed to proceed in spite of all this, as Tillich would say, is that treatment decisions are being made by the thousands daily anyway; that they are being made very badly for the most part; and that nearly any revised approach which is not foredoomed by logical inconsistency, not in obvious conflict with the few facts available now, and which contains a mechanism for continual evaluation and improvement as new concepts develop and new data emerge, can at least do no worse than the methods in effect at the present time—and may some day do a good deal better.

The therapeutic approach to be outlined below begins with the most comprehensive definition of treatment I have been able to conceive, without lapsing into metaphysics or violating too seriously the traditional semantic limits of the term. Treatment may be defined, thus, as *any planned attempt to change disordered behavior for the better.* Whatever else one may do, however one may go about his work, the essential task of psychological treatment is to change behavior. This may be done singly or in groups. It may be done in a total institution or in a private office. The changes may be instigated by verbal stimuli or in some other way. The behavioral changes may be overt or covert. The change agents may be highly trained professionals or they may not. But the goal always is to change some aspect of behavior. Such a definition places disordered behavior as the condition to be altered, behavior theory as the conceptual system within which disordered behaviors are to be understood, and behavior change as the goal of treatment, at the center of the definitional system.

Methods for modifying behavior, however, vary enormously and procedural specification is needed. In the statement to follow, fundamental inquiries are addressed to the behavior which treatment is designed to change and to the external conditions under which the behavior occurs. But the behavior is enacted by a person, and not all the behavior of persons is explicit and observable. Covert processes and methods for changing them must be studied as well. People frequently interact with one another; some of their major problems arise in the transactions which occur and the relationships which form with other people, and treatment may sometimes be accomplished best in group settings. Furthermore, people function in societies which are systematically organized in certain ways. Changing the organizational structure of a social system is frequently the most general and lasting way to alter the behavior with which clinical inquiry began. The treatment approach to be outlined here as a basis for effective clinical assessment thus partakes of behavior therapy, individual psychotherapy, group therapy, and social psychiatry; and the material which follows is an attempt at preliminary synthesis of these procedures. Despite necessary variations in form and level, they all have the same goal and are functionally all alike. This permits the conceptual unity and methodological coherence required for rational choice of specialized procedures and for the orderly development of an effective clinical technology.

CHANGING INDIVIDUAL BEHAVIOR

Behavioral therapies have been available for many years. The mental exercises Aretaeus and other Greco-Roman physicians employed to improve faulty memory in their patients were direct efforts toward remediation of a functional learning disability. Alfred Binet not only constructed an intelligence test, he attempted to develop means of improving intellectual performance. Burnham's book, *The Normal Mind* (1924), describes many of the procedures which are sometimes distinguished as novel innovations in modern behavior therapy. In 1924, Mary Cover Jones reported success in the treatment of children's fears by direct conditioning procedures. A decade later, Knight Dunlap (1932) popularized the treatment of maladaptive habits by negative practice. In 1938, Mowrer and Mowrer described a highly effective conditioning procedure for the treatment of enuresis which is still in widespread use today.

Starting around 1960, however, the professions concerned with behavior disorder began to witness a renewed and heightened interest in behavior therapy, which was most forcefully spurred by the publication of Wolpe's *Psychotherapy by Reciprocal Inhibition* in 1958.

The Modification of Anxious Behavior

Salter (1950), Dollard and Miller (1950), Shoben (1949), and others before Wolpe, had attempted to redefine psychological treatment procedures in terms of learning theory, but these efforts amounted for the most part to a description of rather traditional psychotherapies in the language of learning. Salter's conditioned reflex therapy, for example, consisted mainly of advice and exhortation to replace timid social reactions with assertive behavior. The method was loosely based on some Neo-Pavlovian concepts of excitation and inhibition, but the relationships between theory and practice were not very completely articulated, the differences between the actual behavior of a Salterian therapist and any other directive psychotherapist were not clearly visible, and the effectiveness of the treatment was never very fully documented.

Wolpe's procedures, by contrast, are more firmly rooted in established principles of learning, the actions of the therapist depart significantly from those which characterize traditional evocative psychotherapy, and the methods appear to be highly effective. Wolpe assumes that all treatable disturbed behavior stems from anxiety, that the anxiety originates historically in the conditioned experience of the disturbed individual, and that the essential task of the therapist is to replace the anxious reactions of the patient with more acceptable and adaptive behavior.

Treatment is based on the single, and to Wolpe, sufficient principle of reciprocal inhibition.

If a response antagonistic to anxiety can be made to occur in the presence of anxiety-evoking stimuli so that it is accompanied by a complete or partial suppression of the anxious responses, the bond between these stimuli and the anxiety responses will be weakened. (Wolpe, 1958, p. 71)

The essential task for the therapist is to identify the stimuli which arouse anxiety and then to present these to the patient, either directly or more commonly by means of induced fantasies, in such a way that some reaction other than anxiety will be experienced by the patient.

Many reactions are antagonistic to anxiety, in Wolpe's view, and among those which have been most successfully employed are deep muscle relaxation (cf. Jacobsen, 1938), sexual behavior, and assertive action. The replacement of anxiety by these responses is of course no simple task for a clinician, but in such procedures as systematic desensitization the diagnostic and therapeutic measures are at least explicit and consistently grounded in learning principles, they represent clear departures from the usual psychotherapeutic practices, and they evidently work.

Shaping Operant Behavior

The second major current in the contemporary development of behavior therapy is the application of operant conditioning procedures in changing disordered behavior. The principles of learning which Skinner and his colleagues have developed in laboratory experimentation have found wide applicability to the problems of modifying clinical symptoms.

As in the work of Wolpe, the operant behavioral approach entails a fundamental change from traditional conceptions of disorder, a basic change in the procedures employed to assess and treat disorder, and a reasonably clear interrelation of principle and practice.

The fundamental principle is that behavior, disordered or not, is controlled by the stimulus conditions under which the behavior occurs, particularly the reinforcing stimuli which follow the behavior. In applying the principle to behavior disorder, the major clinical task is to identify the stimuli involved in their functional relationships with the behavior under consideration, and then, by systematic alteration in stimulus-response regularities, to modify behavior in whatever direction is desired. The disarming simplicity of the principle is badly matched by the technical complexities which can arise in clinical shaping, for instance, of bizarre verbal

behavior by successive approximations. But the principle itself is
clear enough and its utility in the modification of disordered behavior is quite amply documented (Krasner & Ullmann, 1965;
Ullman & Krasner, 1965).

New variations and embellishments of behavior therapy are
appearing almost daily. Bandura and Walters (1963) have added
the concepts and techniques of social modeling to other procedures
of effective stimulus change. Ayllon has developed token economies
in hospital situations to encourage socially adaptive behavior. Krasner (1962) has analyzed the psychotherapeutic interchange in the
framework of operant learning principles, and has defined the action of the therapist as a "reinforcing machine." Such developments
will surely continue to emerge. If the recent past is any guide, the
new discoveries will frequently be announced with strong enthusiasm, and attacked with equally enthusiastic fervor. The introduction of a thoroughgoing behavioral viewpoint in the analysis and
treatment of clinical disorders requires some wrenching changes
in conception, and the abandonment of some attitudes and beliefs
both familiar and dear to many clinicians. The outcome research
for behavioral therapies is less than fully definitive, but the signs
of effectiveness are favorable (Krasner & Ullmann, 1965; Wolpe,
1958; Eysenck, 1960; Paul, 1966). In one form or another, and most
likely in specific forms too numerous to anticipate, behavioral treatment procedures seem to be here to stay, and appear to offer a
particularly appropriate point of departure for development of a
useful system of clinical assessment.

Changing Beliefs and Attitudes—Psychotherapy as a Procedure for Behavior Modification

There is a considerable tendency for those who become en-
amored of behavioral treatment methods to reject psychotherapy
entirely. This is unnecessary and unwise. There is no inherent in-
compatibility among the methods. With some redefinition they can
all be seen as facets of a single treatment enterprise.

Redefinition can proceed most coherently, however, if psychotherapy is regarded as one set of procedures among many for use
in changing behavior, rather than considering the behavioral pro-

cedures as variants of psychotherapy. Viewed in this way, individual psychotherapy can be most usefully defined as a set of treatment procedures in which two people, one of whom is a therapist and the other a patient or client, communicate with each other in an effort to examine and change the systems of belief and attitude of the client. The most troublesome terms in that definition are *communication, belief,* and *attitude.* Communication is a form of social interaction in which information is mutually conveyed from each person to the other, largely though not exclusively by verbal means. The term is neutral as to which member of the communicating pair takes the major responsibility for initiating the messages, and is noncommittal regarding the exact way in which the information is encoded, transmitted, decoded, interepreted, made-use-of-in-living, and so on. A belief system is an ordered set of concepts a person employs in guiding his own behavior. Belief systems are made up of personal and social constructs (Kelly, 1955), rules of personal and interpersonal behavior (Mischel, 1964), in part of the things people say to themselves (Ellis, 1964) as they plan, enact, and recall behavior. An attitude is the way an object, such as the self, another person, or some act or characteristic of the self or another, is evaluated. Colloquially, this amounts simply to the goodness or badness attributed to the object. More formally, an attitude is a generalized implicit evaluative response which mediates favorable or unfavorable actions toward the object (Osgood, *et al.,* 1957; Fishbein, 1967).

The focus of psychotherapeutic attention on beliefs and attitude, and on cognitive and affective processes in guiding behavior seems preferable to the traditional search for insight. The pursuit of *insight* in the psychoanalytic sense, i.e., the recognition and verbalization of the unconscious motivational bases of symptomatic behavior, involves a factually inaccurate or at least badly overgeneralized proposition about the origins of disordered behavior. The search for insight in the sense of total self-discovery or an oceanic oneness with the universe is impossible to define. But the historical durability of psychotherapy and some laboratory data persuasively indicate that beliefs and attitudes play an important role in behavior and offer a critical target for therapeutic intervention.

At a rather simple level, the importance of cognition in learning is well documented. No noncognitive theory of learning has ever adequately explained the facts of latent learning which Blodgett (1929) and Tolman and Honzick (1930) presented more than 30 years ago. The more recent flurry of research on learning and awareness (Dulany, 1961; Spielberger, 1962; Eriksen, 1962) shows that awareness can facilitate learning dramatically and radically. As suggested in Peterson and London (1964), the proposition that awareness is necessary to learning is difficult to support. Planaria and earthworms can "learn" to do fairly well at certain kinds of tasks, but it seems unlikely that they cognize very actively about their own behavior. It may be possible to shape behavior in ways unknown to the subjects. But human beings, being human, are remarkably adept at certain kinds of symbolic activity. And there is no advantage in failing to make use of this fact. If efficient, general, and lasting changes in behavior are to be brought about, it seems likely that the cognitive and affective processes of persons must be taken into account. The account may profitably go beyond designation of reinforcement contingencies on the part of the client and behavioral prompting by the therapists to a detailed consideration of the nature and structure of generalized beliefs and attitudes toward the self, toward others, and toward the actions of all concerned.

The emphasis has been on the role of cognitive change rather than emotional insight in this discussion, because recent evidence suggests that the two are very intimately related, and because cognitive functions are easier to define and manipulate than emotional reactions. Festinger (1957) and Hunt (1963) particularly have shown the extent to which cognitive incongruities can have a motivating emotional aspect. The extent to which attitudes, i.e., affective evaluations, can be influenced by communication and resulting changes in beliefs has been known to social psychologists for some time (Hovland, Janis, & Kelly, 1953; Fishbein, 1963). However badly he may want to change motives directly, a therapist does not have any clear means at his disposal to accomplish this end. But the therapist can inform, and if the information which he supplies is somehow dissonant with the beliefs which the client has about his own state of affairs, then the client may be motivated to change something in his own system of thoughts or other actions, and this may have favorable emotional repercussions. The therapist may find, incidentally, that the best way to change cognition is by way of changing some kind of overt behavior. More people, it is said, behave themselves into new ways of thinking than think themselves into new ways of behaving. But from laboratory evidence and clinical impressions alike it seems likely that some kinds of cognitive change can be made quite directly by way of psychotherapeutic communication (cf. Ellis, 1964). We should avoid substantive commitment on issues of primacy at this point. It seems plausible to surmise that such covert events as ideas and affects as well as discriminative stimuli and extrinsic reinforcers influence subsequent behavior, and that changes in any of these may be useful in helping people get along with themselves and others.

Psychotherapy has traditionally been valued in Western society because it assigns first importance to the individual patient and his welfare. His problems, his dynamics, his history, his treatment, his well-being are of ultimate concern. And in the sweep of a *Zeitgeist* where treatment is increasingly designed to shape the behavior of the individual to meet someone else's demands, a call for the rights of persons may not be out of place. Justification of psychotherapy on grounds of protecting individual freedom seems ill-based, however. The paramount task for all clinicians is to help the individuals they see and improve the societies they all live in, with the most effective means at their disposal. Individual psychotherapy in which the client is required to assume responsibility for the direction and substance of treatment is not necessarily the best way to do that. Talk about the integrity of the individual and assignment to him of primary responsibility for defining the course of treatment is frequently no more than pious rationalization. Therapists who do not know how to proceed blithely "leave it all up to the patient." This way nothing much is likely to happen and if something goes wrong it is the patient's own fault.

The only legitimate reason for including psychotherapy as a treatment procedure is that it may be useful in inducing some of the cognitive and other changes which are important in general behavior modification. The kind of psychotherapy which lends itself most readily to this kind of treatment approach is one in which information is introduced by the therapist to facilitate cognitive changes, and thereby to influence other forms of behavior. It thus resembles most closely the rational-emotive therapy of Albert Ellis

(1964) and the directive therapies which Thorne (1950) and others defined some years ago.

As one method among many, however, behavioral psychotherapy loses its unique quality as a psychological treatment procedure. In redefining the clinical task as behavior modification, and insight as a means rather than an end, the clinical repertoire of available procedures is considerably extended. One is no longer limited to sitting in an office talking to patients, although, at times, talking to a patient may be the most valuable measure one can possibly take. In changing individual behavior, clinicians must define some changeworthy action and the conditions under which it occurs, and then set out to alter that by the most effective means available. Induction of fantasy, manipulation of social reinforcement, and verbal communication may all be employed, as may any other procedures a rapidly expanding technology will in time provide.

CHANGING SOCIAL TRANSACTIONS

Group therapy arose from a need to treat large numbers of patients in more efficient ways than individual treatment could allow. As the reasoning went, a therapist who treated ten patients at a time could increase his total therapeutic effect tenfold. The first treatment groups were conducted much like classes. Pratt (1907) trained groups of tubercular patients in principles of physical hygiene and psychological well-being. Emerson (1910) instructed groups of "delicate" children in the essentials of diet and good health. It is hard to say whether these efforts constituted group therapy in any of the modern senses. The problems involved were basically medical, the methods were purely didactic, and the collective structure was employed more as an expedient than as a rationally justified essential of treatment.

Hunt (1964) has identified the work of Greene in 1917 (see Paine's introduction in Greene, 1932) with stutterers as the first attempt to employ specified and controlled group interactions to ameliorate the behavior disorders of individual members. But even in this case the problem was of a rather focal kind and the methods were based on the prototype of the classroom. With the work of a number of psychoanalytically minded clinicians in the 1930's and 1940's (Bender, 1937; Schilder, 1936; Slavson, 1943), group treatment became more clearly a form of psychotherapy. Insight, and the release and working through of dynamically troublesome material, were construed as the goals of treatment, and the methods were largely those of individual psychotherapy transposed to a collective setting. Group procedure was still justified principally by emphasizing improved efficiency over individual treatment, so it came more as an unexpected dividend than as a planned profit when the therapeutic effects of the group were seen to go beyond those of the therapist himself. In the work of Slavson (1943) particularly, Lewinian principles of group dynamics were intermeshed with psychoanalytic conceptions of individual dynamics; the group as such was seen as the effective treatment unit, and the interactions among group members were regarded as the central events of the therapeutic process.

Group therapy flourishes today in many forms. Married people share their problems with other troubled couples in family service clinics. Neurotic adults and disturbed children and lonesome old people are collected in groups where they interact and communicate and hopefully help each other to achieve more satisfactory ways of living. T-groups meet to train participants in sensitivity and interpersonal competence. Families, ward mates, basketball teams, and work crews are set to the task of analyzing and resolving their problems in getting along with one another. The therapists may try to foster a permissive atmosphere for individual growth (Hobbs, 1951), or to facilitate insight into intrapsychic and interpersonal dynamics (Ezriel, 1950) or to expose and understand the games people play in daily living (Berne, 1964), or to encourage integrity in human dealings within and beyond the group itself (Mowrer, 1964). Variations seem to appear along all the dimensions which matter in describing treatment groups.

Any attempt to develop assessment procedures to accommodate all the events, processes, and structural characteristics which occur in all forms of group therapy would obviously be hopeless. Restriction of the field and some approach toward more rigorous definition of crucial aspects of the field appear to be required. In this attempt, it will be useful to focus discussion on treatment in natural groups and to define essential treatment parameters by extending the definition of treatment outlined above for the modification of individual behavior to the transactional regularities of interpersonal relationships. The conjoint family therapies of John Bell (1962), Jackson and his colleagues (Jackson and Weakland, 1961), and Ackerman (1958), as well as the quasi-therapeutic action groups which Fiedler, *et al.* (1959) have discussed, furnish prototypes for the kinds of group procedure which lend themselves most readily to the general treatment approach now being defined.

A particularly informative illustration of the kind of group treatment which can be developed within a behavioral conception of the origins and treatment of disordered interaction is provided by the family group therapy of John Bell (1962). Bell regards the nuclear family as many social scientists regard any group, as a collectivity of individuals formed by action processes to accommodate the conflicting as well as the complementary demands of all members. The action processes may be specified by the purposes or motives from which they originate, by designating the media—verbal or nonverbal—by which actions are expressed, and in regard to the mechanisms by which transitive actions are accomplished. Families are healthy (function effectively) when a means for evaluating action patterns has been built into the action process, and when a variety of mechanisms can be flexibly employed to fulfill the complementary purposes and resolve the competing demands of the people in the family.

In this framework, symptoms are said to arise mainly as primitive preverbal efforts to convey otherwise uncommunicable messages from one person to another, but once enacted, symptomatic behavior may be misinterpreted and perpetuated as a recurrent habitual pattern of transitive action. Bell cites the case of a young boy who misbehaved during a ride in the family automobile and as punishment was put out of the car a short distance from home. In his anxiety and chagrin, the boy became nauseated and later expressed his symptomatic behavior as a generalized car-sickness. The parents then began to define a new partial role for the youngster—that of car-sickness-prone child—and reorganized relevant aspects of their family life around the child's disorder. They avoided occasions in which the boy would enter an automobile and thus guaranteed that he would become ill when the necessities of a vehicular culture required him to ride in a car. In family group therapy, the family (parents and children alike) had as one task to recognize the communicative intent of the car-sickness and develop other means of coping with it, as well as accommodating the more general needs to which the symptom was related. In this case as in others, discrete symptomatic behavior was seen to arise in part as a preverbal communicative action, but had become stabilized by complex patterns of social reinforcement into a rigidly habitual way of acting.

With chronicity, in Bell's formulation, verbal communication is replaced by more primitive media, and indeed communicative actions of all kinds may be reduced in frequency. Rational evaluation is disrupted and the mutual satisfactions of family members are curtailed. Family group therapy usually begins with the referral of an individual family member who displays behavioral problems of some kind. In Bell's practice, this is immediately translated into a need for extended change in the family, and he reports that most people accept this redefinition quite readily. The therapist initiates a new group process which includes the entire family and the therapist himself. The therapist forms a working relationship with each and all family members, and among the family members themselves, to help them discuss the way they have been treating each other, to communicate more clearly the messages they have been trying to convey to one another, to perceive new possibilities for complementary action and conflict resolution, and then to proceed with the more effective actions themselves. The participants are organized more as a task group than as a maintenance group in the traditional distinction between those terms, and the tasks are to communicate more intelligibly, act more effectively, and interact more harmoniously than before. In this form of treatment, as in individual behavior therapy and behavioral psychotherapy, the central task of the therapist is to determine the recurrent patterns of dysfunctional transitive action people are displaying, and then to exercise appropriate changes in the conceptual, motor, expressive, and communicative behavior which is the core of the problem. Bell is anything but passive in his practice.

The therapist's overall activity may be described . . . as an effort to promote social interaction through communication within the family unit, permitting it thereby to experience, appraise, define, and reorder its relational processes. . . . He *promotes* . . . new evaluations within the family of the potentialities and skills of the individual members. He *encourages* reassessments of the past, of the responsibility for earlier difficulties, of the meaning of symptomatic behavior, and of the family climate within which it grew. He *prevents* any family members from evading the implications of the relationships with him and others. He *demonstrates* forms of relationship that can be transferred to other interactions in the family. . . . Family group therapy is . . . a treatment method which depends on the presence and control of the therapist. (Bell, 1962, pp. 10–11) [1]

Bell's contributions and those of other innovators in conjoint family therapy are well and justly recognized, but the potential of this form of treatment can be greatly enhanced by application of the same general principles to natural groups of all pertinent kinds. Suppose we assume, as was contended in the preceding chapter, that situational influences play a critical part in determining behavior. And suppose we further assume that other people are particularly influential in therapeutic learning processes. A change in the behavior of one person might thus be facilitated most effectively by producing a change in the stimulus characteristics of another, and if the two are interacting in a coherent and durable interpersonal relationship, changes in the behavior of each should mutually occur.

To anticipate the conceptual suggestions made in the next chapter, the essential objects of change in group therapy are the relationships which obtain between members of the group. But relationships are most meaningfully defined through stipulation of the *recurrent transactional patterns* which characterize the dealings of any two people who influence one another. That is, the way any two people get along is the matter of dominant concern in natural group therapy. The way they get along depends on the relationships between them, and the relationship is ultimately defined by the behavioral interchanges in which both participate—by the things they do to each other.

But if this very general view of group process is adopted, the focus of therapeutic action extends immediately beyond the family to any primary group whatever in which disordered behavior has occurred, in which it is maintained, and in which it might be

[1] Italics added.

altered. The group of primary concern for a troubled child may or may not be his family, though most clinicians would presuppose some *a priori* salience for the family as a likely scene for disordered interpersonal behavior, a probable source of many disturbances, and a particularly useful agency through which beneficial changes might be effected. The disturbances of a troubled child might arise predominantly in school. While entire classes are rarely available for anything approaching group therapy, the selective actions of selected members, particularly teachers, may often be modified in helpful ways. The essential concerns of a troubled man may arise in his dealings with others at work, and it may be possible to examine and improve, far more than has been done to date, the transactional interbehaviors which go on there, not only by changing the individual but by altering the social climate in which the disturbed transactions take place (cf. Fiedler, *et al.,* 1959). How to change a social climate is not so clear, but when one begins to think in broadly behavioral terms about the functions of groups, treatment action is immediately directed toward the patterns of interpersonal behavior—affective and cognitive as well as motor, covert as well as overt—which characterize the relationships and reciprocal actions of people in groups of all kinds.

A major characteristic of the behavioral group methods being proposed here is that the therapist behaves more like an experimental social psychologist than as a friendly purveyor of warmth and permissive climate. He need not be harsh in his performance of that role. He need lack neither compassion nor interest in the welfare of his clients. But his task is to assess, with the essential help of group members, the patterns of disordered transaction which characterize the processes of living in natural groups, and then to initiate or encourage appropriate changes. He must plan the actions he will take on the basis of any knowledge available to him at the time the action is undertaken, and he must evaluate the behavioral effects of his intervention and the repercussive social effects his treatment may generate. In these regards, his task is essentially experimental.

Social interactions comprise a distinguishable class of phenomena from those of individual behavior. Reciprocity of stimulation and effect is involved and any treatment initiated in a group setting entails interactive phenomena, whether the group is a biological family, patients on a ward, or the members of a tank crew. Supraindividual concepts such as relationship and transaction are required for adequate description of events in the domain, but the principles of social learning still apply and the need for detailed *interbehavioral* specification is as great as in describing the action of a solitary organism.

CHANGING SOCIAL SYSTEMS

Changes can be effected in the organization of social systems as well as in the actions of individuals and transactional patterns of group behavior. The professional field of social work has traditionally included community organization, along with individual casework and group work, as an area in which useful interventions might be made. The other dominant helping professions in the mental health field, psychiatry and clinical psychology, have only more recently begun to recognize the utility of a sociological view of disordered behavior and the advantages of organizational action in dealing with the social problem behavior disorders represent. Social psychiatry and community psychology have emerged to express this expansion of scope.

Forerunners of modern social psychiatry can be found in the moral treatments of the 19th century and in the "commonsense" psychiatry of Adolf Meyer early in the 20th century, but the contemporary movement was given its most vital force by the work of Harry Stack Sullivan at Sheppard and Enoch Pratt Hospital in Towson, Maryland, only a few decades ago. Sullivan was the director of clinical research there, and as part of his work he developed a receiving service which had most if not all of the characteristics of the better milieu therapy units in operation today. The ward consisted of two three-bed units connected by a corridor, physically housed within a larger building but administratively distinct from the rest of the hospital.

Sullivan himself took charge of the diagnostic and treatment effort, but in his definition of disorder in interpersonal terms and in his use of others in the appraisal and treatment enterprise, the uniquely social character of Sullivanian psychiatry was defined.

The aides particularly played a new and important role. They were selected, that is to say hand-picked by Sullivan, for intelligence, clinical sensitivity, and common sense, and they were trained to take an active role in treatment. To Sullivan, treatment began with the removal of the patient from the interpersonal situation in which his problems were forming and placement in a new situation in which the problems might be resolved. Aides were taught to initiate, encourage, and sustain the resocializing efforts of the patients. They talked with the patients when talk was appropriate; they worked beside the patients when work was needed. They sometimes entered the interviews which Sullivan conducted, moving psychotherapy beyond the private revelation of fantasy to an experience in social communication and interpersonal behavior. Aides became not wardens or keepers but human beings in a social situation designed to help the patients. The ward became an institute in social living instead of a custodial care center or a benign prison.

Sullivan's work, as is well known, was carried forward by Frieda Fromm Reichmann and others at Chestnut Lodge, and converging with other influences led to the development of one important aspect of social psychiatry as it is evolving today (Sullivan, 1962).

At Chestnut Lodge, Stanton and Schwartz (1954) developed a program whose major emphasis was on the structure and administration of the hospital rather than the individual treatment of the patient. In 1954, a symposium was held at the meetings of the American Psychological Association to discuss the mental hospital as a small society. This led to a larger conference in which psychology, sociology, and cultural anthropology, as well as the many professional disciplines involved, all contributed comments about the nature and especially the inadequacies of the mental hospital as a social system for dealing with disordered behavior (Greenblatt, 1957). Working with occupational misfits and quasi-sociopaths in England, Maxwell Jones (1953) developed the concept of the therapeutic community, a situation in which the total resources of the treatment unit and ultimately the community around it are mobilized to help the people toward whom therapeutic concern is directed.

In North America, Cumming and Cumming (1962) defined some relations between "ego and milieu" with a somewhat curious theoretical concatenation of ego psychology and sociological flotsam, but presented a keen descriptive analysis of hospital administrative structure. Goffman (1961), a sociologist, sought to characterize the mental hospital as a total institution, and the view he provided of the lives of patients and staff alike was a revelation to those whose engagement in therapy had previously consisted of 50-minute conversations in the privacy of an office.

Psychologists like Fairweather (1964), and Ellsworth (1964) brought an interest in small group process and an awareness of the importance of incentive systems to the enterprise, and Pratt and Tooley (1964) rooted the efforts of their human actualization teams in the ethics of an "emergent humanism."

By now such phrases as the therapeutic community and the mental-hospital-as-a-social-system are clichés. There is no doubting any more the energy of the sociological movement in the management of disordered behavior, and while outcome research is very limited, some of it is quite compelling (Ellsworth, 1964; Fairweather, 1964). At least people appear to be gaining some grasp of the problems with which they are dealing and are devising some rather promising ways of coping with them.

Of the many sociological strategies which have emerged in the effort to do something helpful about disordered behavior, two major trends can be identified. Change operations have been directed toward the organizational structure of existing mental health agencies, particularly mental hospitals. Milieu therapy as it has been implemented in most actual treatment efforts to date has been dominantly concerned with changes in the administration of mental hospitals. Sociological change operations have also been addressed to the more general organization of social systems in the community at large, and to the preventive and therapeutic effects of the way societies function as a whole. Community mental health and community psychology have been employed as terms to designate social actions of this kind.

A good deal of chauvinistic gamesmanship has been involved in the justification of appropriate terminology. If one employs the term social psychiatry, the field will be within the domain of the medical profession. If such a term as community psychology is employed, the prerogatives of clinical psychologists might be enhanced. Social workers, who have been in this business all along, have not proposed a slogan which consigns the field to themselves alone. The phenomena with which we are concerned are planned changes in the organization of social systems to prevent and ameliorate disordered behavior. The actual operations constitute a kind of clinical sociology. If a comprehensive term is needed, social engineering would appear to be more acceptable than most alternative candidates. Such a phrase focuses semantically on the work to be done and is neutral about professional hegemonies among those who are to do the work.

Milieu Therapy: Changing the Organization of a Mental Hospital

The analysis of any social system begins with study of the collective functional purposes the system is designed to serve, and the organizational means which have been developed to accomplish those purposes. Study of the organization itself is usually directed to the positions and roles of participating personnel, the patterns of authority by which decisions are reached, and the routes of communication by which information is transmitted from one person to another in the system. The entire operation is logically based on some set of shared assumptions about the nature of the phenomena with which all involved are dealing.

The improvement of a mental hospital as a social system, as is attempted in comprehensive milieu programs, involves change in all the characteristics identified above. The basic purpose of the organization must often be redefined. Staff and patients alike may need to be reminded that the purpose of a mental hospital is treatment, not custodial care. The patients are expected to improve, and staff are expected to help them in the search for better ways of living.

The activities which are performed in a treatment center are different from those which serve the aims of protective maintenance. And if treatment is defined broadly as any planned effort to improve behavior, therapy is no longer confined to occasional conversations about intrapsychic affairs with highly trained but impossibly scarce psychotherapists. Concern is addressed to "the other 23 hours" and to the activities of patients in various locations with many different people. Treatment is not dispensed by the physician alone, nor solely by professional personnel of any particular identity. Persons in social systems influence each other, for better or for worse, and appropriate role redefinitions can provide nurses, aides, and the patients with clear responsibilities for helping those about them.

Executive control of the system may be reorganized. The most common shift in implementation of milieu programs is from a hierarchical system of authority to a lateral diffusion of responsibility among professional personnel, nurses and aides, and the patients themselves.

Communication within the system can be changed in amount, direction, and kind. One of the more conspicuous features of most hospital milieu programs is the formation of some kind of patient-staff meeting procedure, as typified in patient-government operations.

Anyone who has attempted to mount an effective milieu program knows how much easier it is to write cheerful descriptions like those above than actually to accomplish the basic changes. People have to alter long-standing ways of thinking and acting, and this comes hard. An attempt to organize a milieu program may have been in progress for a year, and still one may hear a nurse say, "Oh yes, miloo [sic] therapy. We have that every Wednesday afternoon." In some way, a successful milieu program requires that the patients view themselves as active participants in the work of treatment. Yet a patient may say, as he is about to be discharged, "Why are you sending me away? I've tried to be good." Basic change in a mental hospital or any other treatment system requires more than procedural tinkering and organizational gimmicks. A fundamental ideological change may be required and this can usually be brought about only by slow and painful effort. Administrative power is also very helpful.

Community Mental Health: Changing the Larger Society

The community mental health movement is organized to remove barriers between mental hospitals and the communities in which they are located. "Interpenetration" is the slogan and the "open door" is the symbol of the change. Not only do the staff and patients in the hospital function as part of the same basic treatment enterprise, but the relations between the treatment unit and the community as a whole are altered. No longer are the patients cooped up in medieval prisons to be forgotten by those who sent them there and ignored by those who are supposed to be helping them out. In active community programs, the diagnostic staff go into the community to assess needs for hospitalization, engage employers, friends, the family, anyone who can be helpful to the patient, in the treatment effort, and follow him back into the community upon discharge. Patients enter the community for work and recreation, and people from the community, most often as volunteers, do what they can to benefit the people who happen to be in the treatment center at the time. The patients inside, and the people outside, cease to exist as dichotomous classes. A psychological treatment center becomes one agency among many for the fulfillment of social aims and the management of social problems.

The major goals of community mental health are preventive rather than curative. The simple economic futility of individual case-by-case treatment is recognized, and the more general preventive aims of traditional public health are assumed instead. Indeed adoption of a thoroughgoing sociological view of behavior disorder leads quickly afield from the treatment center as the major institutional framework within which desired psychosocial changes can be brought about. One becomes concerned not only with "the other 23 hours" of treatment within the hospital, but "the other 69 years" of the usual human lifespan. We all of us may find ourselves, or get ourselves, in severe psychological difficulty at some time or another. It is usually unfortunate but not necessarily catastrophic when this occurs. When the time arrives, one hopes that decent and effective agencies are available for emergency help. But before that time and after, in all aspects of the lives of all of us, should not society be organized to forestall serious disruption wherever possible and to deal with it as effectively as possible wherever the inevitable problems arise? If so, the school, the church, the court—all social institutions whatever—should have ways of dealing with disordered behavior. This usually means more than attaching a guidance counselor to the staff of a high school with 1500 students, more than assigning a psychological examiner to a juvenile court which serves 700 cases each month, more than training a few Episcopalian ministers in pastoral counseling; though all these may be measures of a potentially useful kind. At its extreme, community mental health becomes indistinguishable from a general program of societal improvement. Social engineering is required—planned changes in social organization to improve the lives of all members of the society. How to accomplish this without creating a Brave New World or a 1984 is the social and moral dilemma of our time. Walden Pond is gone forever and Walden Two is unthinkable. No adequate utopias have yet been proposed. As societies expand, become urbanized, secularized, and progressively more complex, the need for organizational structure and the planned use of power grow more and more urgent. There is no use lamenting a dead past; the changes are inevitable. It is very important that the organizations serve essential functions instead of impeding them, and it is even more important that power be wisely and humanely used.

UNITY AND DIVERSITY IN BEHAVIOR MODIFICATION

As general treatment systems for dealing with disordered behavior are now emerging, individual behavior, group transactions, and organizational functions must all be included as classes of modifiable phenomena. A suitable set of procedures should embrace any available means of accomplishing desired changes in these phenomena. Among present methods, individual psychotherapy, operant and other behavioral procedures, group therapy, milieu programs, and community action can all be employed. For rational applicability, maximal effectiveness, and continually self-corrective growth, a treatment system of very broad comprehensiveness is required.

But loose eclecticism—a somewhat intuitive selection of procedure, and transitory adoption of the theoretical presuppositions and principles which underlie that procedure, to suit the perceived needs of various people and problems—should be avoided. Thus a true eclectic becomes a Rogerian when he feels that is appropriate, thinks and treats like a Freudian on other occasions, follows

Mowrerian ideas with some of his more loosely principled patients, conducts an activity group along Slavsonian lines if he happens to be confronted with the need to treat several predelinquent boys at the same time; indeed he may claim to be able to change his professional identity and accompanying treatment orientation as often as the diverse and changing needs of his patients require.

Eclectics usually justify their methods by suggesting that many authors of treatment procedures have had some truth to say about behavior disorders and ways of dealing with them, but no single innovator of a clinical procedure has ever defined a fully satisfactory position. That is undoubtedly correct, and in a way the faults of eclecticism lie not so much in the professional indecisiveness of clinicians as in the limitations of the systems among which therapists are forced to choose. From Freud to Wolpe, the inventors of psychological treatment procedures seem to have been afflicted by the same kind of conceptual and technological constriction. In all cases which come to mind, assumptions are made concerning a single or very limited class of determinants of disordered behavior, and a single or very limited class of treatment procedures. In most cases, just one method is proposed. With a lack of imagination which seems almost inconceivable now, Freud could only think of one way to deal with disturbed people. Rogers did no better. And for the average eclectic, whose perceptions of clinical reality insistently belie the diversities of human behavior, more than one way is needed. To meet the clinical necessities of disordered behavior, procedural variation is required.

The trouble with the usual practice of loose eclecticism is that it offers no method beyond clinical intuition for choosing among procedures, no clear way of telling if they do any good, and frequently requires sequential adoption of theoretical presuppositions and factual propositions which are logically incompatible. One cannot believe on Tuesday that all neurosis arises centrally from unconscious conflict and on Wednesday that the essential determinants of disordered behavior are external reinforcing contingencies. And something better than whimsy is needed to determine choice among diverse procedures.

If the more effective treatment procedures under development today are to be employed in a systematic way, and if these are to be further augmented and improved, it seems that we need a sufficiently comprehensive conceptual system to accommodate sociological and social phenomena as well as individual psychological events. And we need definitions of disorder and treatment of appropriate semantic scope. Such definitions can be provided in a conception of disorder as deviant changeworthy behavior, and of treatment as the entire set of procedures, available now or in the future, which can be employed to bring the desired changes about. This establishes a behavioral approach to treatment in primacy over psychotherapy, family group methods, social psychiatric programs, community actions, or any other procedures, without restricting clinical technology to the limited procedures of operant conditioning, desensitization, or any of the other specific methods which are sometimes mistakenly identified as behavior therapy. Psychotherapy may be done, but a change in behavior, overt or covert, is the aim. Groups may be formed, transactions may occur and relationships may develop, but the goal of treatment is to change behavior. The authority pattern in a state hospital may be altered, but changes in the social system are engineered for the sake of desired behavior change, not merely because democratic structures are better somehow than authoritarian ones, or because the lateral diffusion of responsibility seems like a good idea. One is required to stipulate the behavior he wants to alter and to state the direction change should take. One must indicate, furthermore, the means by which the changes are to be accomplished, and this requires knowledge of the processes of behavior modification. No conception of personality or social structure, however complete, can provide the principles involved. These are, in essence, principles of learning and they are central to behavior change, inside or outside a traditional treatment setting.

Behavioral definitions of disorder and treatment appear to provide the flexibility and diversity of method which human problems demand, and at the same time offer a guide to the conceptual unity systematic application and improvement of treatment procedures require.

BEHAVIOR CHANGE AND BEHAVIOR ASSESSMENT

If assessment procedures must above all contribute to treatment decisions, and if treatment consists in changing functional relationships between disordered behavior and the conditions which maintain the behavior, then diagnostic inquiry must proceed along different lines from those of traditional psychodiagnosis. No longer are forms of illness, personality traits, or dynamics the crucial objects of study. Basically different questions must be asked.

What, in specific detail, is the nature of the problem behavior? What is the person doing, overtly or covertly, which he or someone else defines as problematic and hence changeworthy behavior? What are the antecedents, both internal and external, of the problem behavior and what conditions are in effect at the time the behavior occurs? What are the consequences of the problem behavior? In particular, what reinforcing events, immediate as well as distant, appear to perpetuate the behavior under study? What changes might be made in the antecedents, concomitants, or consequences of behavior to effect desired changes?

If a behaviorally oriented psychotherapy is to be considered, diagnostic inquiry will turn to the specific behavioral hypotheses and intentions the individual has about the behavior under consideration and eventually will extend to the generalized beliefs and evaluative attitudes the person holds about himself, significant others in his life, and the behaviors they all enact.

If behavioral group methods are to be undertaken, clinical study must extend to the relationships among members of the group as this is defined by recurrent transactions. What transactional sequences characterize the relational patterns of particular concern? What antecedent conditions precede the interbehaviors? What beliefs and attitudes does each participant bring to the transaction? What are the short- and long-term consequences to both parties and to others in a larger group of which both may be members? What can be changed to improve the way the people get along together?

The modification of a social system requires abstractive knowledge of a different order. What collective purpose is the system supposed to be serving and how well are present organizational mechanisms accomplishing those purposes? What are the functional characteristics of the organization itself? In particular, how are the positions and roles of key personnel defined, how are decisions reached, how are orders effected; how is information conveyed throughout the system? On what shared assumptions or cultural beliefs does the whole operation rest? How are all these characteristics expressed in and defined by the actual behavior of the people involved? What changes might be made in the system and hence in the behavior of participants to produce the greatest general benefit?

None of these questions are easy to answer. The procedural difficulties may be impossible to surmount in many cases. But these are the kinds of questions one must ask if assessment data are to be transitive to recommendations in a comprehensive behavioral treatment system. Present clinical procedures are ill-suited to the task, and the need to develop a new clinical technology is clear and urgent.

If one is concerned wholly with the pragmatics of treatment, however, there is some danger that clinical assessment procedures will be elaborated chaotically, as *ad hoc* inventions to meet the peculiar demands of each new therapeutic innovation. This would be undesirable; the systematic development of a clinical assessment technology needs to be guided by a more general conceptual framework. If such a conception can be stated, the clinical methods may be useful not only in arriving at practical decisions, but as operations for defining and examining psychological and social processes, for the description and ultimately for the improved understanding of social behavior.

4

Behavior Theory and
Behavior Assessment

Stipulation of a useful treatment strategy, and the collection of data required for decisions in that strategy, may best proceed in the framework of concepts provided by general behavioral science. Relevant concepts must be designated and an attempt toward operational as well as implicit definition of the concepts must be made. Wherever possible, conceptual interrelations should be stated. For reasons already given, the required body of concepts must take situational as well as personal factors into account and it must yield propositions which have some pertinence to desired behavior change.

FAULTS IN PREVIOUS ATTEMPTS AT
THEORY CONSTRUCTION

The dangers of reification and circularity which have characterized so many formulations in the past must also be avoided. These dangers have been noted with eloquence and wit by others, and there is no need to re-emphasize them here. There may be some advantage, however, in summarizing the major arguments against irresponsible theory invention, for contemporary psychiatry and abnormal psychology consist all too largely of an elaborate set of conceptual fabrications which bury the problems of behavior disorder in the minds of the mentally ill, lull the theorizers into a complacent sense of total *Verstehen*, and provide absolutely no knowledge of any use to a therapist or the person he is trying to help.

Bandura and Walters (1963), among many others, have noted the analogic character of "hydraulic" and "infection" models of disorder and the suggestions for cathartic treatment which are usually associated with such principles. After commenting that most psychotherapists since Freud have operated on assumptions of this kind, they quote a sublimely illustrative passage from Dorothy Baruch's *New Ways in Discipline* (1949).

When pus accumulates and forms an abscess, the abscess must be opened and drained. If it isn't done the infection spreads. In the end, it may destroy the individual. Just so with feelings. The "badness" must come out. The hurts and fears and anger must be released and drained . . . when unwanted NEGATIVE FEELINGS have been emptied out sufficiently then—warm and good POSITIVE FEELINGS flow in. When muddy water, which has dammed up, drains out from a pool, then fresh, clear water can flow in. So it is with these feelings. (Bandura & Walters, 1963, p. 255; from Baruch, 1949, pp. 38–45)

This is the clearest instance in my recall of the reification of concepts which characterizes so much theory in the field of personality and behavior disorders, but other illustrations abound. Ullmann and Krasner (1965), for instance, cite the definition of psychiatric disorders in the standard nomenclature of the APA Diagnostic and Statistical Manual (1952). In that system, a psychoneurotic reaction is defined as a disorder in which ". . . the personality, in its struggle for adjustment to internal and external stresses, utilizes the mechanisms listed above to handle the anxiety created." One is confronted with the interesting spectacle of a *concept* which *struggles* with stresses, *utilizes* mechanisms, and *handles* anxiety.

There is some merit in going beyond the mere summary of relationships between stimulus and response variables in psychological theory development and clinical assessment. Definition of constructs, careful attachment of surplus meaning to these, and systematic examination of the meanings, appear to have some heuristic value in science and practice. But thinking of the kind expressed above goes far beyond those bounds. Analogy is taken for fact. This is the kind of thinking which can have not only theoretical disadvantages but unfortunate practical effects. It is entirely possible, for example, that cultural beliefs about the need to drain hostile feelings from hateful children has led a generation of misguided parents and therapists to train children systematically in aggression and ill will.

Beside the dangers of concretizing concepts lie the evils of circularity. From behavior, constructs are inferred. From the constructs, the behaviors are deduced. The performance of this exercise may lead to a feeling that all has been explained. A patient is neatly dressed and polite, though a bit punctilious in his manner. He lines up the pencils on the desk in order of size as he is talking, and at an opportune time presents the examiner with a list of symptoms, which include some obsessional ideas and compulsive rituals. He is diagnosed "obsessive-compulsive reaction," and the presence of this neurotic condition is then used to explain the symptoms and the interpersonal behaviors he displays.

There are conditions under which response-based inference of psychological dispositions is a logically legitimate act. The basic condition is that the inference lead to behavioral propositions other than those from which the inference was formed, and that the latter descriptive statements be testable, and preferably tested. But psychological "diseases" are rarely diagnosed from symptoms in this way, and the practice of conducting psychiatric examinations and attaching diagnostic labels has led all too many practitioners into the comforting but illusory belief that when a mental disease has been specified the explanatory problem has been solved.

B. F. Skinner (1953, 1959) has been more vehement than most in his criticism of loose theorizing. As is well known, he argues that the explanation of behavior by reference to central events fails to account for the behavior itself, and instead of encouraging thoughtful inquiry may impede scientific enterprise by creating an unwarranted satisfaction with the status quo. Skinner's views have had considerable impact on psychology in general, and have had a particularly forceful effect on clinical applications of general psychology. In fact, a quasi-Skinnerian behavioral view seems at present to be the foremost candidate to replace the dynamic views which dominated thought about behavior disorders for the first half of the twentieth century. In many efforts (Krasner & Ullmann, 1965; Ullmann & Krasner, 1965; Bachrach, 1962; Staats & Staats, 1963; Bijou & Baer, 1961), disorders are defined in behavioral terms, the study and treatment of disorders are placed in the context of general behavioral science, stimuli and responses are examined, and the inner lives of persons are ignored.

From the work of Skinner, of Watson and Kantor before him, and through the efforts of numerous younger theorists, a new Radical Behaviorism is forming. Almost entirely an American invention, it is vigorously anti-subjective, strictly scientific, and often very effective as a basis for clinical action. To psychologists weary of the conceptual obscurity and practical futility of traditional views, it is charged with a powerful appeal. But Radical Behaviorism is not the only alternative to ineffectuality and confusion, and it has some serious limitations as a basis for the clinical technology we need to construct. It may therefore be worthwhile to examine the major premises of the system before suggesting a different one.

There is something of the straw man in the following. The premises are stated in an abstract idealized form, and this means that no given Behaviorist, living or dead, would actually subscribe to all the propositions exactly as they will appear. This does not matter because the purpose is to isolate as clearly as possible the main arguments of a generalized systematic position which in one aspect or another is seriously espoused by a rapidly growing highly vocal group of proponents as the only acceptable basis for a new clinical psychology. In examining the premises themselves it may be possible to define the logical bases of a more sensible conception of social behavior to be developed gradually in the years to come.

Radical Behaviorism contains at least six basic theses. The first of these is an *epistemological cliché: The ultimate data source for psychology is observation of the behavior of organisms.* In one sense, this proposition is purely tautological. Psychology is defined as the science of behavior, hence behavior is the object of study for the science. In another sense, the premise goes beyond definitional circularity to a stipulation of the means by which the science is to be constructed. That is the observation of behavior. The epistemological thesis of Radical Behaviorism is perfectly acceptable, but we have all agreed about this ever since the abandonment of purely philosophical rationalism as a means for constructing any science.

The second thesis of Radical Behaviorism is a *metaphysical absurdity: Mind does not exist.* Of all the Behaviorists, Watson is the only one who said this and it is doubtful that he really meant it, so there is probably no need to spend much time dealing with the problem. Purely as logical argument it may be enough to say that if behavioral definition of the subject matter of psychology makes internal constructs meaningless—asserting the nonexistence of mind is just as foolish as asserting its existence.

The third premise of Radical Behaviorism is a *causal presumption: Behavior is strictly determined.* In most arguments about this point a deterministic assumption is contrasted with a doctrine of free will, and since the latter is then made to imply circumvention of natural law and ultimate chaos, determinism comes in an easy winner. There is of course nothing a scientist can do but assume order in nature. Conjoined with an anti-subjective metaphysics and an epistemology which deals solely with observable external events, however, the determinism of the Radical Behaviorist can have a seriously constrictive effect on scientific and clinical activity. If all events occurring in the life of any organism are determined by external events in the history of that organism, and if the present time is in principle no different from any future time, the destiny of the organism is really settled now and there is nothing he can do to change it. This is fatalism in its deadliest form, and it follows inescapably from a strict determinism which leaves the autonomous decisional capabilities of human beings out of account.

It is unfortunately impossible to settle the ontological issue of determinism in a fully decisive way. The subjective sense of autonomy (we all *feel* that we can decide what to do) is no guide. A sense of freedom and a sense of determinism may be equally illusory. Empirical evidence cannot solve the problem. The facts of influence are sure and compelling. Events of many kinds do influence human behavior in a very dependable way, so we are obviously functioning in a somewhat orderly universe. But empirical proof of total determinism would require perfect predictability and that has never been found in the human case.

The systematic position one adopts can only be vindicated pragmatically. Alternative assumptions may have alternative consequences, and these can be evaluated apart from the truth or falsity of the assumptions themselves. Viewed this way, the consequences of a strict determinism may not be the best ones we can manage in developing a powerful clinical technology. We must assume order and influence, but we may need to conceive of Man Deciding as well as Man Reacting, to conceive of autonomous processes in human beings which go beyond the press and tug of external influence, if we are to go as far as we can in dealing with disordered behavior. It may be exactly when man spurns the baubles of external reinforcement, when he willingly endures the pain of punishment, when he takes the basic responsibility for all he is and all he can become, that he fully emerges as a human being. At any rate, the pragmatic consequences of these assumptions are different from those of a strictly behavioral determinism. Skinner's *Walden Two* and Fromm's *Sane Society* are very different worlds.

The deterministic assumption of Radical Behaviorism is a necessary premise of the system. Indeed an assumption of order is necessary for any viable system. But coupled with the exclusion of internal psychological processes and with disdain for any hope that man can elect his own destiny, a narrow determinism may have very unfortunate effects.

Beyond this point, the systematic position of Radical Behaviorism consists wholly of preferences or opinions, not scientific dicta, not logical necessities. The fourth element in Radical Behaviorism is a *theoretical preference: Psychological science should be restricted to stimulus-response relationships.* Constructs relating to inner function are excluded. Only stimulus and response events and relationships between these are admissible. Thus objectivity and precision are gained, and according to the Behavioristic argument there are no real losses, since all legitimate constructs must ultimately be defined by reference to stimulus and response events anyway. It was suggested above, however, that constructs may have potent heuristic value. An idea of what is going on derived from observation of behavior may suggest that other things are going on, and these ideas, when tested, may turn out to be substantively correct. The ideas may never have emerged without the construction.

The principal dangers in positing constructs are those of cir-

cularity and reification. But both can be avoided if the constructs
are stated in such ways as to generate testable predictions and if
these in fact are tested. Cronbach and Meehl (1955) have written
persuasively to this point, and the works of Festinger (1957) and
Piaget (1954) offer two examples of systems in which inner mental
functions can be examined and understood in scientifically acceptable ways.

To be useful, statements about human behavior must always
move from discrete accounts of singular events to general propositions of some kind. Scientists and clinicians are always concerned
with classes of events and classes of conditions which determine
those events. The statements which result are probabilistic, not
declaratively certain, and this holds for classes of strictly observable
stimuli and responses as much as for covert events. There is no
escape from the uncertainty of generalized description and prediction. The only relevant question is a pragmatic one. Can useful behavioral propositions be arrived at more effectively and efficiently
by introducing mediating constructs or by omitting them? For the
kinds of events of concern in this book there is no clear answer at
the present time.

It is well to remember that the Behavioristic prohibition against
constructs is a theoretical preference and no more. It is an opinion,
not a law. It offers a gain in objectivity at the possible risk of less
than optimal generative power. The supposed gain in parsimony by
which Radical Behaviorists justify their position rarely accrues and
the tortured efforts to explain thought process in strict S-R terms
are usually ludicrous. There is little scientific profit in developing
a complex chain of S-R propositions to explain events which can
be much more simply accommodated by simple verbal inquiries
and sensible inference of central events.

The fifth element of Radical Behaviorism is a *methodological
preference: Scientific knowledge in psychology should be accumulated by the experimental analysis of behavior.* Response frequencies
are determined by stimulus events. The functional relationships
between these are examined by altering stimulus conditions systematically and observing the response changes which occur.

The clinical pertinence of experimental methodology is only
slowly being realized and once the full meaning of functional be-

havior analysis is grasped, the way to an extremely powerful technology is open. A major section of the following chapter on clinical procedure is designed to make this clear.

But again, the Behavioristic emphasis may be unnecessarily restrictive. The general methodological proposal stated above can take two specific forms: (a) the experimental analysis of behavior constitutes a scientifically acceptable method for introducing new substantive propositions in psychology, and (b) the experimental analysis of behavior is the *only* scientifically acceptable way of gaining confirmatory knowledge in psychology. The weak form of the proposition (a) is obviously acceptable; the strong form (b) should be questioned. To use an ancient but pertinent analogy, astronomy is not an experimental science but that does not remove it from the realm of science. The prime necessity is not for experimental definition of terms but for operational definition of terms. In psychology, observation of responses with no experimental manipulation whatsoever can be employed to gain useful information, and restriction of the discipline to experimentally manipulatable responses excludes from study all phenomena for which the effective stimulus manipulations are unethical, unknown, or otherwise inapplicable.

The experimental analysis of behavior is an exceedingly powerful method in psychology. But restriction to that method at the present time seems neither necessary nor desirable.

The sixth element of Radical Behaviorism is a statement of *logical preference: The organization of theories in psychology should be restricted to the formulation of functional relationships between stimulus and response events.* The resulting theory is an aggregation of laws, not an interrelated set of postulates. Many contemporary theories, especially most dynamic personality theories, seem to consist mainly of elaborate hypothetical relational structures among unconfirmable hypothetical entities. But there is a difference between noting and deploring this excess, and discouraging efforts to formulate the logical as well as empirical relationships among psychological concepts. Systematic interrelation of propositions, however difficult to accomplish and however unsystematic present formulations may be in this regard, still seems a legitimate and feasible goal, and this work may proceed before all the functional relationships are fully known and rigorously examined. Any relationships between concepts which can be stated should be stated if conceptual coherence is desired.

The logical, methodological, and theoretical preferences which guide Radical Behaviorism, like those which guide the present formulation, must ultimately stand or fall on empirical merit, not on *a priori* argument. To a clinician the ultimate test is pragmatic, and only history can provide it. There is no firm way to evaluate eventual utility now. The test is made by one means only, by developing conceptions and procedures along various lines, and seeing over the course of time which work best.

The Scope of a Useful Conceptual Framework

An adequate set of concepts for clinical assessment and treatment should accent behavior, but the internal psychological functioning of persons who behave need not be excluded, and some attempt may profitably be made to examine the behavior of individuals in relation to others and in context of the systems which form society.

A conceptual framework of the necessary scope has no business being Skinnerian—or Hullian, or Freudian or Frommian, or Lewinian or Heiderian, or Parsonian or Mertonian, or called by the name of anybody else. No one man has the vision to elaborate principles of the needed comprehensiveness. The basic concepts and principles are those of *behavioral science*, particularly those forms and aspects of behavioral science which are concerned with man in society.

An ostensive definition of the relevant theory can be given very simply. With one hand pick up a good introductory textbook in general psychology. With the other hand pick up a good introductory textbook in general sociology. Hold both books aloft and say, "Here are the concepts we need." Here also are the methods with all their range, and the logical rationale which places these sciences in relation to others, and the sciences in relation to other truth-seeking enterprises. We need no special *ad hoc* system. Let us use the science we have, continue to improve it, and try to grasp its pertinence to the problems before us.

So far, that grasp is very loose and light and takes in only a little of the whole. But some concepts and principles are now seen to have clear implications for clinical treatment, and hence for clinical assessment, and the immediately following sections represent one effort to select, define, and synthesize a set of concepts in behavioral science which appear particularly useful for clinical practice at the present time.

No single concept discussed below is necessary for the explanation of social behavior. Even the principle of reinforcement, which figures so large in most behavioral formulations, has its faults (such as circularity) and can be dispensed with, as Guthrie and others have shown. The concepts below are surely not sufficient to explain all behavior of interest to clinicians. They merely appear useful, and offer one plan within which still more useful theory building might sensibly proceed.

Three classes of phenomena will be analyzed. The first of these is the *action* of individuals. This has ordinarily been the province of individual psychology. The second class of phenomena is composed of the *interactions* of two or more individuals. Historically this has been the concern of social psychology. The third class of phenomena relates to the *organization* of social systems. This lies within the traditional realm of sociology. It is obvious that an attempt to consider individual psychology, social psychology, and sociology in the space of a single chapter will permit only the barest of conceptual frameworks to be erected. The fine theoretical details within each discipline will have to be omitted and only the most pertinent concepts and principles can be selected and put in place. But the clinical problems we face are as large as all behavioral science, and the theoretical basis for an adequate technology to deal with those problems must be equally comprehensive.

THE ANALYSIS OF ACTION

The unit of concern for individual behavior is the *act*. An act is a sequence of behavior which begins with an organism in a situation, proceeds over time to the occurrence of behavior on the part of the organism, and is followed by consequent changes in the situation, in the organism, or both. When relatively durable changes take place in the dispositional tendencies of the organism, *learning* has occurred.

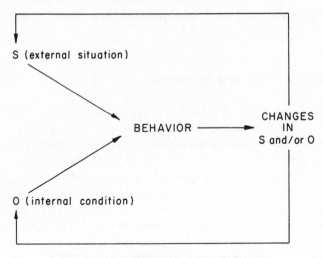

Figure 4.1. A model for individual action.

Acts are complex. The situation may involve a widely hetero-
geneous variety of social and nonsocial stimuli. Human organisms
reveal that many processes are in operation at the time behavior
is initiated and throughout the action involved. The consequences
may be primarily in the nature of a change in the environment
of the organism with little residual effect on the organism itself. Or
the organism may change considerably with no particular shift in
the situation. The effects of action may be immediate or remote,
and any action of sufficient importance to warrant clinical attention
is likely to have both short-term and long-term consequences. Some
of the effects of behavior may be evaluated favorably by the actor
and unfavorably by others, or different aspects of a single act may
be evaluated differentially by a single judge.

From this welter of describable events, however, it is possible
to abstract two general sets of concepts which are especially useful
in comprehending what goes on in human action, and appear to be
of particular importance in planning and generating clinically desirable changes. The first group of concepts revolves about the idea
of *reinforcement* and the psychological process complements of
reinforcement which have usually been subsumed under the general heading, *motivation*. The second group of concepts have to do

with *information* and the related psychological process complement, *cognition.*

Reinforcement and Motivation

If one principle of behavior is more important than any other for clinical treatment and assessment it is the well-known idea that behavior is affected by its consequences. The principle has of course taken many forms; Thorndike's law of effect, Hull's principle of reinforcement, Skinner's principles of operant conditioning, Freud's pleasure principle, etc. In a rather crude form suitable for present purposes, the principle may be stated as follows: *The probability that one response rather than another will occur in a given situation depends on the consequences of those responses on past occasions.*

It is useful to distinguish between two general classes of consequent stimuli, those which in the absence of any external constraint tend to be approached by the behaving organism, and those which tend to be avoided. Stimulus consequences of the first kind may be called *incentives,* and those of the second kind may be called *deterrents.* Incentives and deterrents can be manipulated in two basic ways, i.e., they can be presented or they can be withdrawn. The terms *reward* or *positive reinforcement* can be used interchangeably to designate the presentation of an incentive or the withdrawal of a deterrent, and the terms *punishment* or *negative reinforcement* can be used interchangeably to designate either the presentation of a deterrent or the withdrawal of an incentive. The resulting corollaries of the reinforcement principle then state that reward or positive reinforcement tends to increase the frequency of preceding response, and punishment or negative reinforcement tends to decrease the frequency of preceding response.

Such general principles need not presuppose that the effects of positive and negative reinforcement are simple mirror opposites; that the withdrawal of a deterrent and the presentation of an incentive will have perfectly symmetrical effects, or anything of the kind. One need only assume what the propositions say: response frequencies can be changed higher, or lower, by reward and punishment, respectively. Despite enormous complexities in nature and at least equal complexities in the literature on reinforcement, these principles are as nearly indisputable as any we have in the behavioral sciences.

Clinical application of the principles, however, may be a very difficult task. Application requires one to identify probably effective incentives and deterrents before they are used, and incentive values can differ widely from one person to another. To be sure, there may be some conditions which have universal and uniform effects. Deprivation of oxygen, for example, will likely have a deterrent effect on anybody's behavior, and its supply following deprivation will have a positively reinforcing effect. But it is clinically risky to go much beyond that. Efforts to locate a set of primary incentives and deterrents, whose effects are presumably native to the species and hence universal, have not been particularly successful. Even the use of food as a reinforcer has a severe clinical limitation since humanitarian considerations usually prohibit extremes of control, and since there are such broad individual differences in incentive value within the usually allowable limits of manipulation. The major clinical task in applying a reinforcement principle to behavior change usually lies in finding out what situational consequences can be employed as incentives and deterrents for a given individual, and in this task it is often heuristically profitable to try to figure out what the person wants. Sometimes it helps to ask him. We are led to consider individual motives as these are inferred from verbal reports and other behavior.

A motive may be conceived as an internal stimulus which is effective in the initiation of behavior. Justification for including the concept, aside from the heuristic quality noted above, lies in the obvious fact that behavior frequently varies in the presence of fixed incentive conditions. A person opens the door of a refrigerator one time but walks by it another. This behavioral difference, along with verbal reports, leads to an inference that the person was hungry one time and not the other. In case data inconsistencies arise or there is some doubt about the internal process, multiple operations must be developed and performed for confirming or disconfirming the inference. In the present case, the observations of door-opening behavior and verbal report could be supplemented by information about food deprivation (time since eating) and any measures of visceral events available technology might provide. In any case, one moves logically from observations of discrete events to less than certain general propositions. Justification of the latter is based on multiple operations. How many and what kinds of operations are needed will depend on such factors as the number and complexity of competing hypotheses, the degree of convergence in available evidence, and the cost of making an inaccurate inference.

Motives are frequently expressed as behavioral *intentions*. Persons not only want to engage in some form of behavior in reference to consequent events, but intend, if conditions permit, to do so. When the behavior actually occurs and the situational consequences follow, certain internal effects are experienced by human beings. They usually report feelings of satisfaction upon occurrence of a positive reinforcer and feelings of affective distress and dissatisfaction in consequence of negative reinforcement. Patients will often tell clinicians about these things and the information can be useful in defining the patterns of reinforcement which will be most effective in changing behavior.

Motives, in this conception, are viewed as internal complements of reinforcement. No deep and universal wellsprings of behavior are postulated. The latter are usually so deep no one can get at them and so universal all individual explanatory power is lost. No list of primary and secondary motives is drawn up to account for behavior. These are as variable and as useless as the earlier lists of instincts. One simply assumes that people want certain conditions to befall them and that they will in the usual case execute those actions which lead to desired outcomes. One clinical task is to specify the consequent conditions which matter and the related motives which are important for a given individual.

As a therapist, the clinician is also concerned with changing the motives and the reinforcing conditions which influence behavior. Sometimes the former (motives) can be changed by altering the latter (incentives and deterrents). In general, people want what they have a chance of getting. For example, a young American lawyer may want a new automobile. A laborer in Sicily may want a motorscooter. A vice president of Socony-Mobile may want to buy a yacht. If reinforcing opportunities were changed for any of them, their motives would probably change either way, stronger or weaker, depending on available incentives. There is reason to suppose, furthermore, that the peasant will work just as hard for the motorscooter as the executive for the yacht and their relative degrees of satisfaction will be equally profound when the goals are attained. Incentives and deterrents may not always be under clinical control, but when they are, it is usually easier to change motives by changing external reinforcing consequences than the other way around.

For human beings, social reinforcement often assumes powerful significance. The approval of others can have compelling importance as an incentive and as a positive reinforcer after behavior has occurred. Disapproval of others can be an extremely effective deterrent. This is probably related to the fact of prolonged total dependence in human development and to the constant association in civilized living between social stimuli and the satisfaction of other motives. However the relations are established, the actions of others—even purely gestural and verbal actions—can have very significant effects on behavior, and these are among the most effective reinforcers clinicians have at their command.

It is naive to assume, however, that the same people acting in the same ways will be equally and uniformly effective in modifying all behaviors on the part of all patients. The people who matter to one person may be of no account to another, and the particular social actions which have a strongly positive effect when offered by some people may be negative coming from another. To some delinquent boys, the lift of an eyebrow from a gang leader may be enough to instigate murder, while the sternest admonitions of a judge have no effect at all.

In human beings, verbal stimuli assume great importance as reinforcers. In the apparently simple case of threats and promises, words perform a signalling function. The parent who has regularly or intermittently followed such statements as, "If you don't stop annoying your sister you are going to get a spanking," with an actual spanking when the child continues the behavior, may eventually exert some control over the child's behavior by mere repetition of the verbal statement. The reinforcing effects to a college student of the words "You are going to get an A," are immediate and sometimes very strong, though the real benefits—survival in an academic program, securing a good job upon graduation, earning a high salary, attracting a sexually exciting wife—may be fairly distant and complex. A long history of higher order learning is involved in the establishment of reinforcing consequences of verbal stimuli, but there is no denying their effect in influencing behavior of human beings.

The clinical effectiveness of verbal reinforcers, however, is difficult to assay. Effects appear to depend on the characteristics of the person who delivers them, his relationship to the respondent, the way the words are spoken, and the circumstances under which they appear. It is unsafe for psychologists to assume that they can uniformly change behavior in favorable ways by saying "Good" and "Um-hmm."

The development of signalling and reinforcing effects for verbal stimuli, however, permits another human function to take place. This is the evaluation of behavior on the part of another or oneself. Over the course of time, most people develop a set of *ideals*. These consist of behavioral standards with associated evaluative labels and affective connotations. Congruence between a behavioral ideal and actual behavior tends to produce feelings of satisfaction and well-being. Recognition of severe discrepancy between ideals and behavior can be very unpleasant. This is a little more specific than concepts of congruence between the self and the ideal self as Rogers (1951) and others present it. We are speaking of correspondence or the lack of it between a specifiable behavioral standard and the actual behavior which occurs rather than about qualities of personality. The negative affect associated with incongruence is not necessarily inherent. It is probably related to a conditioning history in which failures to live up to ideals were negatively reinforced.

Ideals, as defined above, can have a potent motivating function. The concept helps make more comprehensible the personal suffering people sometimes endure in order to maintain a sense of self-respect. Although one cannot deny the extraordinary controlling force of direct primary pay-off, neither can one deny the urgent power of other people, verbal stimuli, and one's behavioral ideals in keeping human behavior human.

Information and Cognition

The clinical attempt to understand behavior may profitably include an effort to find out what the patient thinks about himself and the situation he is in, or more specifically to determine the covert hypotheses by which his behavior is guided. An effort to change behavior may proceed by instigating a change in these general beliefs and particular hypotheses through some change in the information the patient has at his disposal.

Many models have been designed to represent the way human beings act on sensory information. There are different ways of talking about the perception and interpretation of stimulus input. Many levels of organization or central processing have been posited, from purely automatic reflex action to the most abstract philosophical thought. Though less attention has been paid to output, there have also been different ways of conceptualizing expressive functions in the patterning of behavior. If one attempts to locate useful features of relevant models, however, it appears that most models specify at least the occurrence of some sort of *decoding* or interpretative operation as well as an *encoding* function of some kind. And most of the models distinguish between low level automatic action, such as reflex behavior, and high level cognitive behavior in the organization of data. Clinically, it appears that some actions occur under clear and definite cognitive control, while others reel off automatically, beyond the reportable awareness of the agent. If one can stipulate and apply a two-level system of this kind, many of the most urgent clinical problems will become soluble, however many levels may really exist. The diagram which appears as Figure 4.2 represents the essential features of a model which will do for present purposes.

Decoding involves the interpretation of data. At a fairly

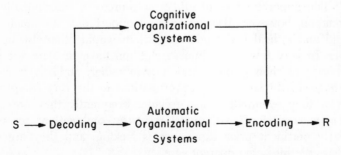

Figure 4.2.   A general model of information processing.

primitive level, this requires the detection of stimuli previously ignored, and discrimination among originally homogeneous stimuli. Generalization from one situation to another may occur. Organisms learn what is relevant and what is not, in coping with the situations which confront them.

In the usual laboratory situations where the phenomena have been studied, the stimuli involved are all external and are made as simple as possible for reasons of experimental control. The behaviors examined are typically unitary explicit responses such as disc-pecking and bar-pressing.

There is no reason to suppose that these principles suddenly become invalid when action is examined outside the laboratory. On the contrary, there is every reason to believe that the basic laws of generalization and discrimination, like the principles of reinforcement and motivation, are fully operative in the actions of clinical patients and in the day-to-day lives of all of us. But the analysis of action in nonlaboratory situations is a good deal more complex than in a Skinner-box, and it is important to realize this, without becoming so overwhelmed by the complexity as to take refuge in meaningless concepts.

In day-to-day living, the most strongly relevant discriminative cues are apt to be social, i.e., the actions of others. The lights in a pigeon-cage stay put. People keep changing. Other people get the discriminative functions of cues and the reinforcing properties of their reactive behavior badly entangled. They use words and gestures whose meanings are ambiguous to the person affected as well as the clinician. All this creates difficult problems for clinical assessment and for the modification of social behavior.

The important role of others as sources of discriminative information, however, also provides an opportunity for much more rapid and radical behavior change than would otherwise be possible. In very few years, human children have to learn the basic folkways of their culture, and it is extremely unlikely that they manage this by successive approximations to the very complex behavior they eventually must execute. Frequently they are called upon to come forth with novel response combinations for which clearly pertinent prior experience is lacking, and they are often able to do this with apparent ease.

As Bandura and Walters (1963) have pointed out, *social modeling* is a very useful concept to employ in characterizing the rapid acquisition of complex social response dispositions. When one child observes another behave in a certain way, he may immediately behave in the same way. Adults in all cultures show the young how to behave, and thus offer the complex discriminative information needed for rapid enculturation.

There is some question as to the theoretical status of modeling. Whether the phenomenon is merely a complex instance of responding to discriminative stimuli or requires new principles is open to dispute. But the pragmatic effectiveness of modeling in the modification of disordered behavior is well documented. The quickest and most effective way to get a patient to behave more adaptively may be to show him, by actual demonstration, the kinds of behavior required, and then to see that the new behavior is reinforced. Two of the major tasks of a clinical assessment procedure which takes cognizance of the difficulties as well as the opportunities of social cues are to determine what models are important in providing discriminative information to guide behavior, and to find what changes in present models or what new models might be provided as guides for more effective behavior.

Human beings also make good use of words, in the present language verbal discriminative cues. They not only show other people how to do things; they tell them. The general effectiveness of verbal instruction is assumed in the general Western educational system, and the value of verbal interchange is obviously acknowledged in psychotherapy. Indeed the clinical utility of verbal instruction in operant conditioning has recently been demonstrated by Teodoro Ayllon, who showed a moderate change in behavior under operant shaping procedures to accelerate abruptly into extreme behavior change when verbal instructions were used.

Verbal stimuli have many functions. They can serve to evaluate behavior and to reinforce its occurrence, as noted in the section above. Words can also *signal* the impending occurrence of any circumstance, and they can function simply to *label* objects or events, to describe what something is like or what is going on, with no obvious portent of good or evil to follow.

Once an individual has acquired verbal capability by the precept and tutelage of others and by his own practice, he can enact verbal behavior implicitly, and this ability forms an important basis for cognition. Words are not the only elements in thought processes. Visual, auditory, and other sensory images also seem to form a significant part of internal cognitive affairs, whether these can be adequately described or not. But verbal functions are easier to examine than most of the others, and play a very important role in the covert mental activity of civilized human beings.

In the usual action sequence, implicit cognitive stimuli can play a particularly significant part at the time a response is initiated, and form, along with the discriminative cues in the external stimulus situation, the basic informational guides to action. People will often discuss this, if careful inquiry is made to get them to describe in detail the events leading up to a behavioral occurrence. If asked what they were thinking about at the time behavior occurred and just before that, they sometimes can tell, and this can be clinically useful in planning a change in cognitive behavior for its own sake or as a mediator of some subsequent explicit behavior.

It is a mistake to assume, however, that thought always precedes motor action. Motor behavior is overt and accessible to direct visual observation. Cognitive behavior is covert and is not accessible to direct visual observation. Both are functional activities of the human organism, and may occur discretely, sequentially, or simultaneously. One may think without moving, and he may move without thinking. He may think before he moves, or he may move before he thinks. He may carry out some complex sequence of explicit behavior with thoughtful attention to every movement. Or he may engage in behavior automatically, while he is thinking about something else entirely. Covert and overt behaviors may occur in any order and combination whatsoever.

There appear to be some fairly stable and consistent individual differences in the extent to which people behave planfully (Kagan, 1965). At one extreme quasi-psychopathic people can be found who characteristically leap into action without much care in figuring out what they are going to do and with little apparent regard for the consequences of their behavior. At the other extreme one may observe people who spend most of their waking moments ruminating over past events and covertly rehearsing events in the future. Obsessive thinkers behave in this way, and so in a sense do many schizophrenic patients, though there would presumably be major differences between schizophrenic and obsessive patients in the degree of organization which characterized thought and in the extent to which the covert images and verbal stimuli corresponded to observable stimuli in the external world.

Either extreme may result in inappropriate behavior, and clinical treatment may take the form of making impulsive people more thoughtful or vice versa. In the context of the treatment and assessment orientation presently being defined, however, it would be more useful to identify and change specific relationships between covert and overt behavior than to attempt elevation or depression of a general trait of planfulness-impulsiveness. This requires the detailed analysis of particular action sequences, in their covert as well as overt aspects. If a patient typically engages in some behavior thoughtlessly, and then lives to regret it, it may be useful to persuade him to think more about that, whether he is generally impulsive or not. And conversely, if someone thinks so hard about his behavior in some particular setting that he never quite reaches the point of doing anything, it may be possible to get him to go ahead and act, without any general decrease in a ruminative trait of any kind.

Once we abandon the assumption that thought and overt behavior are necessarily related in any particular sequence, it is possible to conceive of action in which people cannot designate the external discriminative cues to which they are responding, or their motives, or the incentives to which they are oriented, as arising through a failure to acquire or to employ descriptive labels for the objects and events involved. There may, furthermore, be motivational influences which make appropriate sign-learning very difficult. This approaches a behavioral definition of unconscious motivation. Defining it this way does not imply that the unconscious motives can always be "brought under ego control" by the simple expedient of conveying verbal labels directly to the patient. The definition does suggest the need for carefully conducted multiple operations to make the best determination possible of both covert and overt aspects of disordered behavior, and for changing any facet of action necessary so that the patient knows what he is doing and behaves accordingly.

A good deal of clinical time and energy have gone into the assessment and improvement of insight on the part of patients.

Insight is usually presumed to mean self-knowledge of some kind, but as the term "insight" is actually operationalized in many mental hospitals, it means consensual agreement between patient and staff at a conference that the patient is "mentally ill." As the term is operationalized in many psychoanalytically oriented clinics, it actually means consensual agreement between analyst and analysand that the real reasons for the latter's problems lie in hitherto unconscious motives. In neither case does the generation of insight or its assessment seem to be a particularly useful clinical procedure. There is a sense, however, in which the examination of insight may be helpful. This is the extent to which the patient has accurate knowledge about the determinants of his behavior, both antecedent and consequent, both external and covert. This is more accessible to change and more significant than quantitative degree of insight. The objective for clinical assessment is to stipulate the specific knowledge a client has about specific behavioral regularities, especially those clinicians call disordered and may wish to alter.

There is also reason to examine the way individuals organize beliefs about themselves, the situations they enter, and the behavior which goes on there. As many theorists have noted, human beings tend to interrelate knowledge into systems of constructs, schemata, or cognitive structures. In general, the principles of organization appear to emphasize conceptual consistency (e.g., Lecky, 1945; Rogers, 1951; Festinger, 1957) and involve the establishment of ordinal relationships among concepts (Kelly, 1955). Some ideas, that is, are supraordinate to others, and a shift in the ordinal system can have far-reaching consequences for other ideas and for the explicit behavior related to those ideas. Thus a patient who initially thinks he has some symptoms of a mental illness may come to think of the symptoms as ways of avoiding responsibility. If this cognitive change occurs, significant aspects of overt behavior may change. If his therapist, for that matter, comes to think of the clinical task as one of assessing and modifying behavior rather than the treatment of illness, his own system of beliefs about clinical psychology and his own behavior as a clinician may shift considerably.

The most elementary principles underlying change in belief systems are only beginning to grow clear. For a considerable time prior to the twentieth century, man was regarded as a rational animal and his beliefs were presumed to depend upon reality and logic. With Schopenhauer and Herbart and of course with Freud, some relationships between ideas and motives were seen. The importance of human needs in determining the fantasies and other thoughts of men were recognized. Like any discovery, the importance of this one was probably exaggerated. Thoughts became the slaves of unconscious motives, and it was not until the ego psychologies were developed around the middle of the twentieth century that cognitive processes as such were again paid due regard in psychoanalytic theory.

Now behavior scientists are beginning to discern other relationships between cognition and motivation. Heider (1958), Osgood, et al. (1957), Festinger (1957), and others have emphasized the motivating effect generated by cognitive incongruity. In one formulation of the most relevant principle, incongruity between information coded and stored in the brain and information entering by way of receptors is posited to have motivating properties in and of itself. When the incongruity is too great, organisms tend to reduce it by cognitive operations, such as redefinition, or by explicit behavior such as withdrawal. When a situation offers too little incongruity, that is when input and stored information are too much alike, boredom results, and organisms tend to seek greater incongruity, or novelty, or stimulus change (Hunt, 1963).

The clinical implications of this principle have been implicitly recognized by many psychologists, but are only slowly coming into explicit formulation. One of the most effective ways of motivating human beings appears to be to introduce new stimuli which challenge their conceptions of themselves or the situations in which they are functioning, to create dissonance in their beliefs, and if some guidance and perhaps some reinforcement is offered, the altered beliefs and behaviors which result may be preferable to those which have been replaced. If this sort of thing is done as a treatment procedure, clinical assessment must be directed to the initial concepts covertly maintained by the individual and periodically displayed in overt behavior.

Difficult as such content is to study, clinicians may usefully seek to discover the basic beliefs each person holds about himself and his behavior, and about the world, especially the social world in which he is functioning. When that knowledge is fairly clear the process of challenge and change may begin.

THE STUDY OF INTERACTION

Consider now another class of situations, namely those in which people interact with one another. Interaction occurs whenever the action of each person in a situation reciprocally influences the action of one or more others. In the dyadic case, each member of a pair forms an essential part of the external stimulus situation for the other. In his motives and cognitive beliefs, each person takes the other, who has his own motives and beliefs, into account, and when action occurs there is a mutuality of effect. When relatively stable patterns of interaction develop between two individuals, a *relationship* has been formed.

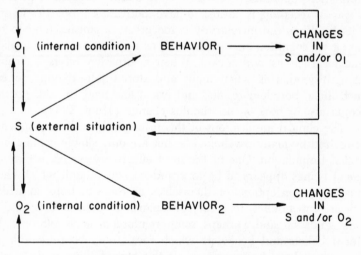

Figure 4.3. A model for dyadic interaction.

Concepts of interaction and relationship are useful for the same reasons social psychology has been useful in general social science. Groups of people interacting can be studied as emergent units. A different class of phenomena can be examined, and with this a new order of comprehension may result. Let us say an attractive young woman comes to see a clinician for psychotherapy. She expects and receives certain actions from him and he from her which define their relationship from the beginning as that of therapist-patient. Then one day she says, "You are a very warm person. I would like to know you better as a man." Suppose he says, "I'm getting a little tired of all this clinical stuff too. What say we go out and have a drink?" Be assured that their relationship has changed radically at that point. Anyone familiar with concepts of transference and counter-transference knows this, but in a behavioral view it is apparent that a sudden shift in incentive values, cognitive definitions, and conceivable actions has taken place. It is extremely important for therapists to have a perfect grasp of interactions like these, both to avoid interpersonal disasters and to foster relationships which are of maximum therapeutic benefit to patients.

It is the abruptness of change and the mutuality of stimuli and effect which make the concepts of interaction and relationship useful if not essential to understanding social behavior. There are dangers in the concepts, however, and ideas of a social-psychological kind need to be introduced with some care if maximum theoretical gain is to be realized.

One of the principal dangers in any interaction concept is that it may lead to neglect of main effects. If the behavior of patients in a mental hospital ward for instance, is under the direct aversive control of a sadistic aide, it may be silly to talk much about the relationships among patients. A second limitation is that interaction concepts may fail to specify the directions of effect. The aide, in the example above, has a great deal more to do with the destiny of patients than the other way around. A third major difficulty with interaction concepts in clinical use is that they may encourage the belief that labeling relationships is sufficient to help people. A clinician, after careful inquiry, may decide that the relationship between a mother and child is one of rejection-insecurity, but that is not very helpful unless an effort is made to change the interactional pattern somehow. An especially pernicious belief among some psychotherapists is that formation of a warm, accepting relationship is necessarily beneficial to patients, and that if a therapist can manage to be kind his responsibilities have been discharged.

The evidence which supposedly supports this view is not impressive, and it is theoretically more plausible to presume that therapeutic relationships should be accommodated to the particular needs of particular patients as these may change over time.

The way to avoid such pitfalls is simply not to ignore main effects, not to neglect the directions of effect in social behavior, not to rest in smug contentment when relationships have been named, and not to assume that general benevolence is necessary and sufficient to treatment gain. That is, psychologists have to study action too, and the study of interaction should complement rather than replace investigation of individual behavior.

If action is complex, interaction is naturally more so. In dyads, all the complexities of action analysis are multiplied by two, and as groups get larger the increase in complexity is exponential. The kinds of reinforcement people afford each other can be quite indirect. The kinds of cues they offer to guide social interchange can be extremely subtle and may involve aspects which are unlabeled and unrecognized by any of the people involved. Even in dyads, interaction may extend over long periods of time. The schematic diagram in Figure 4.3 suggests parallelism of behavior on the part of both persons represented. It looks as if analogous actions and reactions of both people take place at the same time. In rare cases, temporal simultaneity of this kind may occur, as when two people try at just the same moment to apologize for something that has happened. Such interactions are usually experienced as uncomfortable at first and if extended they are comical, but in any case they are rare. Most social intercourse proceeds by way of action-reaction sequences. Explicit behavior by O_1 serves as a stimulus to O_2, who reacts in some way. This either terminates the interchange or leads to a further reaction on the part of O_1 and perhaps to an action-reaction chain of indefinite length.

The unit of concern in interaction analysis is often referred to as a transaction, but other terms have been employed. Some sorting of the major concepts involved may help avoid unnecessary confusion. The term transaction has been used to denote both a particular unit of social behavior and a general epistemological framework within which these and other phenomena may be examined. In the latter usage, man-in-action is seen not as an entity operating outside an environment, nor even merely in an environment, but of and by the situation in which he, as a person, is an essential and integral constituent. This viewpoint has been defined and fostered by the philosophers Dewey and Bentley (1949) who trace it historically to the works of the physicist Clerk Maxwell, *circa* 1875. In more recent times, the general viewpoint has been influential in social psychology, particularly in the study of social perception (Kilpatrick, 1961), and has found expression in clinical extensions of social psychology (Berne, 1961, 1964; Pratt & Tooley, 1964). The present work is an effort to define some problems of clinical inquiry from the viewpoint of a modified transactional epistemology, without getting lost in ideas about the oneness of man and his universe.

As a noun, transaction denotes an interchange of social stimuli terminated by a mutual effect of some kind. More precisely, a transaction is a time-limited action-reaction sequence involving an exchange of social stimuli and leading to a mutual terminal effect. Thus *transactional viewpoint* refers to an epistemological position from which man can be studied as an active agent in and of a formative society, *interaction* refers to a class of social phenomena involving mutuality of stimulation and effect, and *transaction* as a noun refers to a unit of interaction terminated by a consummatory exchange.

Transactions and Games

In recent years a number of efforts have been made to examine clinically significant forms of social behavior from a transactional viewpoint. With numerous redefinitions, embellishments, elisions and other changes, one of these formulations (Berne, 1961, 1964) is discussed below in some detail, because it represents a very useful kind of conceptualization for the study of social behavior.

Human beings, according to this view, enter any social situation in a certain dispositional state. They are motivated toward given incentives, they have certain beliefs about the situation as they approach it, and certain patterns of explicit behavior tend to be related to the beliefs and motives. One enters the social situation in a certain state of mind. Each individual has a limited repertoire of dispositional states, and the states change from time to time, depending on individual motives and beliefs about the social situation.

The predominant states, in Berne's formulation, are those of the *adult*, of the *parent*, and of the *child*, and he believes that most transactional analyses can be conducted with no more extensive a list than that. Functionally considered, adult states are related to sensory data-processing and the rational solution of problems, parental states are related principally to social domination and critical evaluation, and the child-like state has mainly to do with the relatively spontaneous expression of individual motives and ideas. The conceptions are more than vaguely reminiscent of classical Freudian conceptions of ego, superego, and id, though there are some differences. In any case, it is the functional translation which matters and some of the functions of major concern are rational information-processing (adult), evaluation (parent), and direct behavioral expression (child).

There is nothing inherently good or bad about any state as such. Creative spontaneity is as necessary as executive control to personal well-being and social gain. Communication between one person and another, furthermore, will proceed smoothly as long as people do what is expected of them and get what they want, whatever the level of the transaction or the nature of the dispositional states involved. If both members of a dyad interact in expected, mutually satisfying and cognitively explicable ways, a *complementary* transaction is said to occur. If one person or another behaves in an unexpected or inappropriate way, the exchange is disrupted and the transaction is likely to culminate in something other than mutual gratification. In Berne's opinion, most of the interpersonal troubles in this world come about when an adult transactional stimulus emitted by one person (e.g., "Let's try to find out why you're drinking too much,") elicits a child-like response from the other (e.g., "You're always criticizing me"). This is one form of "crossed transaction," and adult interchange can go no further.

The clinical study of disordered transactions amounts largely to determination of the dispositional states of the participants and the way these change as the transaction proceeds. In terms of the action principles outlined in preceding sections, one needs to examine the critical motives, beliefs, and explicit behavioral expressions of each person, as these occur in action-reaction chains to the point of mutual consummation. There is no need, from the viewpoint of general behavior theory, to restrict consideration to the particular constellations Berne has identified, though if summary labels like adult, child, or parent happen to fit there is no reason not to use them.

The clinical study of disordered transactions may also be addressed to the games people play (Berne, 1964). This requires consideration of some intermediate concepts, particularly the idea of an *ulterior transaction*. Transactional stimuli often convey more messages than one. One is an *explicit,* mutually acknowledged, socially acceptable meaning. But there may also be an *implicit,* possibly unrecognized, less acceptable meaning. In the one-upmanship of a tea party someone may say, "That is a lovely hat—I had one a lot like it last year." In seduction games, "Let me show you my etchings," has become a trite paradigm for which the originally implicit meaning is now universally known.

Decoding implicit messages in transactional stimuli is an important task for clinicians, and the accuracy with which decoding is accomplished in general social intercourse is a major determinant of the effectiveness of interpersonal behavior. From the view of thought and action outlined in the previous section, where automatic behavior organizations are posited along with cognitive organizations, and where the essential independence of thought and action is assumed, it is clear that two-level and possibly multi-level transactions may occur with all possible degrees of awareness on the part of all the people concerned. Both parties in a dyadic ulterior transaction may be quite aware of what is going on. Cowboy: "Let me show you the barn." Visitor at the dude ranch: "I've loved barns ever since I was a little girl." Or maybe only one party is cognizant of the implicit meanings involved. Salesman: "This one is better, but I suppose you can't afford it." Customer: "I'll take it." In many clinical cases, transactional behavior takes place at a purely automatic level. I recall a marital pattern in which the wife would seduce her husband, criticize him as a clod all through the foreplay, and then laugh at the failure she helped determine. The husband in his turn would ask for rather elaborate dishes at mealtime and criticize his wife before the children when the meal fell short of his standards. Neither party, so far as I could tell, was very keenly alert to the meanings of the messages they were sending and receiving, nor the essentially damaging outcomes of their own behavior.

In one kind of ulterior transaction, the explicit and the implicit message contain incompatible behavioral demands on the person who receives the message. This is the double bind situation which Bateson, Jackson, et al. (1956) have identified as a common pattern in families of schizophrenics. Even if a person manages to decode a stimulus of that kind there is nothing he can do to suit the other partner in essential transactions. There is no way a fully complementary transaction can be carried out.

A *game*, in Berne's conception, is an ongoing series of ulterior transactions progressing to a well-defined predictable outcome. More colloquially, it is a series of maneuvers with a concealed motive. A game is thus distinct from a *ritual* (a stereotyped series of simple complementary transactions programmed by external social demands), a *pastime* (a semi-ritualistic simple complementary transaction, arranged around a single field of material), and a *procedure* (a series of simple, complementary, adult transactions directed toward problem solution). Many activities which are legitimated in our society as procedures turn out on closer study to be rituals or games.

A game in this sense need not be fun. Suicide, addiction, and war can be viewed as games. And the human capacity for inventing games appears to be limitless. Berne offers a titillating lexicon of some of the more common ones in Western society, such as *Kick me* (Transactional Stimulus, "Don't you dare kick me"; Transactional Response, "Of course I'll kick you"; Reaction, "Why did you do that?"), *Schlemiel* (Forgive me for being such a bumbling idiot), "If it weren't for you" (I could be successful, admired, etc.). Some of the games of major interest to clinicians are *Wooden leg* (Since this terrible crippling disability happened to me I am not responsible for my failures or my behavior), *Alcoholic* (a complex, usually five-handed game in which the alcoholic "child" is either begging or daring other people to stop him from drinking), *Suicide* (Now you'll be sorry), and for marriage counselors, *Frigid Wife* (Stimulus, "See if you can seduce me"; Response, "I'll try"; Reaction, "What a rotten lecher you are."). Anyone who spends much time in committee meetings should be familiar with the game "Why don't you? Yes, but," in which suggestions for action and the reasons for their unfeasibility circulate in endless rounds. And it might be profitable for any busy professional person with middle-class status aspirations to pay close personal attention to the game of "Harass," in which a person successfully makes his life so complicated and difficult that he cannot possibly accomplish anything others might criticize.

The clinical analysis of games is directed diagnostically to clarification of dispositional states and related behavior as these occur in transactional sequences. In treatment, one strives to approach game-free authenticity as closely as possible and it may be possible to do a good deal more than this, though work of the needed kind is only beginning. That is the experimental control of transactions, an extension of the procedures and principles of experimental social psychology to clinical behavior modification in groups, as discussed in the preceding chapter.

Recurrent Transactions and Relationships

Transactional sequences tend to become stabilized in time and become related to other transactions with the same individual. The constellation of stable transactions which take place in the association between two people defines the *relationship* between those people. Relationships can usually be grossly characterized by a hyphenated noun, with the terms on either side summarizing the dominant role of each participant. Thus we speak of parent-child relationships (not always between people who actually are parents and children), student-teacher relationships, husband-wife relationships, employer-employee relationships, lover-lover relationships, salesman-customer relationships, therapist-patient relationships, and so forth. A reciprocity of behavioral expectation and performance is assumed, and the social rights and duties of both participants may become very firmly fixed, as is clear when either person fails his obligations or assumes rights the other does not acknowledge.

The rights and obligations, in fact, are in the nature of *social contracts,* and some theorists (Pratt and Tooley, 1964) have suggested that the contracts to which any individual is party define his essential social identity. The investigation of behavior from this viewpoint requires study of the significant contracts a man has formed with others in his world. Clinicians should examine the agreements, explicit and otherwise, legal and otherwise, which define any person's rights and obligations to the people he deals with, and their rights and duties toward him. Treatment should be directed mainly toward renegotiation of the agreements which are troublesome to the person or the others in his world with him. A general change in the contracts of a social system may have far-reaching effects on social behavior in the system, and this provides one basis for linkage between the social psychological phenomena of interaction and the sociological phenomena of system organization.

Linkage in the other direction, between the concepts of social interaction and those of individual behavior, can be formed by defining interbehavioral abstractions in specifically behavioral terms. Whatever else it may be, behavior in social situations is still behavior. The principles which govern individual activity do not suddenly cease to operate in primary groups, and all abstractions drawn from classes of interbehavioral events must ultimately be definable by reference to behavior per se. The clinical study of relationships and the contracts which form the obligational basis of relationships requires the detailed investigation of transactions. The essential qualities of interpersonal relationships are abstracted from the facts of transactional behavior sequences. There is no way to divine directly the nature of the relationship between two people. One must examine by any means at his disposal what people *do* to each other in the give-and-take sequences of daily living. That is where the relationships are. That is where the contracts are broken or fulfilled. That is where the meaning of interactive social behavior resides. The phenomena of social interbehavior can be distinguished from the phenomena of individual action, but both must be behaviorally defined.

THE STUDY OF SOCIAL ORGANIZATION

A comprehensive theory of social behavior must deal not only with individual action and social interaction but with the sociological mechanisms by which behavior is collectively controlled. Even the skeletal conceptual framework presently being assembled may profitably include ideas relevant to social organization, if for no other reason than that changes of a cultural kind can be of much more general and lasting benefit than any individual treatment, however effective the latter may be. Over all, society influences the individual far more than any given individual influences society. If a benevolent cultural practice becomes traditionalized and organizational machinery becomes a genuine institution, people may come and go, generations may succeed one another, and the effects of the practice will continue until some other institution replaces the first one. Conversely, a cumbersome or pragmatically malevolent social institution will extend beyond the lives of any people in the system at a given time, and only evolution or revolution can change the organization and the effects it has.

A functional sociology of disordered behavior may begin with the conception of *disordered behavior* itself, as socially defined. To be crudely operational about that, one may designate the behavior under consideration by three criteria, namely statistical deviance, identifiability by social judgment, and changeworthiness. Any behavior likely to instigate a special control mechanism has to be different from the mode, hence a basic condition of deviance is essential to the definition. A crucial factor in instigating formal sociological control machinery, furthermore, appears to be a negative consensual judgment of the society and particularly of acknowledged experts in the field. Men in primitive societies inquire of witch doctors; we ask psychiatrists. The people in society who define deviant behavior as disordered also imply that it should be changed, and changeworthiness is the third component of the definition.

In fact, the severity and frequency of disordered behavior excite a *collective public concern* (cf. Rhodes, 1965). People demand that something be done, and this leads to *organized social action* to deal with the problem. Figure 4.4 shows these concepts schematically, and indicates in addition the loci of action for most of the major forms of control systems modern society has developed to cope with disordered behavior.

One solution to the problem of disordered behavior is simply to lock the patients up in isolated mental hospitals, give them custodial care, and wait for medical science to find a cure for mental disease. This is pretty much what has been done in Western

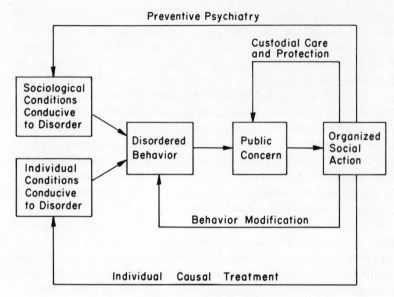

Figure 4.4.   A model of social action for the control of
disordered behavior.

society for the past century, and from the short range viewpoint of the larger nondeviant society it is not a bad solution to the problem. Social protection is assured, lots of jobs are made available to the economy, immediate financial costs are fairly low, maybe the patients aren't treated too badly, and the people outside can console themselves with the belief that they and medical science are doing the best they can for the mentally ill. Figure 4.4 indicates that the major sociological effect of custodial care and protection in the traditional mental hospital system is to assuage public concern over disordered behavior. It has not really done much to change the behavior itself or to help the patients who display the behavior.

Until recently, the only other large scale organized system for dealing directly with disordered behavior was the exercise of individual psychological treatment, usually psychotherapy of some kind. The experts who have organized therapeutic practices, training systems, and all the rest it takes to form a culture usually have justified their professional existence by proposing that psychotherapy was directed to the dynamics, the causes of the behavior, and hence could offer a relevance to the real problems at hand and a permanence of change other treatment systems could not provide. Action was, and of course still is, focused on the individual determinants of disorder.

Recently preventive psychiatry has burgeoned to deal with the sociological conditions which foster disordered behavior. The most critical determinative influences are seen in anomie, poverty, early cultural deprivation, unemployment, social disorganization, and the other conditions which make our society less than great. Basic prevention of behavior disorders, to say nothing of such problems as crime and delinquency which are not always defined as disorders, are seen to lie in the general social community, and as the flaws of social function are corrected, so will the problems of disorder be resolved.

One other social action is indicated in Figure 4.4. This is the development of mechanisms for the relatively direct modification of behavior. Systems are established in schools, clinics and other centers for behavioral re-education. Professionals engaged in this enterprise are not predominantly concerned with palliating public concern, nor are they primarily moved to alter the presumed determinants of symptoms. They try by all available means to modify changeworthy behavior for the better, and they do this as directly and effectively as possible.

The sociological study of disordered behavior requires introduction of the concept of the *social system*. From a functional viewpoint, *a social system is an organization of personnel and practices designed to accomplish a collective purpose.* The personnel in the system generally share a set of assumptions or beliefs about the nature of the task they are attempting to deal with, and the procedures which are instituted for accomplishing collective purposes are very closely related to these assumptions. Thus mental hospitals are organized about the belief that mental illness is a disease, and the mechanisms established to cope with mental illness are generally consistent with that belief. In the history of procedures for dealing with disordered behavior, operational practices have always been rooted in the basic conception of disorder prevalent at the time. A person displaying hallucinatory behavior in 14th century Leipzig was apt to be identified as one of Satan's legion and burned at the stake. Today he might be put in a mental hospital and given drugs and psychotherapy in hope that that will cure him. The cultural assumptions underlying procedures in social systems may not always be explicit and they may not always be correct, but they form critical guidelines for major characteristics of operational procedure and go a long way toward determining the organizational structure of the system itself.

The organizational structure of a system is partly defined by the characteristics and interrelations of the *positions* which personnel in the system occupy. Positions are specified primarily by statement of the central functions occupants are expected to perform, and by the rights and duties related to the performance of function. The behavior patterns associated with positional expectations are called *roles*. Most social systems are also characterized by an authority structure of some kind, a status hierarchy usually correlated with authority, a communication system which specifies the channels through which information is to be passed, and an incentive-sanction system by which role conformity is enforced.

It is sometimes said that any social system has a life of its own. This sentence has many implications, some of which are sufficiently vague to be useless and some of which are probably incorrect. But some of the implications appear both true and illuminating, and it may be useful to identify these meanings to avoid both uncritical acceptance of inappropriate surplus meanings and overgeneralized rejection of useful concepts.

The major implications of the proposition are that systems have certain organic qualities, like individual organisms, that the components of the system function interdependently, and that social systems operate in a conservative self-maintaining way to preserve the identity and stability of the system.

There is little advantage in generalized attribution of the qualities of living individual organisms to social systems. This is analogy, and like most analogies leads to a spurious sense of comprehension derived from inappropriate surplus meanings. Propositions concerning universal subsystem interdependence—propositions which assert that anything happening anywhere in the system will affect all other components of the system—are factually untrue. It is, of course, semantically possible to reserve use of the term "system" for those organizations in which the condition of total component interdependence is met, but in complex systems many changes can take place in one sector without any visible effect on function in other sectors, and it is still useful to speak of the whole as a system.

There is a sense, however, in which propositions about systems having lives of their own appear to be appropriate and informative. These statements refer to the relative permanence which social systems tend to exhibit. In general, social systems are much more durable than are individual action tendencies or interactional expectations. A culture is established either from the beginning, when a new system is formed, or gradually over the course of time. This is transmitted from one generation to the next, and formal procedures for the education of new members are sometimes written into the charter of the system itself. The acculturation of newcomers is basically accomplished by rewarding conformity and punishing deviance. Positive and negative sanctions are imposed to encourage members to respect positional bounds and faithfully to enact the role behaviors required for smooth organizational operation. Social systems are therefore inherently conservative, and any effort toward change is likely to meet resistance of some kind.

It is possible to stipulate creativeness and change-directed action in defining some positions in certain systems. Thus many industrial firms explicitly reward inventiveness on the part of workers in research and development, and psychology professors are esteemed for new ideas and procedures. It is also possible to establish a self-evaluating subsystem within any organization, so that changes may proceed from an orderly base of information. But most of this is secondary to some more central function which demands conformity, and most of the encouragement for change is directed outside the system itself. Professors in the sciences, for example, are expected to be creative, innovative, inventive, and desirous of continual change *in the subject matter of their science.* But let any of them try to change the academic culture in which they themselves are situated, let them try to change incentive values or the criteria according to which professors are evaluated, and they will soon discover how rigid academia can be.

With disordered behavior defined as broadly as it is here and in general usage, the social problem presented by disordered behavior is bound to be enormous. The social systems which have evolved to cope with disordered behavior are therefore numerous, diverse, and complex. Because disordered behavior often runs athwart the law, the legal-correctional systems of our society are necessarily and intimately involved. Because all children in our society go to school, and because deviant disruptive behavior there is inimical to the basic function of the school, the educational system is involved. Special class mechanisms, counseling and guidance operations, psychological personnel services of many kinds are now being instituted plentifully in the educational system, with heavy support from the political-governmental system, which is also enmeshed in the problem of behavior disorders by way of funding operations, administrative control of high level positions, and in many other ways. The psychological problems of men may have a moral and spiritual side, and the religious systems of our society are involved. Social welfare agencies continue to flower, new institutions are invented it seems every week, and when none of the professional systems work, people form their own. Thus Alcoholics Anonymous and Synanon emerge when professionals fail to deal with alcoholism and drug addiction.

Over all, then, the social systems involved in the control and remediation of disordered behavior constitute a very large network of interrelated agencies and operations. The complexity of this network is considerable, and for reasons of comprehensibility the discussion will be focused on one system, namely the medical hospital-clinic system which is the predominant sociological mechanism for dealing with disordered behavior in Western society at the present time. Let us analyze that system briefly, within the theoretical framework outlined above. The framework, as has been stated above, contains as essential conceptual elements the functional *purposes* of the system, a set of operational *procedures* for accomplishing those purposes, an *organizational structure* within which the procedures are carried out, including definition of positions and roles of personnel, where operational functions, authority relations and communication rules define major aspects of the various positions, and the basic *cultural assumptions* on which the whole system rests.

The mental health systems of our society have two major purposes, custody and treatment. The larger society is protected from the actions of the mentally ill, and the mentally ill are protected from damaging themselves. In hospitals and clinics, treatment is given to cure or at least alleviate the illness.

In discussing the purposes which guide a social system, however, it is important to remember that the purposes exist only on the part of people in the system and in the larger society the system is designed to accommodate. And then it is important to ask whose purposes are being served, for many people are involved and their needs may not always be identical or even complementary. Is it mainly the patients whose purposes are served in a mental hospital? Or is it the aides, or the physicians, or the political office incumbents of a state which requires patronage positions for its own maintenance? Is it possible that incompetent but prestigious medical figures have joined in a gigantic but dimly recognized and publicly unacknowledged collusion with the larger society to control deviants and care for misfits in a way which cannot possibly benefit the patients they lock within the walls? Or do the patients all want to get well? For which of them is the major purpose of hospitalization the attainment of a tolerably comfortable existence where no one sets unattainable requirements for competence in living, and the meals are regular and the wards are warm enough? Within the broad bounds of protection and treatment the many purposes of many people have to be considered, and a comprehensive sociology of mental health must explore them all. In addition to accurate identification of purposes, the very legitimacy of the purposes can be examined ethically, logically, and empirically, and the need for this kind of scrutiny is becoming increasingly clear.

Most of the procedures in present mental health agencies are officially defined as treatment operations of one kind or another. Playing volleyball in a hospital is called recreational therapy. Outside it is no more than a pleasant diversion. Tubs and packs are called hydrotherapy, though their functional use may be more in the nature of an aversive device for behavior control than an instrumentality for cure. If protection and custody are legitimate purposes for a mental health system, as well they may be, then restrictive measures may have a place in operating procedure, but neither the methods nor the purposes they are designed to serve should be misstated and confused.

In addition to the basic procedures for remediation and control, a superstructure of bureaucratic procedures is usually developed to facilitate accomplishment of the fundamental aims of the institution. At least that is the initial goal. But as time goes on and Parkinson's First Law inexorably proceeds, the expanding bureaucracy may usurp primacy of function. Under these circumstances, procedures in mental hospitals may be designed to maintain and enhance personnel offices and business management to the neglect of the patients. People in the system at all levels may devote more of their time to writing reports and attending committee meetings than they give to helping the people they are hired to treat, while the patients sit idly around with occasional breaks for meals and bedtime.

The organizational structure of most mental hospitals and mental hygiene clinics is hierarchical as to administrative authority and communication. That is, the ultimate responsibility for treatment decisions rests with the people in upper administrative echelons, actions proposed by people at any level can be vetoed by anyone higher in the system, and messages conveying essential information are expected to go through the proper channels. At all levels of the structure, but particularly at lower levels, a microdivision of labor prevails, and the rights and duties which define various positions, and hence role behavior, are quite finely drawn. Psychotherapy belongs to the doctors, lately the psychologists, and maybe the social workers. Woe betide the nurse who tries it. And woe to the activity therapist who tries to perform a nursing function, for the lines of responsibility may be very closely drawn and very jealously guarded. For their part, patients are usually expected to be docile and cooperative. Trouble is to be avoided at any cost. In general, patients are expected to adopt the values of the professional and subprofessional staff as closely as possible, though since they are mental patients, wide eccentricities of behavior are expected.

The basic assumption supporting the organizational structures, defining the functional procedures, and legitimating the basic purposes of present mental hospitals and mental hygiene clinics is that behavior disorders are forms of illness. The error of this assumption has been discussed in detail elsewhere (Szasz, 1961). The assumption is strongly rejected in the present formulation. But that does not lessen the importance of the assumption in defining social practices. The collective actions and institutional systems evolved to deal with the problem of disordered behavior are rooted in pervasive cultural beliefs. We need to examine present assumptions very closely. And we need to examine the assumptions designed to replace present beliefs with equal care or we may only trade futility and hypocrisy for chaos.

UNITY AND DIVERSITY IN BEHAVIOR THEORY

The conceptual framework outlined above contains terms of many kinds and at many so-called levels of organization. Both implicit and explicit individual actions are included. Time-limited transactions and the recurrent transactional patterns which define relationships are considered. Ideas related to sociological organization are also considered. Presuming some merit in unity, questions arise about relationships among concepts. These questions are not easy to answer, and some of the most common answers are not easy to defend.

An attempt is often made to reduce the concepts at one level to those of another. This practice is associated with a pyramidal model of science, which in the limited segment of concern for social behavior usually places individual behavioral psychology at the bottom, interactional social psychology above that, and sociology at the top. It is ordinarily proposed that the laws comprehending behavior at one level plus appropriate principles of organization will ultimately explain the phenomena at the next higher level.

Of course satisfactory reductions never appear. However much is known of molecular physiology, molar behavior must still be analyzed, and however clearly individual behavior may be understood, new concepts are needed to describe and explain behavior in groups. I think the failure to generate effective reductionistic explanations of social behavior lies in the basic unsuitability of the pyramid analogy to the relationships among social sciences. The concept of levels has been misleading, and it ought to be replaced by the notion of *classes of phenomena*, each of interest in its own right, each deserving distinct conceptualization, but each related to the others by way of empirical interactions and by a basic unity of method.

In studying individual action, one may be concerned with such covert events as experience of anxiety and cognitive disorganization, as well as overt behavior. Individual action, as defined in a preceding section, constitutes a class of phenomena. In the study of interaction one examines another class of events in which two or more people exert reciprocal influences on one another. If the investigator, clinical or otherwise, fails to observe people interacting, he may never know what the people are doing to each other, and the relationships between people will escape him. In studying social systems one needs to watch institutions operate over time in reference to the social functions they are supposed to perform, and observation of one individual or any unorganized collection of individuals is insufficient. This is a third class of phenomena, and the proper understanding of sociological phenomena requires that they be viewed sociologically. Perhaps no further emphasis is needed. The historical survival and current prosperity of individual psychology, social psychology, and sociology augurs a favorable future for them all and suggests a complementary rather than a competitive relationship among them.

To disavow reductionism, however, is not to deny a need for specification and it is in this latter regard that so many abstract conceptualizations, particularly at the higher levels, fail. All concepts, at any level, of any phenomenal class, must be operationally definable, and in the case of the behavioral sciences, must be defined by reference to specific behavior itself. Thus the organizational concept of the communication system must ultimately be defined by (not reduced to) statements concerning who-says-what-to-whom-under-what-conditions-to-produce-what-effect. Until that is done, the communication system is a paper concept and of no use in science or practice. The concept of position must be defined in terms of the behavioral expectations one set of people have for another set of people, and the laws of role conformity must be defined by stipulating the behavioral actions people in a group exert toward one another or toward other groups to encourage conformity. Position and role are powerful abstractions. They deserve a place in behavior theory and are particularly useful in sociological concepts of organizational structure. But they must be given full behavioral specification for their use to go beyond filling pages in theoretical books.

If behavioral specification is demanded of all concepts referent to all classes of phenomena, the relationships among concepts may slowly grow clear and a comprehensive understanding of social behavior may begin to develop. Consider such a concept as authority which may be applied with minor formal modifications to individual, social, and sociological phenomena alike. A clinician may find a patient, for instance a foreman in an industrial plant, to be authoritarian in his treatment of crew members. If the clinician wants to say what that means, he must obtain detailed behavioral information regarding actions of the man in reference to those about him. Additional study may show that some employees have sought this particular supervisor out and have established some mutually gratifying if interpersonally difficult relationships with him. Defining such relationships also requires behavioral specification, but once the specification has been made and transactional regularities are clear, new light may be cast on the individual authoritarian behavior of the foreman. From still another view, the authority structure of the industrial organization itself may be of interest. Problems of this kind may be very common in the plant. Knowing that and determining what the authority structure is may illuminate the individual behavior of the foreman as well as the relationships which form between foreman and crew; but determining what the authority structure is and redefining, in any conceivable way, a sociological position in reference to authority must be accomplished by reference to behavior.

In a comprehensive theory of social behavior there is a place for diverse concepts referring to different classes of phenomena, but they all must be operationally definable for acceptance in science and they all must be behaviorally specifiable for inclusion in behavior science. The necessary specification, however, is itself a difficult problem. One must provide a set of operations by which theoretical concepts may be defined and clinically useful information may be obtained.

The next chapter is concerned with directions, problems, and some accomplishments in developing the needed clinical-scientific procedures.

5

Methods for Studying
Social Behavior

Once treatment strategies have been defined for the modification of behavior and a conceptual framework has been outlined for
the understanding of behavior, assessment procedures must be developed for the clear description of behavior in relation to the
conditions which influence it. If the definitions of treatment and
theory proposed in the preceding two chapters are provisionally
acceptable, clinical procedures must be formed within the traditions
and according to the rules of behavioral science. And if this is done,
the so-called clinical method is entirely deprived of special status
as a mode of inquiry.

As clinical methods are sometimes defined, a number of distinctive features are alleged to set them off from the observational
and experimental procedures on which general behavioral science
is based. In a typical formulation (Garfield, 1963), the following
basic and unique characteristics are noted. First, clinical methods
are said to rely on the observations of the clinicians to a degree and
perhaps in a way other methods do not. The clinician is supposed
to be especially sensitive to the behavior of his patients, to have a
good third ear (Reik, 1949) or third eye (Meehl, 1960), and with
these extrasensory advantages to detect signals other less acute
observers might miss. Second, the clinical method is marked by the
extent to which the clinician's own personality: his abilities, skills,

perceptual tendencies, motivational dispositions, etc., play a part in the observations which are made and the formulations which result from observation. Third, the clinical method is distinguished by its flexibility. The clinician may proceed in any direction he chooses and follow any line of inquiry which seems appropriate in his efforts to understand his clients. A fourth distinctive characteristic of the clinical method is its emphasis on individual uniqueness. Only secondarily is the clinician concerned with general nomothetic relationships. His primary task is to understand each person as an individual. Related to the idiographic viewpoint in clinical study is a fifth characteristic, that is, emphasis on holistic conceptions of personality. An effort is made to understand the individual in his totality, and Gestalt concepts of homeostatic balance and global interdependence of part-functions are usually assumed. Closely related to this feature is the sixth and final hallmark of the clinical method, that is, reference to dynamic concepts in explaining overt behavior. Free association, dream analysis, and projective methods have emerged as special clinical procedures designed to uncover the hidden motives which presumably lie beneath the surface of disordered behavior.

Affirmation of value for behavioral science is already quite emphatic in this book. Little would be gained by another tedious discussion of the shortcomings of present clinical procedures and the virtues of science. But there is nothing very special about clinical methods, where clinical procedures deviate widely from the general methods of behavioral science they tend to be bad procedures, and the utilities of such absolutely fundamental scientific methods as experimentation have been very inadequately realized in clinical assessment practice to date. These comments are extended below as a general basis for the procedural suggestions to follow.

Consider first the proposition that clinicians either have or need to develop special sensitivity in order to accomplish the task of clinical assessment. Aside from some engaging anecdotes, there is no evidence to support the idea that professional clinicians are more sensitive to the nuances and shadings of human behavior than anyone else. The few pertinent studies which exist have yielded equivocal or contrary results. In one of the earliest investigations of this problem, Hanks (1936) found no relationship between training in psychology and the ability to predict answers to inventory questions from biographical and other data. Estes (1938) found psychologists to be significantly poorer than a wide variety of other judges in assessing personality characteristics from expressive behavior. Luft (1950) compared the ability of clinicians (social workers, psychiatrists, and clinical psychologists), graduate psychology students, and students in the physical sciences to predict the responses of subjects to various test stimuli. The physical science students came out at the top of the distribution. Kelly and Fiske (1951) found no difference between mature staff clinicians and clinical trainees in accuracy of assessing promise in clinical psychology. There are some ambiguous results, but Taft (1955), who conducted a general review of the literature on the ability to judge people, concluded that physical scientists and other nonpsychologists appeared superior to psychologists in this regard.

There is also reason to be skeptical about efforts to enhance general clinical sensitivity by special programs of instruction. Though some evidence supports the contention that ability to make certain specific kinds of behavioral judgments can be improved by training (see Taft, 1955), there is no proof that the sessions in sensitivity training which have become so popular lately affect general sensitivity in the way and to the degree needed for improved clinical effectiveness. The required documentary data would have to show that individuals who had undergone specified training experiences could detect and react appropriately to stimuli which before were ignored or misinterpreted, and that this ability extended to a general class of novel situations beyond the training condition itself. So far as I know, such data are not to be found, though I suspect any group experiences as intense as some of the sensitivity training experiences are said to be may well have lasting effects on something.

There appears to be little or no evidence that special courses, professional training or prolonged clinical experience improve sensitivity. In the course of professional training and experience people naturally learn some facts, conceptions, and technical *modi operandi* which they did not have at the start of training. They will therefore be alert to some relationships and forms of behavior that an untutored layman might ignore. That is what clinical training is all about. But that is not what some people mean by clinical sensitivity. The idea that clinicians have or can develop some special kinds of antennae with which they can detect otherwise subliminal interpersonal stimuli and read from these the intrapsychic condition of another person is a myth which ought to be demolished.

The second allegedly distinctive feature of the clinical method is the extent to which the clinician's personality influences observations of and formulations about the person under study. If personality means what it often means to clinicians, i.e., the constellation of dispositional characteristics (perceptual tendencies, motives, traits) which characterize the unique individual, then it would seem that every available effort should be made to eliminate the role of the clinician in observing and explaining the behavior of another, for all the clinician's eccentricities can possibly contribute to the final output is noise of his own creation.

If the influence of the clinician's personality in the assessment operation consists only of an examiner effect on client behavior in clinical diagnosis, then this must simply be accepted as a fact of life. The previously cited studies of examiner influence on test performance are clear about that. Given the fact, two courses are open for improving clinical inquiry. We must try either to minimize clinician variance by getting all clinicians to behave alike or we must try to take examiner influence into systematic account in developing assessment strategies. The former course is probably unavailable to us for the practical reason that it is impossible to get all clinicians to act just alike and because the desirable flexibility of clinical assessment might be lost in any thoroughgoing effort to standardize clinician influence. A more profitable and feasible course would appear to lie in the systematic study of the clinician himself as an instrument of inquiry. There has been a lot of talk about this without much accomplishment because most of the efforts have been on the wrong track. Exhortations to study the clinician often end with the declarative statement that the clinician is (and should be) a participant observer in and of the situation he is examining. Where to go from there has not been clear. Efforts to study relationships between the professional participants' personality traits and various characteristics of the diagnostic output are doomed to failure for the same reasons traditional personality appraisal has failed in clinical assessment generally. A much more profitable approach, in keeping with the principal message of this work, might be found in a focus of attention on the behavior of the clinician, and the experimental study of changes in clinician behavior on the behavior of clients. If we can begin to determine what clinicians do to the persons they examine and what the effects of the action are we may begin to move beyond the vague truth that examiner and client affect each other in all their interchanges to more definite knowledge of relationships between clinician and client behavior.

This would permit retention of the third distinctive feature of the clinical method, one which appears to offer some genuine and important advantages over other forms of investigation, that is, flexibility. It is factually the case that not all the decisions which have to be made in clinical assessment can be made at the time the inquiry begins. Sequential contingencies arise, and information gained at one point may influence the choice of assessment procedures at a later point. It is both the curse and the blessing of clinical study that it is ordinarily conducted as a stochastic process. The decisions are usually made informally on the basis of highly fallible principles and very uncertain instantiative knowledge, but only by allowing the clinician to make such choices can the gains of richer understanding be obtained.

At this point in our professional evolution, and perhaps indefinitely, it seems advantageous to retain the flexibility of clinical inquiry, but it is important to distinguish flexibility from aimlessness and idiosyncrasy. The clinician does not have license to proceed in any direction he chooses, especially if choice is determined by his own personality (cf. Garfield, 1963). The intuitive pursuit of clinical hunches is not a satisfactory general rationale for clinical assessment. The kind of clinical skill which needs to be taught might be construed more accurately as a form of tracking behavior, in which progressive inquiries are conducted in sensitive reference to the condition of the patient and the information which has been accumulated about him at any given time. This kind of behavior cannot be totally preplanned, but it can be programmed in a way intuitions cannot.

The fourth distinctive feature of clinical methodology, and the most important one to many writers on the subject, is focus of study on the individual case rather than on group trends of any kind. Clinical assessment is said to be idiographically rather than nomothetically oriented. This is undoubtedly true—most useful clinical decisions do require idiographic formulation—but clinical methods are not therefore set off as separate or different from the methods of general behavioral science.

Suppose the clinician is called upon to develop an educational program for a twenty-three-year-old colored man who appears to have some fairly strong mechanical skills but who lost two fingers in an industrial accident some time ago. Let us say the client is married and has two children. He has a history of enrolling in a number of training programs but dropping out before training is completed, and there is reason to suppose that this is related to some dependent trends on his part, or maybe to some reinforcement contingencies, for whenever he is out of work his wife and the Government manage to provide the necessary financial support for the family.

The clinical study of such a person will ordinarily involve some instruments developed on large populations, and general behavior principles apply as much to his behavior as to that of any man. But using this information in clinical assessment, counseling, and remedial effort is another matter. From the viewpoint of the person making the choice and of the clinician helping guide the choice, the problem is one of relating multiple forms of possible action to multiple opportunities, taking the multiple characteristics of both person and situation into account. The clinician and the man he is trying to help are not asking "How likely is Person X to succeed in Training Condition A?" The question is "Of all the $A, B, C, \ldots n$ training opportunities available to X, who displays k characteristics, which offers the best chance of success?" Success, furthermore, is complexly defined. Most counselors and clients are not only concerned with such simple parameters as work proficiency, but with such matters as prestige and job satisfaction.

Given this complexity, the nominal identification of relevant variables, to say nothing of their assessment and combination in a predictive statement, is exceedingly difficult. The research literature most likely does not carry any studies on the success, consequent to diverse training experiences of twenty-three-year-old, eight-fingered, colored, mechanically adept, married fathers with possible dependent inclinations and a history of educational dropouts. Even the flood of research with which our journals are now being engulfed will never provide the necessary information for every conceivable clinical problem. This is so in principle, not only in fact. There is no real alternative to idiographic study.

Clinical needs for individualized formulation, however, do not exclude clinical methods from the realm of science, and they offer no excuse for careless procedure or loose thinking. As Ebbinghaus and Skinner have shown, the functional study of a single organism can be rigorous. Scientific status is conferred upon a method by its dependability and the accuracy of predictions made through its use, not by the number of cases employed in establishing norms. As Allport (1937) proposed some time ago and as Mischel (1964) has recently affirmed, there is nothing logically or methodologically objectionable about the idiographic study of persons. As Tyler (1959) has suggested, we need a workable psychology of individuality, and there is no need in this development to forsake the rules of science. As Kelly (1955) and Renner (1965) have urged, there is need for an experimental approach to idiographic formulation. The study of an individual should lead to testable propositions about that individual, and these should then be tested in the evolution of a partially confirmed reformulation, which generates another set of testable propositions, *ad infinitum*. The population of events in the kind of idiographic formulation proposed here will consist of functional relationships between disordered behavior and determinative influences both inside and outside the organism. The basic requirements of science will be met if these relationships are described in testable form, and the accuracy of the formulation is then examined by experimental changes or converging observations free of manipulative interference. Useful clinical methods need to be idiographic, but they need not therefore be unscientific.

The other allegedly distinctive properties of the clinical method are not at all necessarily components of clinical investigation. One of these obfuscating irrelevancies is the assumption of holistic conceptions of personality on the part of clinical psychologists, and the belief that this is the only way in which people can be fully understood.

"Only from a holistic point of view, from seeing the individual as a totality, can one fully understand his behavior, his motivation and his conflicts. Worthwhile predictions for the individual can ensue only when one attains this understanding" (Garfield, 1963,

p. 486). That is absolute nonsense. No clinician ever knows another person totally. What kinds of conceptions lead to the most worthwhile predictions is of course a matter for careful test, not pontifical declaration.

Dynamic conceptions of personality, which are often mentioned as the only proper theoretical basis for a truly clinical method of studying human beings, have already been discussed in detail. It might further be noted here, however, that the relation of observed phenomena to psychodynamic theory in clinical practice is historically comprehensible and statistically common, but not logically necessary.

In summary, clinical methods need have no special properties beyond those of sound procedure in behavioral science. Individuals must be studied individually and clinical inquiry must ordinarily proceed in a flexible way. But no special sensitivities are required of the clinician, his personality should not contaminate the data any more than necessary, and resultant formulations need not be stated in the theoretical terms of psychoanalysis or Gestalt psychology.

PROCEDURES FOR GATHERING CLINICAL DATA

The basic methods of science are observation and experimentation. Instead of relying on the mythical sensitivity and errant personality of the clinician, let us exploit the methods of science more fully, enriching them as the necessities of human problems demand by verbal inquiry as a means of eliciting clinically important behavior. We need not convert clinicians into machines to do this. There is still need for all the creative intelligence and all the interpersonal skill any man can muster if he is to do the unified work of clinical assessment and treatment well.

The suggestions to follow identify observation, interview, and experiment as the most promising methods now available for clinical inquiry. Some comments will be made about the role of tests in clinical assessment. Throughout, emphasis will be placed on individual action. No special procedures will be proposed for examining group interactions and social systems. The investigator must still watch, and inquire, and test his ideas, whatever the classes of phenomena with which he may be concerned.

Observation

A completely omniscient view of a person's behavior would have to be drawn from total notation by an undetected observer of all covert as well as overt activity in all settings over the lifetime of the individual under study. The closest available approximation to such a Godlike accomplishment is probably to be found in the behavioral ecology studies of Barker and his colleagues (Barker & Wright, 1955). Observing behavior in the natural settings of a small midwestern town, these investigators discovered over 200 behavior settings which one might enter and some 1,200,000 objects with which one might have commerce. The numbers of distinguishable acts or behavioral episodes were equally enormous. They pursued one little girl from the time she got up until she went to bed, and found that she used 571 different objects, a new one every 1.6 minutes on the average, and engaged in a total of 969 behavior-environment episodes over the course of the day (Barker, Schoggen & Barker, 1955). Even then there was no record of covert behavior, and some people think these are the most important events of all in the life of a person.

The sheer abundance of human behavior is overwhelming, quite apart from its complexity. Some basis for reducing and simplifying behavioral data is essential. Persons themselves, of course, simplify their lives by entering only a limited number of available settings and exercising only a restricted set of potentially available behaviors (Tyler, 1959). The child mentioned above, for example, used only 571 of the 1,200,000 objects in the town and the actions which actually occurred probably represented a considerable curtailment of her total available behavior repertory. But even this restriction leaves a hopelessly unmanageable remainder for the clinician. Gross abstraction, massive simplification, merciless exclusion of some classes of behavior, and very narrow focus on the phenomena which matter most appear necessary if comprehensibility is ever to be attained and helpful clinical action is ever to be initiated. It is impossible, for practical reasons if for no others, to know any patient in his totality for so much as a single day. Any attempt to understand him totally over his lifetime is absolutely absurd.

To clinicians, the most obvious starting point for observational scrutiny is the symptomatology of patients, and a number of checklists and rating schedules have been developed to facilitate observations of this kind (e.g., Lorr, *et al.*, 1963; Wittenborn, 1955; Peterson, 1961). Scale content is usually derived from the clinical lore on symptomology or from empirically frequent symptoms. The ratings are usually made by nonclinicians in close and extensive contact with subjects, data are typically factor analyzed somewhere along the line, and the basic record which is developed for each patient is a profile of scores on the resulting factors.

Observations recorded on such symptom schedules offer an advantage over the usual kind of psychiatric office diagnosis in providing decently reliable information about behavior of clear clinical importance and stating this in dimensional rather than typological terms. The utility of such procedures, however, is severely limited. This is not so much a consequence of faulty instrumentation as of basic limits in dimensional trait concepts of all kinds and in the lack of relationship between observed behavior and the circumstances surrounding its occurrence. The unique symptomology of the individual may be lost in the general trait system, and no clear direction is given for changing anything that matters.

The initial focus for clinical observation clearly falls upon the unique *problem behavior* of each patient and the *situations* in which the problem behavior occurs. The goal in such an inquiry is a *functional analysis of behavior* in a sense very close to that originally intended by Skinner, related specifically to problem behavior defined either by the patient or someone passing social judgment upon him. Skinner's first statement of the relevant definition appeared in his *Behavior of Organisms* (1938), but a more direct statement appears in *Science and Human Behavior* (1953), from which the following is quoted:

The external variables of which behavior is a function provides for what may be called a causal or functional analysis. We undertake to predict and control the behavior of the individual organism. This is our "dependent variable"—the effect for which we are trying to find the cause. Our "independent variables"—the causes of behavior—are the external conditions of which behavior is a function. Relations between the two—the "cause and effect relationships" in behavior—are the laws of science. A synthesis of those laws expressed in quantitative terms yields a comprehensive picture of the organism as a behaving system. (Skinner, 1953, p. 35)

Precise stipulation of the effects (behavioral symptoms) and causes (external antecedents and consequences) in clinical situations is a highly diversified affair, and it has remained for others to extend Skinner's general rationale to the problems of disordered behavior. Many attempts have been made along these lines (see Krasner & Ullmann, 1965; Ullmann & Krasner, 1965), and it will be neither profitable nor necessary to go into all of them here. It may be useful, however, to summarize a report which places major emphasis on the observational-experimental analysis of behavior (Bijou, 1965) to show what some of the details of a functional assessment procedure look like.

A six-year-old boy was brought to a clinic by his mother to see if something could be done about his overdemanding behavior. The mother was told about the plans for gathering and analyzing data and accompanied her son to a playroom where she was asked to play with him the way she would if she were at home. Two observers monitored activity in the room by means of a microphone and one-way glass, and recorded all of the child's behavior, verbal and nonverbal, and all of the mother's behavior, verbal and nonverbal, occurring immediately following the child's behavior. Data collected over two sessions were classified as deviant or normal, with deviance defined by the mother's complaint. In this case, commanding behavior, "Now let's play checkers!" "You go over there and I'll stay here!" was designated as deviant. Behaviors incompatible with the deviant behaviors, in this case cooperative actions, were considered normal. Data on the mother's reactions to the child's problem behavior were also classified and analyzed to provide information about the kinds of social reinforcers the mother used.

Two more sessions were then held in which the mother was again instructed to play with her child as she would at home. The observers now recorded only three classes of behavior—cooperative and commanding behavior for the child, and the response of the mother to either of these. Recording was done in five-second intervals on an appropriate checklist, and the resulting data provided a measure of the frequency of occurrence of the two critical forms of child behavior and the frequency with which the mother responded to them. Data were plotted on two separate cumulative curves, one showing the frequency of commanding behavior followed by mother's response, and the other showing the frequency of cooperative behavior followed by a response from the mother. The rate of the function for commanding behavior was much greater than that for cooperative behavior.

At this point an experimental measure was introduced both by way of treatment and to test the hypothesis that the mother's reactions were reinforcing and hence maintaining her child's overdemanding behavior. There is further discussion about this in the section on experimental assessment procedures below, but to document the essential unity between observation and experiment the rest of Bijou's operation is described here.

During the next two sessions, lasting 20 minutes each, the mother was instructed to ignore her child completely except on signal from the investigator. A flashing red light visible only to the mother was used as a cue, and the mother was told to respond to her child in any way that seemed natural, except that she had to limit herself to one statement or action each time the light was on. The investigator turned on the light whenever cooperative behavior was displayed by the child. When commanding behavior was emitted, the light was turned off. This signalled the mother to ignore her child and hence deny him social reinforcement. Under these conditions, the rate of commanding behaviors decreased and the rate of cooperative behaviors increased over the original baseline values.

As a further test, the experimenter then asked the mother to revert to the behavior she had shown during the baseline phase. In the following two 20-minute sessions a marked increase in commanding behavior occurred and cooperative behavior sharply declined. This was followed by a return to the treatment condition under which commanding behavior was ignored and cooperative behavior was reinforced. In the sessions that followed, efforts were made to teach the mother more refined perceptual discriminations between the two classes of behavior, thus reducing her dependence on the investigator and allocating control of the child's behavior to her.

Variants of this general procedure have been described by Ayllon (1965), Ferster (1965), Staats (1965), Patterson (1965), and others. The central features of the method are (1) systematic observation of the problem behavior to obtain a response frequency baseline, (2) systematic observation of the stimulus conditions following and/or preceding the behavior, with special concern for antecedent discriminative cues and consequent reinforcers, (3) experimental manipulation of a condition which seems functionally, hence causally, related to the problem behavior, and (4) further observation to record any changes in behavior which may occur.

The power of functional analysis in the clinical study of disordered behavior is only beginning to be realized, and it seems highly desirable to extend the rationale and procedure as far as it will go. In most clinical settings, however, and in dealing with any but the simplest clinical problems, direct systematic observation has serious limitations. The behaviors of fundamental concern may be either so infrequent or inaccessible (e.g., sexual impotence, criminal behavior) they cannot be observed in the laboratory or under the quasi-laboratory conditions of the clinic or hospital. Some of the most important events may already have happened and hence be unavailable to observation in principle. Others, such as a possible suicide attempt, may be in the future. Furthermore, as was emphasized earlier, the most important symptomatic behavior from a clinical viewpoint may be highly specific to the circumstances under which it occurs, and the situation may not be reproducible in the assessment setting. These difficulties call for naturalistic observation; but this may raise problems of a different kind, frequently by way of exerting observer influence, altering the real life occurrences in crucial ways, and thus introducing a genuine epistemological indeterminancy. A partial solution to some of the problems may be found in persuading the clients themselves to keep systematic records of their own behavior. A mother can record frequencies of her child's behavior as well as her own reaction to it, a teacher may find time to note occurrences of aberrant actions if they are sufficiently troublesome to her, a nurse may tabulate frequencies of psychotic behavior on a ward, a husband and wife may keep records of the interbehaviors of one another if it means enough to them to do so. But observations of all kinds, systematic and naturalistic, direct and indirect, have their drawbacks and need to be complemented by other methods.

Interview Procedures

In addition to observation, the procedural standby of most clinicians is the interview. As Sundberg and Tyler (1962) have said, "In trying to learn about the behavior of other persons . . . we either 'ask 'em' or 'watch 'em' " (p. 102). The ways clinicians do the asking, however, differ widely. A completely discrete polarity seems to exist between dynamically oriented, existentially inclined interviewers and traditional psychiatric examiners. Existentialists emphasize the relationships which allegedly develop in the encounter between each person and the other, the need to let the patient define the direction the interchange takes, and the unstructured nature of the clinical transaction. Traditional psychiatric interviews are not too popular any more. Those who still complete mental status outlines of a classical kind tend to conduct interviews much as an internist would examine for any other disease, that is by means of a straightforward, highly structured, often rather brusquely delivered series of questions. The patient's answers are recorded, and from these the nature of his illness is inferred.

We need alternatives to these procedures, and some of the more useful alternatives should not just offer a middle course between the extremes briefly caricatured above. More than compromise is needed because the problem goes beyond the degree of structure in interview procedure. Three basic facets of clinical interviewing need to be considered, namely the *form* of the interview, with emphasis on the issue of structure, the *content* of the interview, and the interpersonal *relationship* within which the verbal inquiry proceeds. In the course of the following discussion, some ways are suggested in which the interview might be developed as a scientifically respectable, clinically useful method without turning it into either a cold-blooded, question-and-answer game or a sentimental orgy.

Forms of clinical interview. Most of the early attempts to define procedures for psychiatric interviewing (Henderson & Gillespie, 1946; Noyes & Haydon, 1940; Preu, 1943) were founded on Kraepelinian and Meyerian concepts of mental illness, and recommended quite systematic coverage of history and contemporary mental status. By as uniform a procedure as possible, the examiner was to elicit anamnestic information about social and personal history, and in the examination of the patient, sensorium and intellect, mental content, emotional tone, thought process, and other components of the mental status were to be evaluated by standard question-and-answer procedures. Little heed was given to the relationship between doctor and patient beyond recommending that some attention be devoted to putting the patient at ease, the content was such as to imply a descriptive psychiatric diagnosis, and fairly rigid formal structure was maintained throughout.

Under the impact of psychoanalysis and in reaction to the attitudinal condescension frequently associated with this kind of "psychological thumping" (Menninger, 1952), some writers have proposed complete abandonment of outlines, guides, and structure-defining props of all kinds. To these clinicians, the psychiatric interview is in its essential nature a human encounter and the task of the interviewer is to foster the growth of that encounter as creatively as he can to encourage spontaneous unfolding of the patient's inner being and the relationship between participants. The free associative interviews of existentially oriented psychoanalysts and the client-centered interviews of Carl Rogers (1951) epitomize this view, though of course Rogers has expressly disavowed a diagnostic aim for his procedures.

Most writers position themselves somewhere between the extremes. Indeed it is difficult to conceive of a completely unstructured interview, and one that becomes a rigid exchange of questions and responses ceases to be an interview. Since the early days of alienistic psychiatry, it has ordinarily been assumed that deposition tends to yield more complete but less accurate information than narration, and conversely that the relatively spontaneous narrative account offers an advantage of validity at the expense of the uniform completeness which can be gained from an oral questionnaire.

The relationships between interview structure and the kinds of information gained from interviews needs systematic study—like nearly everything else we have been talking about. At the present time we do not know just how structured clinical interviews should be. Nor, for that matter, is the central question one of optimal structure, but a more diversified and qualified question, namely, what degree of structure has what effect on what characteristics of the information· gained by means of interview procedures? It is likely that different degrees of content preselection and procedural specification are appropriate to the accomplishment of different aims in clinical assessment. We will never know until we move beyond statements of opinion (like this one) to systematic research.

A fairly strong rational case can be made, however, for an intermediate degree of structure in most clinical interviewing. If total client spontaneity is allowed, it is difficult to see how an interview strategy can be defined, taught, used, tested and improved at all. If rigid interview structure is imposed, the most important features of the clinical problems may be overlooked and the clinician may leave the interview secure in the knowledge that he has covered the predefined schedule, but totally ignorant of everything that matters to the client. It seems reasonable that the advantages of flexibility can be gained at minimal sacrifice in clarity and strategic uniformity by conducting *guided* interviews of some kind, though it must be re-emphasized that the seeming reasonableness of a general course of clinical action is a fairly weak basis for proposing it.

Content of clinical interviews. If any structure is imposed at all, if the interviewer is to guide the exchange in some way, the basis for guiding needs to be specified, and this must be done by reference to content rather than form. That is, certain kinds of information must be sought. If the client does not volunteer the information it has to be elicited in some way, and some kind of substantive outline must be stipulated.

I once took the trouble to review representative literature on content for interviewing in psychiatry, clinical psychology and social work. I collated the material in nine outlines and found rather strong consensus on some of the kinds of data included. Three kinds of information, namely identifying data such as age, sex, marital status, the presenting problem, and family history were included in all nine of the outlines I considered. One kind of data, on physical health and illness, was to be sought in six of the inquiry forms. The remaining items which were included in three or more of the outlines are shown in the accompanying table.

COMMON CONTENT IN NINE INTERVIEW SCHEDULES

Kind of Information	Frequency of Inclusion
Identifying data	9
Presenting problem	9
Family history	9
Medical history	6
History of physical (mainly motor) development	5
History of sexual development	5
History of personality development	5
Social relationships with others	5
Educational history	4
Occupational history	4
Marital history	4
Major conflicts	4
Major defenses and controls	4
Emotional dispositions	4
Self concept	4
Cognitive and intellectual dispositions	3
Stream of thought	3
Thought content	3
Memory	3
Present life situation	3
Values and moral tendencies	3

Many clinical investigators thus appear to ask about the same things, but from the present veiwpoint the consensus which has evolved is beside the point. Interview content appears to be guided by a somewhat muddled mixture of wishes to find out (a) what disease the patient has and (b) what the person is like, all around, in his holistic totality. The first goal is inappropriate and the second is unattainable. If the most important clinical information to get about a person is that which defines the problem behavior he is displaying and the conditions which influence the behavior, then a radical shift in emphasis is required. Much more detailed information about the presenting problem is needed. One needs to determine specifically what the person is doing, in the general sense of doing which includes cognitive and motivational-emotional behavior as well as explicit motor activity. And one needs to examine in fine detail the antecedent, concurrent, and consequent conditions under which the disordered changeworthy behavior occurs. In the framework of social learning theory, the environmental conditions of dominant concern are the actions and reactions of other people; but study of these needs to go beyond vague, behaviorally unspecified statements of relationships which hold between the client and those who matter to him. One must find out not only what the patient does to and with others, but what they do to and with him, and infer relationships secondarily, as suggested in the preceding chapter, from recurrent patterns of interpersonal transaction.

If a serious effort is made to study social behavior in a diversity of situations, the needed inquiry can be long and arduous. The interview strategy immediately extends beyond the client himself. Others, in many or all of the situations where disordered behavior occurs, are also examined, in part as informants who can provide independent data about the client's behavior, but not only as informants. In one aspect, the significant others who are studied in a thorough behavioral inquiry are examined directly to determine their own action tendencies, including the beliefs, behavioral expectations, and motives they may have in reference to the client. Frequently, as with parents of disturbed or disturbing children, the most important treatment changes a clinician can effect will be with some other person rather than with the client himself. Since this is the case, the others may require careful study in their own right.

Clinical behavioral inquiry by means of interview is no quick and simple matter. Finding out what people are doing to each other with any degree of accuracy can be a very difficult, time-consuming job. Given the usual practical constraints of the professional situation, this implies that many of the kinds of data typically collected in clinical inquiry, accounts of motor development, psychosexual development, and the like, will simply have to be ignored, and it will remain for appropriate research to show whether any loss results. I am willing to guess that we can dispense with three-fourths of the material that is usually covered by social workers, psychiatrists and psychologists in their interviews with no loss whatever to the patient. Only rarely do the conventional data have anything to do with treatment, and we can do just as well without them.

Systematic inquiry about disordered behavior and the situations in which it arises can be an extremely exhaustive and lengthy affair, even if the inquiry is limited to strictly observable explicit behavioral events. In behavioristic writings, the exclusion of covert activity is usually justified by considerations of parsimony. But it is important to note that the parsimony which results from strict attention to observable stimulus and response events is conceptual rather than procedural. The gain in clinical efficiency which results from restriction to overt S-R events may be negligible or nonexistent. In studying clinical problems we are more often dealing with *reportable* behavior than with *observable* behavior. The reportable behavior of concern may be overt or covert—it doesn't matter—the only data available are reports. In the economic calculus of clinical procedure, one may gain treatment-relevant information more efficiently by direct inquiry regarding covert events ("What were you thinking about when you did that? How did you feel?") than by exclusive concern for S's and R's. Indeed the kinds of treatment proposed above, and the kinds of theory related to treatment are stated as if this were the case. But there is no more point in pressing this opinion than in pressing a radical behavioristic opinion. From a pragmatic view of clinical assessment, what goes into a guided interview schedule and what comes out must ultimately be decided by data rather than logic.

The interview strategy which some of us have been employing at the University of Illinois begins with a *scanning* operation. This is a very straightforward inquiry of the client and referring informants about the nature of the problem behavior and the circumstances which precede and follow it. This is followed by an *extended inquiry* which includes a more detailed and individualized study of the client and others most centrally involved, as well as an extension of the scope of the inquiry by interviewing other people whose significance has been noted in the initial scanning. The procedure is not unlike the Sullivanian reconnaissance and detailed inquiry (Sullivan, 1954) except that substantive focus is much more finely drawn to the problem behavior of the patient and the conditions under which the behavior occurs, systematic interviews are conducted directly with the significant others involved as well as with the patient himself, and the interview operation is embedded in a more general observational-experimental assessment procedure. The third phase of the interview sequence *per se* consists of *periodic reappraisal* following introduction of treatment measures. The same basic questions which were asked initially to find out what the problem behavior was, are asked again in slightly modified form to determine the amount and direction of any changes which may have occurred. From the knowledge thus obtained, a revised conception of the functional relationships between situation and behavior may be entailed, new independent variables (treatment measures) may be introduced, and another later descriptive appraisal may then be required. The exigencies of clinical demand usually dampen hopes for the inquiry beyond termination of the case, but as treatment becomes more and more a matter of programming significant others to act and react differently to the client, the need for a fourth phase of inquiry, namely *follow-up study*, becomes increasingly clear.

The basic content of one possible guided interview outline is given below. Whatever the limitations of this particular form, it focuses directly and immediately on the problems of concern, and on the functional determinants of problem behavior, as these are defined by the various people to whom the client's behavior matters. It thus provides a framework for the scanning operation with which behaviorally oriented clinical study begins.

A. Definition of problem behavior
   1. Nature of the problem as defined by client
      As I understand it, you came here because . . . (discuss reasons for contact as stated by referral agency or other source of information).
      I would like you to tell me more about this. What is the problem as you see it? (Probe as needed to determine client's view of his own problem behavior, i.e., what he is doing, or failing to do, which he or somebody else defines as a problem.)
   2. Severity of the problem
      a. *How serious a problem is this as far as you are concerned?* (Probe to determine perceived severity of problem.)
      b. *How often do you . . .* (exhibit problem behavior if a disorder of commission, or have occasion to exhibit desired behavior if a problem of omission. The goal is to obtain information regarding frequency of response.)
   3. Generality of the problem
      a. Duration
      How long has this been going on?

    b. Extent
    Where does the problem usually come up? (Probe to deter-
    mine situations in which problem behavior occurs, e.g., Do you
    feel that way at work? How about at home?)

B. Determinants of Problem Behavior
    1. Conditions which intensify problem behavior
      Now I want you to think about the times when . . . (the prob-
      lem) *is worst. What sort of things are going on then?*
    2. Conditions which alleviate problem behavior
      What about the times when . . . (the problem) *gets better?*
      What sorts of things are going on then?
    3. Perceived origins
      What do you think is causing . . . (the problem)?
    4. Specific antecedents
      Think back to the last time . . . (the problem occurred). *What
      was going on at that time?*
      As needed:
      a. Social influences
        Were any other people around? Who? What were they doing?
      b. Personal influences
        What were you thinking about at the time? How did you feel?
    5. Specific consequences
      What happened after . . . (the problem behavior occurred)?
      As needed:
      a. Social consequences
        What did . . . (significant others identified above) *do?*
      b. Personal consequences
        How did that make you feel?
    6. Suggested changes
      You have thought a lot about . . . (the problem). *What do you
      think might be done to . . .* (improve the situation)?
    7. Suggested leads for further inquiry
      *What else do you think I should find out about to help you with
      this problem?*

Analogous interviews are then conducted with the other people
who appear to influence or to be influenced by the client's problem
behavior. With each informant obvious modifications of wording are
required and some of the elements of content may have to be
changed. We are stuck with a need for clinical judgment. But the
basic focus is sustained. In all cases, with everyone interviewed,
the goal of clinical inquiry is to obtain two fundamental kinds of

information, namely what the problem is, and what causes it. The fact that the patient did not walk until he was two, or that his grandfather was a drunkard, or that he wanted to play the piccolo when he was in high school, or that he had a dream about flying the night before, may be interesting, but there is no way to tell beforehand which, if any, of these classes of information will be important. We all *know* the problem behavior the person displays is important. It is the clinician's task to find out what that behavior is and to determine the functional influences, antecedent and consequent, internal and external, which determine the behavior. If the search leads to revulsion toward a sodden grandparent or basic sexual conflicts of some kind, then he must proceed in that direction. But if he has spent all his clinical time inquiring after dreams and abstract interpersonal relationships without ever finding out what the problem is, without every inquiring what might be done to change it, he has failed to obtain the most important knowledge of all.

Interpersonal relationships in clinical interviewing. The nature of the transaction which occurs as a clinical interview, and the relationship which is formed and sustained between interviewer and client during the period of clinical assessment, are of utmost importance in determining the amount and quality of information gained. Maybe I should have mentioned this first, before talking about form and content, because the relationship between interviewer and client may be of greater significance than any other factor in identifying the distinctive properties of the interview and establishing the power of the method as a data-gathering procedure. It is this which confers a unique advantage upon the interview as a method of inquiry. The other obvious advantage is flexibility, but one can assume that on-line computers will continue to grow more sophisticated with the passing years, and that many intermediate procedural decisions may eventually be made by machine. Machines do not smile much, however, and they do not care at all. Fortunately or unfortunately, no computer is able to offer clients intelligent interest in their welfare, and a sense of this interest on the part of the client probably has much to do with the extent and the accuracy of the information he provides. It is this, more than anything else, which distinguishes the interview from questionnaires and other mechanical means of getting information.

In order to define the kind of relationship most strongly conducive to obtaining ample and honest reports from others, however, the caricatures begun earlier in discussing polarities of interview structure should be extended further. In regard now to the interpersonal relationship between client and interviewer, recommended transactional characteristics seem to range all the way from the brusque interrogations of psychiatric internists to the mystical harmonies of analytic existentialists. Since the people who talk most about relationships tend toward the second extreme, most should be said about that, after which the interview relationship which seems appropriate to the task of clinical assessment will be defined.

A vivid statement of the kind of relationship many clinicians recommend has been offered by Carl Rogers in his article "Persons or Science" (Rogers, 1955), where he tried to delineate the apparently incompatible interpersonal relationships which evolve in psychotherapy and in scientific research.

I launch myself into the therapeutic relationship having a hypothesis, or a faith, that my liking, my confidence, and my understanding of the other person's inner world, will lead to a significant process of becoming. I enter the relationship not as a scientist, not as a physician who can accurately diagnose and cure, but as a person, entering into a personal relationship. Insofar as I see him only as an object, the client will tend to become only an object. . . . I let myself go into the immediacy of the relationship where it is my total organism which takes over and is sensitive to the relationship, not simply my consciousness. I am not consciously responding in a planful or analytic way, but simply in an unreflective way to the other individual, my reaction being based (but not consciously) on my total organismic sensitivity to this other person. I live the relationship on this basis.

The essence of some of the deepest parts of therapy seems to be a unity of experiencing. The client is freely able to experience his feeling in its complete intensity, as a "pure culture," without having it bounded by knowledge of contradictory feelings; and I am able with equal freedom to experience my understanding of this feeling, without any conscious thought about it, without any apprehension or concern as to where this will lead, without any type of diagnostic or analytic thinking, without any cognitive or emotional barriers to a complete "letting go" in understanding. When there is this complete unity, singleness, fullness of experiencing in the relationship, then it acquires the "out-of-this-world" quality which many therapists have remarked upon, a sort of trance-like feeling in the relationship from which both the client and I emerge at the end of the hour, as if from a deep well or tunnel. In these moments there is, to borrow Buber's phrase, a real "I-Thou" relationship, a timeless living in the experience which is *between* the client and me. It is at the opposite pole from seeing the client, or myself, as an object. It is the height of personal subjectivity. (Rogers, 1955, pp. 267–268)

Rogers was talking about therapy and he was not necessarily recommending this particular form of therapeutic relationship as an ideal. But Rogers has provided an especially well written statement of a clinical position regarding relationships, and there is much talk among humanists about the merits of this kind of relationship for all clinical transactions.

The following is a prototypic statement by Buber:

TO MAN THE WORLD IS TWOFOLD, in accordance with his twofold attitude.

The attitude of man is twofold, in accordance with the twofold nature of the primary words which he speaks.

The primary words are not isolated words, but combined words.

The one primary word is the combination *I-Thou.*

The other primary word is the combination *I-It;* wherein, without a change in the primary word, one of the words *He* and *She* can replace *It.*

Hence the *I* of man is also twofold.

For the *I* of the primary word *I-Thou* is a different *I* from that of the primary word *I-It.*

THE LIFE OF HUMAN BEINGS is not passed in the sphere of transitive verbs alone. It does not exist in virtue of activities alone which have some *thing* for their object.

I perceive something. I am sensible of something. I imagine something. I will something. I feel something. I think something. The life of human beings does not consist of all this and the like alone.

This and the like together establish the realm of *It.*

But the realm of *Thou* has a different basis.

When *Thou* is spoken, the speaker has no thing for his object. For where there is a thing there is another thing. Every *It* is bounded by others; *It* exists only through being bounded by others. But when *Thou* is spoken, there is no thing. *Thou* has no bounds. (Buber, 1958, pp. 3–4)

Within the limits of my own completeness as a person, I believe I know what Buber means. I have lived these relationships. I have even entered such relationships some rare times in psychotherapy. But I have *never* conducted a clinical inquiry as an *I-Thou* relationship and I think a relationship of this kind is absolutely unsuited to the task of clinical search. To quote Buber still further:

IF I FACE A HUMAN BEING AS MY *THOU*, and say the primary word *I-Thou* to him, he is not a thing among things, and does not consist of things.

Thus human being is not *He* or *She*, bounded from every other *He* and *She*, a specific point in space and time within the net of the world; nor is he a nature able to be experienced and described, a loose bundle of named qualities. But with no neighbour, and whole in himself, he is *Thou* and fills the heavens. This does not mean that nothing exists except himself. But all else lives in *his* light.

Just as the melody is not made up of notes nor the verse of words nor the statue of lines, but they must be tugged and dragged until their unity has been scattered into these many pieces, so with the man to whom I say *Thou*. I can take from him the colour of his hair, or of his speech, or of his goodness. I must continually do this. But each time I do it he ceases to be *Thou*. (Buber, 1958, pp. 8–9)

Buber seems to be saying this: reflect upon an *I-Thou* relationship and it vanishes, analyze it and it is destroyed, plan it and it never forms. But how can intelligent clinical inquiry be conducted without planning? How can comprehensible information be gained without reflection and analysis? If *I-Thou* and *I-It* are the only alternatives, then *I-It* has to be the one—the clinical search must be made in the world of objects. There is no other way, for only by reflection, plan, analysis, and abstraction can useful comprehension, as apart from direct existential experience, be derived.

Of course there is an alternative. In discussing the secularization and urbanization of men in modern society, Harvey Cox (1965) has introduced the concept of the *I-You* relationship between people who have important transactions to conduct with one another but who neither can develop nor need to develop intimate oneness in all their dealings. These contacts can be mutually satisfying and decidedly human, but certain role boundaries of the relationship are maintained throughout. The association which develops is still interpersonal, it is more than a clanking together of two objects. It need not be barren. There need be no ill effect on either party. Condescension need never occur. In clinical inquiry, mutual respect seems always to be required, and something akin to empathy may be strongly involved. Understanding the anxiety of a man ready to talk about a painful marriage, knowing the anger of a child whose misbehavior somebody insists on changing, compassion for a person who has just started to face himself and is beginning to see the pettiness of his own ways; these are part of an effective clinical relationship. So are intelligence and competence on the part of the investigator. The most fruitful relationship between interviewer and client is simply that between a somewhat experienced, knowledgeable, respectful, and interested clinician, and a person who comes to the clinician for help. It is the relationship of expert and client as Sullivan defined it, if the expertise of the clinician does not make him arrogant and if the status of the client does not dispose him to the kind of medical passivity which has him, by the end of the hour, leaning back and waiting for a cure.

There is a good deal of sentimental sham in clinicians' talk about relationships. It is a desecration of the other relationships in which authentic lives are lived. Buber says again: "The man who leaves the primary word unspoken is to be pitied; but the man who addresses instead these ideas with an abstraction or a password, as if it were their name, is contemptible." (Buber, 1958, p. 14)

The quality of information from an interview appears to depend on the confidence and trust the client has in the interviewer. But the conditions which foster trust are not easy to identify. They probably have something to do with the nature and purpose of the transaction itself. Thus accurate information is more likely to be provided by a voluntarily interviewed depressive than by a suspected criminal sent by a court. The personal qualities of the interviewer seem to count. It probably helps to have an "honest face." There are constraints on the efforts a clinician can make to promote a relationship of free informational exchange. If he tries too hard to appear worthy of trust and confidence clients may get suspicious and guard their comments all the more closely. The sorts of homely advice offered by Menninger (1952) in his 15 points of counsel for interviewers or by Sullivan (1954) in his comments on the formal inception of the psychiatric interview, are probably the soundest guides available. The inquiry begins before the client ever appears, with thorough study of referral information and other available knowledge about the person and his situation. Nothing is more clearly indicative of a lack of basic interest in the person and hence more disruptive to his relationship with the interviewer than failure on the interviewer's part to determine simple facts about the client's identity and the reasons given for his appearance in the examiner's office. Much of the rest of the interchange during the inception of an interview is no more than human courtesy. One greets the client by name and introduces himself, invites the client to the office, offers him a seat, and takes the initiative in starting conversation. Gill, Newman, and Redlich (1954) comment with some amazement on the degree to which the extension of common courtesy to patients has to be stated as a basic principle in definitions of interview procedure. During the interview itself, the basic principles of social behavior are operating, and candor and authenticity are likely to be increased if the interviewer models candid, authentic expression, and reinforces or otherwise encourages an honest and complete account by the client of his problem and his situation. It is difficult to say just how far one ought to go in this. Whether modeling should extend to a personal confession of one's own trials and past misdeeds (Mowrer, 1966) is a moot point. Just how to go about encouraging and reinforcing honest output is difficult to define, especially since the interviewer ordinarily lacks any hard factual information by which the accuracy of report can be judged. But some clients patently begin playing a game of *Poor me* (I am not responsible for any of the misfortunes which have befallen me) or *Tom Thumb* (See what a good boy am I) as soon as they enter the office, and it is probably wise to begin gently discouraging that kind of show as soon as it occurs.

I have recommended development of clinical interview procedures which are guided or programmed but not completely structured as to form, addressed to problem behavior and the conditions which influence problem behavior as to content, and conducted as a professionally appropriate form of I-You relationship. But the clearest need at the present time is not further advice on how to conduct interviews, it is for research on the interview as a data-gathering procedure. The interview is no sure way to truth, no X ray of the mind any more than projective tests are. It is a flexible interpersonal procedure in which an extended transaction occurs, and from which a good deal of useful information is frequently said to be obtained. The verbal utterances and other behavioral events which occur (Matarazzo, 1965) are data, probably but not necessarily related to other important behavioral facts, and they should be subjected to the same critical scrutiny any data require. If we are concerned about the predictive validity of client's statements, we need to study predictive validity. If we are concerned about methods for eliciting and reinforcing some kinds of verbal behavior we need to define that behavior with all possible clarity and then conduct the necessary experiments to determine the functional relationships which matter. We are not justified in extolling the virtues of the interview as a clinical procedure at the present time. It is widely used. It makes sense. But its merit as a clinical procedure needs far better documentation than is available to date, and its improvement as a procedure awaits appropriate experimental investigation.

The Experimental Analysis of Behavior

Along with observation, experiment is the basic method of natural science, yet its acceptance in social science has been slow, and its utilization as a method of clinical inquiry has been very slow indeed. This is probably so, in part, because the word experiment calls to mind a stereotypic image of the experimenter, who is intellectually brilliant and obsessively curious, but totally unconcerned about the welfare of his subjects. Untrammeled by humanistic motives, guided only by a madness for truth, the experimenter is willing to sacrifice the dignity and well-being of his patients on the altar of his own insatiable curiosity. This is *I-It* with a vengeance, and clinicians, it is said, must have other kinds of relationships with their clients.

But ultimate *I-Thou* communion is impossible in clinical inquiry. When the clinical relationship is stripped of mysticism and sentimentality, all that remains is the responsible interest of a competent professional, doing the best he can to help a person before him. The motive to help the client must come before all others in a clinical relationship as opposed to a purely scientific one, and this rules out all actions which might be injurious to the welfare of the patient. It places the concerns of the client above those of the clinician, indeed above those of the general community who may use scientifically gathered information for all time to come. This is the basic nature of the clinician-client contract, and change in the terms of that contract can ethically be made only with the full knowledge and express consent of both parties.

There is nothing in the contract, however, which prohibits introduction of noninjurious conditions to determine functional relationships between those conditions and behavior. In fact, most clients fully understand that the clinician will conduct such tests as he must, even if some of them are uncomfortable and possibly downright painful, to gain needed information for the benefit of the client himself. It is furthermore the obligation of the examiner to admit his own uncertainty where crucial uncertainty prevails, and to conduct such tests as are needed to provide data potentially beneficial to the client. The difference between the usual clinical tests and the experimental tests suggested here is that behavior is deliberately and systematically changed in the latter. Clinicians sometimes appear reluctant to do this, but accepting the position of therapist already requires function as a change-agent, and the demands of useful clinical action require extension of the concept of the experiment to assessment as well. It is not merely the right of the clinician to perform experimental analyses of behavior, it is his duty, and no irrational horror of manipulation should keep him from doing his job.

George Kelly (1955) was one of the first to adapt fully the viewpoint of a modern philosophy of science to the process of social living itself and thence to the process of clinical inquiry designed to assess human action. Clinical diagnosis, in Kelly's way of thinking, became an on-going process of appraisal, hypothesis-construction, validational investigation, and unlimited reformulation of hypotheses.

His emphasis on implicit personal constructs in the formulation of theory, however, and on psychotherapeutic and quasi-psychotherapeutic activities in treatment, limited the extent to which a thorough going experimental attitude could be maintained in assessment. Even in fixed-role therapy, where specific courses of role behavior were prescribed and enacted, the interrelation between systematic behavior modification and diagnostic knowledge about the patient was unclear. That is, the clinical construction of the patient-in-his-milieu was effectively used to recommend different kinds of roles he might enact in the process of living, but this was never clearly defined as a basic method for testing the adequacy of the original statement of functional relationships. The functional relationships between stimulus and response events were never fully articulated in Kelly's theory, and human behavior, though it admittedly occurred in dominantly social milieux, was still mainly a function of the complex internal systems of constructs by which events were to be anticipated and behavior guided.

It remained for B. F. Skinner, along with his colleagues, students, and sympathizers, to develop a clinically useful approach to the functional analysis of behavior. Once disorder was defined as socially adjudicated learned behavior and the pertinence of general behavior principles was made clear, the treatment of disorders was identified with a change in effective stimulus conditions; and the clinical assessment of behavior became a matter of relating systematically administered stimulus events to the changes in behavior which formed the goal of clinical treatment. Both rationale and technique of clinical functional analysis have been presented in detail elsewhere (see especially the chapters by Ferster and Bijou in Krasner & Ullmann, 1965), and has already been the subject of brief discussion here. The essential features of the method may be reiterated as follows. First, inquiry is conducted and observations are made to determine the frequency of behavior under some specified set of stimulus conditions. A behavioral baseline is thus obtained. Then the stimulus conditions are altered in some defined way and changes in behavior are recorded. Variations on the theme can be very complex, but that is the central theme itself.

There are, of course, limitations to experimental methods in the clinical study of social behavior. The first limitation is mainly practical, and it has to do with the stubborn fact of complexity in human behavior. Anyone who seriously attempts to conduct functional analyses of behavior in actual clinical settings will soon find that one of the most difficult problems he faces is one of identifying the effective stimuli maintaining the disordered behavior he wishes to change. It is all very easy to say that clinicians should locate the functional determinants (causes) of disordered behavior, modify those systematically and observe related changes in behavior. It is usually less easy to determine what the causes are. Saying they are outside rather than inside is not always too helpful, and it may often be untrue. Once a possible set of influences has been identified, for instance by means of interviews of the kind described above, the stimuli appear to be multiple, covert as well as external, and related to multiple disordered behaviors in complex ways. There seems to be some gap, that is, between the marvelous simplicity of the behavior of pigeons in cages and even schizophrenics in controlled ward settings, and that of intelligent ambulent outpatients. I have yet to meet a patient with a single problem uniquely related to a single stimulus condition. Infrahuman organisms may behave that way in laboratories, and the demonstration cases described in books seem to come that way, but if my experience is any guide, clients do not come that way as unselected applicants for clinical treatment at outpatient psychological service centers, and unless there is some highly arbitrary clinical selection of behavioral problems displayed by people in hospitals. I do not believe most inpatients come so simple either.

The complexities of clinical reality do not diminish the pertinence of an experimental approach to the study of behavior. Complexity makes careful functional analysis all the more necessary. But the nature of the problem clinicians face is typically that of relating a *number* of possibly influential independent treatment variables to a *number* of dependent symptomatic behavioral variables. This qualifies the usual sort of experiment required as multivariate, or more properly canonical in its nature, not univariate as some presentations of the rationale for functional analysis might lead one to believe. Whether professional ethics demand it or not, most clinicians who are trying to help their clients will do all they can, exercise every hopefully helpful measure they can think of, to bring about desired treatment effects. So the assessment problem which confronts the clinician is that of evaluating a canonical functional relationship in a single case over time. That does not qualify even as a quasi-experimental design, in the Campbell-Stanley sense (Campbell & Stanley, 1963), though this construction of the clinical assessment problem is methodologically superior and practically more apt to benefit clients than any of the traditional nonexperimental approaches.

It is also likely to be more helpful and revealing than so-called therapeutic shotgun approaches which are sometimes misidentified as experimental procedures. In shotgun treatment, a barrage of measures that someone thinks might be helpful are indiscriminately directed at the patient in the hope that something the clinician does will improve something that is wrong with the client. Detailed planning is involved in the multivariate experimental approach suggested here, and by a subtractive design if no other, it may be possible to find out what conditions influence the behavior of the client, that is, if n social treatment measures are mounted to influence k disordered behavioral tendencies and an effect occurs in some subset of the k behaviors, it may be possible by judicious abandonment of first one and then another treatment measure to determine the remainder which finally are of direct functional relevance.

A second limitation on the experimental analysis of behavior in clinical settings is ethical rather than practical, and has already been touched upon above. However interested the clinician may be in gaining scientifically veridical knowledge about his patient, however badly he may want a good demonstration case for a class or a book or his own illumination, he is morally restricted to experimental changes which in his most careful judgment are likely to be beneficial or at worst neutral in their effects upon the client. "Putting symptoms back in" after they have been removed and then eliminating them once more, as Bijou has done, presents no problem, for at the worst, the patient is as well off as he was at the beginning of treatment. Deliberate intensifications of symptomatology might conceivably be attempted at the very outset of the assessment-treatment enterprise, where both clinician and client are honestly in doubt about the conditions maintaining undesired behavior, and they mutually agree to exaggerate some possibly negative condition to see if this has an incremental effect on the behavior in question. But in general both external constraints and the clinician's professional concern for helping people will limit experimental measures to those which are likely to be of positive benefit.

The functional analysis of behavior in clinical assessment can thus be viewed as an experimental operation in which a restricted class of predictably beneficial stimulus changes are exerted and multiple changes in behavior are observed. The kind of experiment performed can rarely be of a one-shot kind, in which a treatment is effected, a change is recorded and the patient is discharged. Repeated treatment changes are usually required and clinical assessment becomes an experimental *process* in which evaluation, experimental change, re-evaluation and revised experimental changes proceed continuously until the case is administratively terminated. The high promise of functional behavior analysis as a clinical assessment procedure lies in definition of the treatment measures themselves as experimental independent variables, and the unification of assessment and treatment, and of science and service, which this may help provide.

The concept of functional analysis can be extended to the clinical study of social behavior. Almost all of the literature on the subject is concerned with the behavior of individuals, but the same basic rationale is also applicable to the clinical study of groups and social systems. In the case of primary groups, one may extend the methods and concepts of experimental social psychology to a unified assessment-treatment change. In the case of a social system, one may apply an explicit experimental sociology, in which the function of the system is appraised, a social change of some kind is engineered, and the modified function of the system is evaluated.

Consider a natural dyadic relationship, for instance, a marriage, which has gotten disturbed to the extent that a professional clinician is sought to help straighten things out. The first step in clinical analysis of such a problem is to determine in detail the patterns of recurrent transactions, and by abstraction the relationships which hold between the man and his wife. This is usually done by interview of both people at the start, and then it is usually desirable to get both parties to look more closely and systematically at the ways they are treating each other. I mentioned earlier a couple whose sexual transactions consisted mainly of seduction by the wife, criticism of the husband by the wife throughout foreplay, an inadequate sexual performance on the husband's part, and resultant angry displeasure on the part of both. Marriage counselors have traditionally approached such problems in a global verbal way, trying to get the two to communicate better, or trying by talking things out to improve the relationship between them. Without denying the need for verbal inquiry or the desirability of good communication, or even the possible need to change some basic relational belief or attitude if effective clinical treatment is to be performed, some more direct experimental measures seem applicable in cases of this kind both to improve the relationship therapeutically and to determine the functional relationships between the stimuli people in groups afford each other and the interbehavioral effects these stimuli may have. In this case, the husband was encouraged to read a manual on sex technique and wife was persuaded to desist from criticism of any kind before, during, or after sexual intercourse. The next week both reported that they had had "the best affair in our lives." There were other problems in this marriage, as there are in most disturbed marriages. I do not wish to overstate the case for simplicity. But I do wish to propose that a functional approach to the analysis of behavior is just as relevant to the study of group transactions as to the study of individual behavior, and that therapeutically guided experimental measures provide one of the most sharply definitive means available for finding out about clinically important group processes.

The same holds for the study of social systems. For the most part, sociology is an observational rather than an experimental science. But that is changing, particularly in applications to business and industry, where carefully evaluated reorganization may be necessary to economic survival, and in the mental health fields where the engineering measures of so-called social psychiatry are being brought to bear on community mechanisms for dealing with disordered behavior. Although there are formidable technical and ethical problems associated with social engineering of this kind, if we are in the business of exercising power for social change anyway, and are doing it somewhat unwittingly and chaotically as the situation now stands, we are obliged to begin studying the process more carefully than we have before. One way to accomplish this aim may be to apply the rationale of an experimental sociological analysis to the problem of program evaluation in social systems. The task will be easiest if a functional view of society is maintained, so that focal concern is addressed to the way systems *function* rather than the way they *are* in some static topographical sense. If this is done, the basic rationale of functional analysis has a chance of applicability.

I am presently engaged in an attempt to develop a treatment program for some adolescents and children in a state hospital. The youngsters who come there usually have been moved frequently from one social agency to another, through the legal-correctional system, in and out of various welfare offices, and so forth. In the hospital, they are considered sick, but their treatment consists for the most part of medication, some rather scattered activity programs, school in the mornings, and care and keeping by the aides the rest of the time. The nursing staff is short-handed, as is traditional in state hospitals, and the two aides who can usually be assigned to each shift are naturally preoccupied with problems of control. It is clear enough that one likely beneficial change in this system for coping with the problem of disordered behavior in adolescence will be to get larger numbers of aides on the wards and to train them for treatment rather than purely for discipline and custodial care. The matter of program evaluation, of clinical assessment of the ward system, can most effectively be faced by identifying the aide-training program as an experimental measure and reviewing the effects of training on aide behavior toward patients, as well as the ultimate effects on the patients, as the dependent variables under study.

The advantages of an experimental viewpoint in this case are threefold. First, there is clear need to specify the nature of the training involved. Mere education in understanding human dynamics will not suffice. The aides must be taught to do something identifiably different from a previous behavior pattern. Second, the need to specify relevant dependent variables, such as aide behavior, is equally clear. At another level, of course, the actions of the aides become stimuli influencing the reactions of patients, and these functional relationships must be assessed as well. Third, the need for continual re-evaluation is clear. If the neutral or negative actions of the aides have actually had the null or damaging effects they seem to have had, then altering the function of aides by appropriate training and other means should have predictable and desirable effects, and these should be expressed ultimately in improved behavior on the part of patients, higher discharge rates, and the like. The provisional measures of an experimental sociology, however, will be perpetually imperfect and eternally corrigible. As the old mechanisms were studied, found wanting, and changed, so any new measures must be studied and continually improved. That is the nature of an experimental search for functional relationships and it holds as much for the classes of phenomena we commonly identify as social and sociological as for the behavior of an individual subject.

The clinical limitations of functional analysis discussed so far only in regard to individual behavior also hold for groups and social systems, only more so. Again, both practical and ethical considerations restrict the range of feasible action. Social engineers are morally limited to changes which promise to do general and lasting good. They owe to society a public acknowledgement of their roles as social change-agents, the clearest possible representation to others of what they are doing, and frankness about the difficulty in defining the directions and extent of the general and lasting benefits they are trying to achieve. Practical limits on an experimental sociology in studying social systems are set partly by the conservative tendencies of all societies, which make changes difficult to initiate, and by cumulative effects, once changes begin, which make the changes difficult to assess. Social changes frequently have an expanding impact, so that once a particularly crucial change takes place in the system a lot of other changes follow immediately, and establishment of causal relationships, including the identity of the crucial change, may be extremely difficult. An aide training program, for instance, may be accompanied or preceded by an improved pay scale for the personnel, a change in the administrative means by which training curricula as well as job assignments are defined, a variety of other treatment programs for the patients, and maybe a changed conception of the nature of psychiatric treatment on the part of the hospital superintendent. All of these changes may seem desirable on theoretical grounds. And if such changes begin to occur after years of ineffectual effort to get anything at all to happen in the hospital, one may be reluctant to retard the process in any way. Many changes in social systems come chaotically or not at all, and in either case the problem of clinical sociological assessment is a very troublesome one. All one can do is press for order where order seems possible, and accept the realities of the multiple-change-multiple-effect relationships which typically characterize the clinical situation where insistence upon order might stultify and constrain likely beneficial changes. A mental hospital is not a laboratory. Full experimental control is ordinarily impossible in clinical settings. But adaptation of an experimental viewpoint and utilization of experimental procedures to the very limits of their applicability seems the most promising way available to effect desired treatment changes and to know when and how these changes have come about.

The Use of Tests in Studying Social Behavior

In its traditional psychometric definition, a test is a standard situation in which behavior is elicited, comparisons are made with sample norms, and from this information other propositions are implied about the behavior of subjects. Efforts are made to standardize the administration of stimuli as much as possible, so that behavioral variance is a function of the dispositional characteristics of the individuals being tested. An assumption of trans-situational generality lies behind every clinical use of a psychological test, and the legitimacy of that assumption can only be evaluated by some kind of validity index.

In the study of clinically important social behavior, however, it now is grimly obvious that the validities once hoped for and sometimes assumed have not appeared. This holds for all kinds of tests, structured and unstructured, objective and projective, and in spite of ingenious efforts to develop moderator systems of all kinds to improve the psychometric properties of the measures. Many clever men with skilled staffs, elaborate computational facilities, and abundant financial support are working hard to develop new and better personality tests, and newer better ways of improving old ones. It is of course possible that continued effort to refine objective tests, reanalyze questionnaires and develop better projective methods will return rich dividends some day. But hope grows dimmer all the time. Personality test validities have not approached the level required for individual decisions, and it is becoming more and more apparent that the faults lie not merely in the instruments but in the basic rationale on which they all are founded.

If behavior is a joint function of situation and internal disposition, no *standard* stimulus situation can possibly represent the diversity of circumstances in which social behavior occurs. However valid a test may be in its revelation of intrapsychic characteristics, behavior continues to vary with stimulus change and logically, not just empirically, the stimulus conditions must be taken into account. No psychodiagnostic tests designed along traditional lines can do this.

The areas in which psychological tests have shown some utility, notably the areas of human ability, are characterized by two distinctive features. The first is that the tests measure maximum rather than typical performance, and the second is that the situations represented in the test are very close approximations of the situations which confront people in real life. Performance on the best intelligence tests is of the kind required in academic situations, and predictions of academic success are accordingly respectable. Performance on the Illinois Test of Psycholinguistic Ability (Kirk & McCarthy, 1961) is closely representative of the actual functioning required for processing auditory and visual data, and both the diagnostic information and remedial implications are therefore pertinent to the actual data-processing functions we all must perform. There is naturally nothing objectionable about the use of such tests to measure various kinds of ability. But this is a far cry from using tests to measure typical behavior in highly diverse social circumstances.

If tests are to be used at all for the assessment of social behavior, they will have to be developed in ways which can accommodate the situational dependence of social behavior and the idiographic nature of pertinent description. Several efforts have been made along these lines. Kelly's Role Repertory (Rep) test (Kelly, 1955) offers one example. Subjects are asked to select the other people who are significant to them, and then to elaborate social constructions of these others by stating similarities and differences among them. The S-R Inventory of Anxiousness by Endler, Hunt, and Rosenstein (1962) offers another model which fits the actualities of clinical assessment better than the usual trait measures. In the S-R Inventory, particular modes of response are related to particular classes of situations and the descriptions which result therefore express the kind of anxious behavior each subject reports in the presence of each particular kind of anxiety-provoking circumstance. The methods of interpersonal diagnosis proposed by Leary (1957) offer still a third example of a potentially fruitful approach to the study of social behavior. Though the method is hampered by a conception of interpersonal behavior which is fundamentally nomothetic and dimensional, and by an over-simplified identification of levels of interbehavior with the particular instruments employed, behavior in social situations is systematically related to interpersonal stimulus characteristics of the situations themselves, and this permits more effective incorporation of situational parameters than any pure trait system can possibly allow.

But more than this is needed if personality tests are ever to develop utilities comparable to those of effective ability measures. For this, we must begin thinking of personality in terms of behavioral competence. We must conceive of certain kinds of performance required by the society which matters to the individual under study, define the conditions under which those classes of performances are required, and then examine ability to execute the desired forms of action. To do this demands explicit assignment of social values. Some behaviors would have to be judged as desirable and some as undesirable, though the cultural generality of the values could be modified to suit the functions under study and the particular purpose the test operations were designed to serve. A standard set of conditions would have to be specified for elicitation of the behavior in question. Given the situational specificity of behavior emphasized so strongly throughout this book, that would present serious problems, but if some degree of behavioral consistency and situational generality is assumed, tests of social performance could rationally and perhaps effectively be developed. Above all, personality would have to be conceived as a pattern of behavioral competencies, as a set of abilities rather than dispositional "essences" of any kind (cf. Wallace, 1966), and the resulting evaluations would have to describe relative effectiveness in performance of defined tasks rather than typical personality characteristics as these are to occur under all circumstances whatever.

While instruments and test operations of these kinds clearly merit further study, all would ultimately require validation against basic observational and experimental measures of social behavior, and it is a more appropriate ordering of effort in the present phase of professional and scientific development to improve the observational and experimental methods themselves. Most psychological tests have been constructed in the hope of providing an economical way of finding out about general characteristics of personality. With ten inkblots and a couple of hours' time clinicians hoped they might determine the crucially important dynamic facts of a man's existence. With 550 questionnaire items and fifteen minutes of clerical time it was hoped that some useful and objective statements could be made about disordered behavior. Of course plausible dynamic accounts could be written from Rorschach responses. This met the immediate social demand for psychologicals and there was no obvious way to tell whether the descriptions were right or wrong. With a little practice and training in the language, equally plausible accounts could be written from MMPI profiles, and when people did research, the correlations usually were significantly different from zero. But how long can we tolerate a descriptive situation where our measures account for ten percent of accountable variance? How long can we go on seeking and failing to improve that score? How long will it be until we decide that there is no cheap way to study human behavior and begin looking as directly as possible at the behavior itself?

6

Three Cases: A Person, a Group, and a Social System

Let us turn now from the relative freedom of rational argument to the harsh and humbling discipline of clinical trial. It is far easier to suggest a procedural innovation in a book than to develop one that works in clinical practice. But clinical application is needed to test the feasibility and to estimate the potential value of the method.

Three cases will be discussed, one to represent each of the classes of phenomena defined in preceding chapters. The first account concerns a person, a fifteen-year-old boy who was having and causing some troubles at home and at school. The second concerns a group, in this case a family whose problems originally came to notice because of the misbehavior of one of the children, but which were later seen to extend more broadly to other relationships within the family and which were then treated clinically as group problems. The third account concerns a social system, in this case a state hospital, and in particular a program for children and adolescents within the hospital.

Though three distinguishable classes of phenomena will be considered, the problems and procedures merge into one another in ways which cannot and need not be sharply differentiated. Thus the first discussion concerns a person, a boy, and defines his as an individual case. But his problems arose and were treated in relation to the behavior of other people. During one phase of the clinical process, conjoint interviews were held with the father and his son. Their relationships and their interbehaviors came to the focus of attention and both conception and clinical activity at this time were in the domain of social psychology. In discussing the state hospital as a system and its programs as procedures for accomplishing collective aims, there must be constant note of the behavior of the people who pursue the goals and conduct the procedures. Their individual and social actions are the raw events from which organizational concepts are abstracted and in reference to which these concepts must be defined. For expository convenience and innovative fruitfulness, distinctions among individual, relational, and organizational phenomena seem worth maintaining; but the distinctions should not obscure the basic unity of behavioral fact and observational-experimental method which keep them all together.

I have taken some liberties with literal truth in the reports to follow. Each account grows from the facts of a particular case and the dominant theme is of that case, but some uniquely identifying events or characteristics have been omitted or changed in every instance. Composite experiences with other individuals, groups, and institutions have occasionally been introduced. This course, rather than that of literal description, was chosen in part to preserve the anonymity of the people involved and in part to improve the illustrations. Changes in the stories have not been made to prove how effective the methods are. Above all one should learn high respect for the difficulty of clinical problems from these examples, and they are offered as preliminary efforts to apply an approach with certain promising features of design, not as models of clinical perfection. In these accounts as in the entire book, I am defining some directions which I believe clinical assessment practices might profitably take. I am not, as the examples will show, presenting a finished technology.

Most of the case studies in our literature seem to be glossy, well-packaged articles showing remarkable clinical feats accomplished by the authors with apparent ease and unfailingly admirable skill. The following accounts are not like that. They are not glittering success stories in all their facets, and my part in them has not always been particularly heroic. I am painfully aware of major faults in each example. The study of an individual would be more convincing if the account could be buttressed with certain forms of extended *in situ* observations and experimental contingency reversals for which I found neither time nor clinical need. The study of a family will be seen to have similar observational flaws. And in the study of a social system I was not in a position of sufficient power to exercise all the changes a true experimental sociology requires. I hope the accounts will be informative anyway. Despite the limitations which circumstances and my personal shortcomings have imposed, some changes have occurred in each case, I believe I know at least a part of what caused the changes, and could bring the same classes of events to pass again in a reasonably dependable and predictable way.

These three cases are not presented as proof of the validity, efficacy or utility of the methods involved; that will take years and years of research. The cases are illustrative, not documentary. The only proof they are intended to offer is that methods of this kind can be applied to clinically important problems. If the methods have merit, as I believe they may, this will require evidence of a different order. If the methods have faults, as of course they must, then they will have to be studied in other ways to locate the faults and develop still better procedures.

WALTER LILLY: THE STUDY OF A PERSON

I first learned about Walter and his problems from a social worker at a local junior high school, who called to find out if I was able to accept any new referrals. I said I was, and she said she had a particularly difficult case to consider. Earlier that same day, a boy named Walter Lilly had walked out of a ninth-grade physical education class in a state of obvious distress. He was taken to the school office to talk to the assistant principal, and according to a letter I later received from the referring social worker was ". . . hysterical and shaking all over. His thought processes were confused. He was incoherent and rambling in his talk. His conversation had some paranoid coloring involving his feelings about neighbors whom he saw as being in competition with him. . . . He was quite agitated, depressed, and admitted to ruminations about suicide."

This was not the first contact between Walter and the social worker. Earlier in the school year, Walter had been directly re-

ferred to her because he had been coming to the school office during his first period physical education class, "weeping copiously and
continuously," and saying that he just could not go to the class.
The social worker saw him twice thereafter, during which time
Walter talked of being lonely, friendless, and unliked by the other
students, and the social worker formed some ideas about certain
"passive-dependent trends" on the part of the client which were
"not holding up well for him."

The interviews were somewhat rudely terminated when Walter's mother called the school principal and stated that she did not
want her son to see a social worker. For the five months which followed, Walter stayed in school, but according to the social worker's
report, "continued to cry his way through the year, isolated and
passively getting through his classes."

When Walter walked out of the class his parents were called
at once, and that afternoon Walter's father met with two of the
assistant principals of the school. They described Walter's behavior
to Mr. Lilly in some detail and told him how concerned they were
about it. The arrangements for seeing me at the Psychological Clinic
were explained and the need for immediate treatment was stressed.
Mr. Lilly agreed about Walter's need for help, said he would talk
the matter over with his wife, and would contact me at the Clinic.

Several days passed and not a word was received from the
Lillys. Walter still would not appear for physical education and
when urged to do so broke down in tears saying that he knew he
was going to die. After a week of this behavior, the principal of the
school wrote Mr. Lilly, saying that they would probably have to
suspend Walter if he did not either begin to attend classes regularly or get some psychological help. At this point Mr. Lilly called
me and arranged for a meeting the following day. Thus at the time
of the first contact, I was confronted with a badly disturbed, possibly prepsychotic adolescent boy, a rather resistive father and
mother, and some people in the school system who had essentially
forced the boy and his parents to see a psychologist. I met the boy
and his father in the waiting room. When I introduced myself,
Walter took one look at me, lowered and turned his head, and
began to cry. He was a rather large and fleshy youngster and his
shoulders and torso shook with the sobs. I explained to Mr. Lilly
that I wanted to see his son for about an hour, and then to talk

with Mr. Lilly himself the following day. Mr. Lilly scarcely seemed to hear me, but fussed over Walter, saying with a mixture of cajolery and irritation, "Come on, quit that crying." I said, "Come with me, Walter," and led him through the somewhat circuitous maze of hallways and foyers between the waiting room and my office.

Before going into the details of our conversation, I would like to comment on my own clinical beliefs and attitudes at the time of the first interview, and on certain aspects of technique that can be described with greater clarity now than would have been possible in the preceding chapter. In this case as in all cases, I wanted to determine two essential classes of facts, as these were to be defined by the client: (1) the nature of the problem behavior, and (2) the conditions, both internal and external, under which the behavior occurred. I believe I have the best chance of finding out about such matters if I inquire with intelligence, not necessarily cleverness, and listen with genuine interest, not necessarily pained empathy, to what the client tells me. As inquirer and listener my role is dual. On the one hand, I am an evocative stimulus to responses on the part of the client, on the other hand I respond to his behavior, and in the latter transactionally stimulate further behavior on his part. I have found it useful to conceive of four relatively specific techniques which can be emphasized in interviews of this kind. Two of these are of an elicitative nature, namely _questioning_ and _probing_. In direct questioning one simply asks for desired information, e.g., "What sorts of things go through your mind that frighten you so?" In probing, one proceeds from a base of information already gained to a more refined inquiry about the subject at issue. The present client mentioned his neighbors very early in the interview, with no provocation from the interviewer, and it then became important to inquire further about them. "But what about these neighbors, how do they treat you?" Further probing may then follow response to inquiries of this kind. The inquiry process stops when the needed information appears or it becomes obvious that additional probing will be useless or damaging to the relationship.

The other two techniques are of a responsive kind, namely _reflection_ and _provisional restatement_. By reflection I mean pretty much what Rogers meant, only I do not believe one should concern himself solely or even dominantly with feelings as a focus of response. The interviewer, in reflection, simply tries to communicate back to the client the message the client has just expressed, including both cognitive and emotional aspects of the message. For instance:

Client (C). I'm scared I'm going to die. . . .
Examiner (E). Afraid you're going to die. . . .
C. I want to get better like I used to. Last month I was so good.
E. You were feeling better then.

In _provisional restatement_, the interviewer goes a step beyond reflection to a synthetic restatement of ideas and feelings the client appears to have expressed, but about which some interpretative question still remains. In effect one says to the client, "If I understand you, here is what you have just been telling me. Is that correct?" As an actual example later in the present interview:

E. Now that very first time that you were heading for the Fair. Do I understand it? It wasn't so much that you really felt sick, it was just that you thought you might get sick. Is that the kind of idea?
C. Mm hm. . . .
E. And in this case, it's not so much that you have a pain in your chest or anything of that kind. . . . It's just that this terrible fear enters your mind, is that it?
C. (Nods.)

Provisional restatement stops short of interpretation. The aim is to gain information about the client, not to give him any information or insight he did not have before. But it goes beyond reflection in encompassing more than the immediately previous behavior of the client, sometimes to the point of synthesizing most of an entire interview, and in posing a direct request for corrective feedback from the client. Provisional restatement is synthetic reflection presented as a question.

In addition to these rather specific techniques, two more general forms of action have been useful in my experience as an interviewer. One of these is again of an evocative character, and the other is more clearly responsive in its nature. The evocative stimulus is outright social _modeling_. I expect clients coming to see a psychologist to be somewhat defensive during the encounter, but I am very much interested in obtaining a free flow of relatively honest verbal output from them. It is in my interest and ultimately in the interest of the clients if I behave in a rather forthright way myself. It is well to be gentle, but it is no help to be devious, and I have found it uniformly possible and generally profitable to begin talking straightway about the problems that are bothering people, conveying the clearest expectation I can that they will tell me about these, with no apologies and little indirection in the behavioral model I present.

The second general response to use in the encouragement of productive verbal output is social *reinforcement*. There are obvious dangers in this, when the interview is used as a data-gathering procedure. One must avoid the selective reinforcement of content, or he soon may be hearing only what he wants to hear. But the appearance of candor, authenticity, nondefensiveness, honesty as a general class of behavior can be reinforced without necessarily encouraging any particular substance in what the client is talking about. So whenever anyone tells me, by word or gesture, "I have been guarding myself rather closely before, but now maybe I will begin telling you the truth," I am apt to nod, smile, lean forward, or anything else I can think of to keep that very desirable kind of behavior going.

To get back to the case itself, Walter was crying as he entered my office and began to talk.

E. Walter, what's wrong?
C. I'm scared I'm going to die.
E. Afraid you're going to die.
C. I think my heart's not right.
E. It isn't working right?
C. (Sniffs). I'm scared to go anywhere.
E. Mm hm.
C. (Sniffs). I want to get better like I used to be (cries continuously). Last month I was so good.
E. You were feeling better then.
C. I wasn't scared. My heart was beating all right. I went and did things. . . .
E. Yes . . .
C. Now I'm scared. . . . I'm scared I'm going to die, and I don't want to (sobs) die because I . . . I want to grow up and get a job (sobs) . . .

E. And have a reasonably happy life. Sure you do. Of course you do. . . . What sorts of things happen to your heart that make you think it isn't right?

C. It beats slow. And I'm scared to go to bed at night because I'm afraid I won't get up in the morning.

E. Afraid you won't be able to wake up at all.

C. (Sniffs, sobs) Oh God . . . I've been this way all this month.

E. Have you?

C. Scared (cries) . . . get all light feeling in my head, a funny feeling like I'm going to fall over when I get nervous.

E. Just dizzy . . . and you think you just might not be able to stand up at all.

C. And I want to get better and have fun.

E. Sure you do.

C. (Sobs) Everybody's been so good to me. . . .

E. Everybody's good to you, but you're still just as scared as you ever were, aren't you?

C. (Sniffs).

E. What sorts of things go through your mind that frighten you so? What sorts of things are you thinking of?

C. (Sniff) That I'll have a heart attack or something. You think you see people they go uptown and they fall over on the street you know . . . and things.

E. You read about it or you hear about it. . . .

C. Yes. . . .

E. You think this might happen to you.

C. I don't want to die.

E. Of course you don't want to die.

C. (Sniffs). I'm scared . . . I think about our neighbors. They're old you know, and—and I like them so (sobs, sniffs) and they don't care for me, they don't . . . I don't know (sniff). . . . I—I like everybody. I guess I've been too good to everybody. And I help Mom and Dad and things. . . . (sniffs).

E. You try to be nice to people.

C. (Sniffs).

E. But what about these neighbors, how do they treat you?

C. Oh, I think they're . . . I don't know . . . I think they look at me like I'm no good. . . . And we live in a dirty place you know and they got it better than we do . . . and I try to keep it clean, and I work so hard I can't do it any more. . . . I don't eat like I used to. I lost all my weight, er not all of it but quite a bit of it, and (sniffs) ever since my grandma died (sobs) I've been no good. She lived with us, and she'd help me, and she'd be right there when I needed her (sobs). . . .

E. She was very kind to you. . . .

C. And then she went to the home . . . and then she died.

E. You felt a terrible loss at the time she died, Walter. . . .

C. (sobs).

E. She was somebody you had really been close to, you felt you could go to her any time. . . .

C. She lived with us . . . not in the house, and every time they'd scold me, I'd run over there, and she'd help me, or she would baby me, or, well . . .

E. Sort of comfort you. . . .

C. I got one grandma, she don't care about me. I really shouldn't have went up there. . . . Last Fourth of July I went up there, and I didn't want to go, and I got all nervous, and she was sitting there at the table, eating, and they were talking about people getting sick and dying, and things, and she don't care for me . . . and Dad or me and things. And I thought everything was wrong with me. . . . I don't know what it is. . . . I can't go on every day like this, scared every day (sobs, sniffs). I want to get better. I want to grow up and get a job . . . and see things and do things (sniffs, sobs). . . .

E. And be reasonably happy once in a while.

C. I got everything in the world. I got everything I want. Got a good home (sniffs, sobs). . . .

E. But you're still scared, and you're still miserable.

During these early moments of the interview, little active inquiry was required. Walter told me and showed me spontaneously what was troubling him. My principle task was to listen and watch, to understand and to show Walter that I understood his view of the problem.

The material on Walter's fear of dying and the brief partial account of his relationship with his grandmother was followed by a discussion of the way he felt in school—no one liked him there either—a more detailed description of the anxiety experience itself—dizziness, a tight feeling in the throat—and a generalized statement of the idea that no one really cared for him at all. By this time his crying had diminished a bit, and I began to ask him about the duration of his problem.

E. You were saying that last month and last year things were much better. What about the years before that? How long has this kind of thing been going on?

C. What, this feeling I have?

E. Yes, this feeling of being scared that you might die, and the general misery that you have.

C. One summer I went over to the County Fair, and I had that feeling, a funny feeling. I thought I was going to get sick or something. And that was—that was when I was in the sixth grade. And I was scared, and I couldn't go anywhere because I thought I was going to get sick. Then I went . . . I couldn't go anywhere, and the doctor couldn't find anything wrong with me, so he sent me over to the . . . to another doctor. I went there for awhile, and then I was in the sixth grade then, and I was all right.

E. Was that Doctor Harland (a psychiatrist)?

C. Yes.

E. O.K., so then in the sixth grade . . .

C. I was all right then. Everything was happy. . . . but that summer I don't know what happened—I just got scared that I was going to get out and go somewhere and get sick or something. . . .

E. Now that very first time that you were heading for the Fair . . . Do I understand it? It wasn't so much that you really felt sick, it was just that you thought you might get sick. Is that the kind of idea?

C. Mm hm.

E. And you got worried about that . . . that you might get sick.

C. Mm hm.

E. And in this case, it's not so much that you have a pain in your chest or anything of that kind, it's just that you have this terrible fear that your heart might stop or it might go wrong some way and that you might die. And it's not . . . it's not a matter of anything like a little heart attack. It's just that this terrible fear enters your mind, is that it?

C. (Nods).

E. All right. Now that time you had that feeling on the way to the Fair— think back to that for a minute. What happened then, did you go to the Fair anyway or did you go back home, or what happened?

C. I had to go home. I made it miserable for Mom and Dad because they wanted to go and, and ah I couldn't go. I was scared, and the feeling wouldn't go away, and they couldn't find anything wrong with me, and then . . . but then I was afraid I was going to get sick. Now I'm afraid I'm going to die.

E. And that's a different kind of thing, isn't it? I mean it's bad enough to think you might throw up or something of that kind, but to think that you really might not wake up the next morning or that you might have a heart attack and die is a dreadful dreadful thought.

C. (Cries softly again) And I'm scared about going to school too. I went three years of junior high and it hasn't been fun. . . .

E. Well, I've heard that you had a hard time.

C. Everything's been terrible.

E. In what way? How so terrible?

C. Oh. I'm scared of the people. The kids. What they say.

E. What sorts of things do you think they are saying?

C. Oh because I wasn't good in P.E. (Physical Education), and things. They made fun of that. And they spread it all around . . . they said I went around with colored girls. Well, I had talked to . . . (cries) I didn't do that. I wouldn't do that kind of thing. I talked to some colored kids. Gave them some money and some things, and they thought I liked colored people (cries). They were the only ones I could talk to (sobs). It was terrible. I only got one friend, that's all. I just thought the colored kids . . . they'd beg for money, and they wouldn't—wouldn't leave me alone, so I paid them, and . . . I shouldn't have gave them the money.

E. Were they taking this money from you? Did they try to make you give them money?

C. Yes, if I didn't give them the money, they'd beat me up.

E. Yes.

C. They were just doing that to scare me . . . I think.

E. Yes.

C. Until I gave them the money.

E. But then when you gave them the money, was it so they wouldn't beat you up, . . . or maybe just to have somebody to talk to?

C. It was so they'd leave me alone.

E. So they wouldn't beat you up and wouldn't bother you any more.

C. I was always afraid to go to school. Ever since I started I was scared to go (cries). Now I'm (sobs) scared worse (sniffs). Oh God.

Walter then began showing further his fear of dying, telling how frightened he was that his heart would stop, how badly he wanted it to beat more rapidly. This was heard again, with interest, but no particular encouragement. The message was already clear, and it seemed well to get on to some of the consequences of his behavior. If I had been functioning more smoothly as an examiner, I might have managed some kind of transition, but as it was, I simply introduced the next inquiry directly.

E. When you feel scared this way, Walter, and then when you cry, as you do because you feel so scared, what does your father do? What does he do then?

C. Oh, he's loud at me, says there's nothing wrong. To be still and things. But . . . I can't. . . .

E. Just straighten up and stop. . . .

C. Yes, grow up, face things. He says for me to fight it, but I . . . don't know. . . . And Mom, she understands, at least I think she does.

E. What about your mother, what does she do?

C. Oh . . . I think she understands me more, or tries to help me more. . . . Well, he helps, but I mean . . . he doesn't . . . I don't know, she understands things more. She says I'm not going to die. There isn't anything wrong with me. But I don't believe her. I mean I want to, but I just . . . can't.

E. She says that, and the doctor says that, but you still have the same feeling, don't you? . . . And the same thoughts keep going through your mind?

C. Oh. Oh. (cries)

E. You were saying that your father usually tries to tell you to snap out of this. How does your mother try to help you get over your troubles?

C. She's somewhat like . . . the same way he is . . . I don't know. I don't know . . . (cries). They're good parents, but they don't understand (cries). They don't understand.

E. And they don't quite know what to do to help you, do they?

C. They think I'm doing this so they won't get to go anywhere, or it was that way in the summer, then when school would come around I'd be all right. This year it's different. It's worse—it's different. I just feel like a different person or something. Around me it doesn't even feel like it used to.

Walter talked more then about his loneliness at school, of his one good friend, who "always was there beside him." And he talked about the rough treatment he received from the other students. They "screamed" at him in physical education class, played practical jokes on him, put water in his shoes, knotted his clothing—the kinds of torment to which the "goat" in every Army barracks or high school gym class is subjected. "They always did pick on me," said Walter, and I had no reason to doubt him.

But then, for the first time, there appeared some indication that Walter was not uniformly the frightened, pathetic creature he had so far described and had appeared to be in the interview itself. While he had been talking about the way other boys tormented him at school, he reported no anger. But immediately and with no further intervention by the examiner, the following statements appear.

C. At home I get real mad. I have a bad mouth. I mean I get . . . angry and I scream off and I say bad words. I know I shouldn't do that. . . . I get too many things in my head and I have to scream off. And at school I don't say a word to anybody. I just let them pick on me.

The rest of the interview is of less interest, except perhaps for the part in which Walter was asked to state three wishes.

E. Walter, if you had three wishes, what would you wish for?
C. To have some friends (starts to cry).
E. Yes.
C. And to be myself again . . . the way I was (sobs), and to have a grandma that cares for me (cries). Oh little things like that hurt me.

Mr. Lilly was interviewed next, the following day. He came in work clothes, and apologized for that as well as for some mud which had clung to his boots. He was a construction worker and said he had been "down in a hole digging" all afternoon. His interview is not reported in detail. In general, he confirmed Walter's description of the disordered behavior itself. Yes, Walter really did seem to be afraid of dying, and "kept the whole family up half the night, a-crying and a-moaning." Mr. Lilly also gave the same essential view of his own reaction to Walter's behavior as his son had. "Yes, I do get mad sometimes. . . . I've never hit him. Not for that. He's just too pitiful, but gee—I wish he'd stop all that bawling."

Perhaps the most informative material to emerge from talking with Mr. Lilly concerned Walter's grandmother, the one who understood him so well. "I don't want to say anything mm—against her. She's dead now, but it was a mistake to have her around the house. . . . I mean she spoiled him rotten. . . . We'd try to correct him, you know, and he'd run back to Grandma and she'd slobber all over him. . . . We went around and around about that. But I'll tell you Grandma always took care of her baby."

So, apparently, did the parents in some ways. I asked specifically about Walter's tantrum-like behavior, the "screaming off" which he had reported, and what they did when this occurred. Mr. Lilly laughed a bit nervously then and said, "Well to tell you the truth, I guess we always give in . . . so's we won't bother the neighbors. They're sort of old, and I don't think they appreciate the noise."

He was asked for his view of Walter's attitude toward the neighbors and their attitude toward Walter, and Mr. Lilly flatly and completely denied that the neighbors had ever shown any active dislike toward Walter. They had never gone out of their way to make affectionate overtures either and that is probably what Walter would need to feel that they really "understood" him, or even that they did not dislike him. Mr. Lilly further denied that there was anything wrong with their own house or that the neighbors' place was particularly better than theirs.

As we were leaving my office after the interview, I mentioned that I planned to see Mrs. Lilly the next time. Mr. Lilly looked at me very intently at that point and said, "Listen, there's something I want to tell you. When she saw that other psychiatrist he asked a whole bunch . . . a whole lot of questions about sex . . . and— and mm we couldn't see no sense to that. He spent more time nosying around trying to find out about us than he did trying to find out about Walter, and we couldn't see no sense to that. That sex stuff really got the Missus . . . and I think she might be less mm—mm—reluctant . . . if you don't say anything about that." I said I didn't see any need to go into their sex life at this time, though sometimes these matters could influence other problems in complicated ways. I said I was interested mainly in Mrs. Lilly's view of Walter's problem, and indeed that is how our conversation began when she appeared the next day.

E. What I want to know first of all is your view of what the main problem is . . . just how you see it.

C. Well, I think it is this P.E. . . . at school . . . mm . . . four years ago it was the same thing. When he went from Wilson School to junior high. Well see now it's another step . . . from junior high to senior high.

E. And he is terrified, as he told me and as of course everybody else said, of going to P.E. class.

C. Yes, and more so now because you see . . . swimming is . . . mm . . . recommended.

E. I wonder what that has to do with it. Why is he afraid to go to P.E. class?

C. That's something I can't answer. . . . Well, maybe I can too answer it.

E. What are your ideas?

C. Because he has to change . . . clothes . . . to show his body.

E. He doesn't want to undress. . . .

C. Yes.

E. And be naked before the others.

C. Mm hm . . . and I always say, well you're just the same as the rest of . . . the rest of the boys. . . .

E. But then you have to ask the same question again, don't you? Why is he so concerned about undressing before the boys?

C. Well I can't answer that. . . . I won't be able to answer that one.

Mrs. Lilly obviously could not tell me much about these matters in response to direct inquiry. She was becoming reluctant about talking of sexually connotative material so we moved on to discussion of the course of problem behavior.

C. I thought everything was going just fine until Mr. Edwards, the principal at the junior high called. . . . It was in April, I believe, and it just floored me.

E. You really hadn't thought anything was wrong.

C. No, I thought everything was just beautiful. And it just . . . it just floored me. I couldn't get over that. He wanted someone to come just immediately. Of course I couldn't because I don't drive and we live out in the country and I said, well, I'll do the best I could to call him [Mr. Lilly]. It happened to be right at noon, and I said I'd get him, so he came right home and went in. I was just . . . mm . . . I don't know what to say.

E. Well, you were really surprised and upset.

C. Yes, I certainly was.

E. What had Walter done at that time?

C. Well, the way I got it he must have said something pretty bad. Well the fact is I did get it from Walter he did. Walter said he was just so mad . . . that he didn't care what he did, and you know when you get real angry well you don't sometimes care what you say. . . .

E. You might say a few words you wouldn't say in church. . . .

C. And later on you're sorry.

E. So he wasn't just . . . he wasn't just frightened, was he? At that time he was angry too.

C. Yes, mm hm. . . .

In the next part of the interview, some additional information was gained about the way Walter's collapse at school was handled by the parents. Mr. Lilly had gone to school but had not seen Walter there, and then when Walter came home the parents evidently did not mention the problem at all.

C. Harold (Mr. Lilly) went in between the time that . . . ah . . . school lets out at three, between twelve and three there . . . so Walter wouldn't know that his father had been at school. And Walter didn't know that his father had been at school. And Walter didn't know a thing about this for a long long time. He knew of course his dad was home when he got off the bus because he saw the car home, and Walter usually gets home earlier than his father does . . . and he was kind of wondering, but I said oh . . . it had looked stormy, and I said oh . . . I just kind of wanted him home . . . so he wouldn't know about this . . . and we hadn't said anything. . . I believe it was on a Friday . . . Thursday . . . Friday I believe it was. We didn't say anything. I didn't think we should.

We then moved on to a discussion of the generality of Walter's problems.

E. Well Walter has mentioned, and other people at the school have mentioned, that his fear and anger about the physical education situation was one problem, but I suppose there are others. I don't know what all of them are. What do you see as other difficulties Walter is having . . . in his life? The whole problem is not strictly about the P.E. surely. . . .

C. Well, he's having problems of not having friends.

E. Yes.

C. It's very hard for him to make friends. He only has one, and . . . of course he's, this boy he has . . . he's O.K., but Walter needs more. . . . He needs someone a little bit different than this boy because he's so much like Walter, and and mm . . . and I think Walter needs someone that'll say "Well, come on Walt, let's get going doing things," instead of standing back.

E. This fellow is like Walter.

C. He is.

E. In . . . in what ways?

C. Won't go into any activities or anything at school . . . nothing.

E. Mm. He kind of hangs back too.

C. Mm hm. Mm hm. But I like for Walter to be in something. You know, something . . . some activities of some sort.

We spent a few moments agreeing that another kind of friend might offer a better model than the young soulmate to whom Walter had attached himself, and then began considering the behavioral reasons for Walter's lack of friends.

E. Why is he so friendless?

C. I don't know. . . . I . . . it's hard. Mm—mm—I think Walter could have a lot of friends . . . at least I have that feeling. . . . Well, like a lot of times like we're uptown, and various places you come across other boys and they'll say, "Hi, hi Walt!" and Walter will not answer, and I say, "Walter, that's not right." I said he should answer.

E. So they are friendly to him but he's not very friendly in return. What you're really saying is that there are certain ways Walter deals with other boys that either drive them off or cause them to lose interest or something of this kind. He . . . he just doesn't reciprocate their friendly advances. . . . There's something about him so that even though they might approach him in a friendly way . . .

C. Mm hm. Mm hm. . . .

E. He turns them back. So it's a matter of his avoiding others as much as others avoiding him.

Then I asked an open question about other problems, but this yielded no very useful return, so I turned to discussion of the generality of a highly visible form of behavior, Walter's crying.

E. One of the things that was very clear to me as I saw him . . . that would strike me as an obvious problem, is his crying.

C. Mm hm.

E. This is not usual for a boy as old as he is, to break down in tears as he does, and I wonder how much of that kind of thing you see around home.

C. Well, just here recently, yes, well, this July month, it started with him getting afraid. We went through it four years ago, you know, it was the same way. He was afraid of getting sick, and this was, mm . . . a little bit worse, because he was afraid that his heart would stop.

E. Afraid he had heart trouble and would die.

C. Mm hm, and he would die. And oh, I'll tell you, it's hard.

E. It really must be.

C. Oh it is, and he just went hysterical. I says we've got to get him calmed down. He can't sleep, he walks the floor, you know. . . . This has been going on.

E. Does he keep you awake, or how does that go?

C. Yes, well you see our bedroom and his bedroom is connected, and he has to go through our bedroom if he has to go to the bathroom, so I know what he's doing. . . . I don't sleep that terribly sound, unless I just happen to be . . .

E. So he gets up, and he keeps you awake.

C. Oh yes, mm hm, well, he'd cry, as far as that goes. . . .

E. Then what would happen?

C. He'd say his heart was going to stop. . . .

E. You'd ask him what's wrong, and he'd say, "I think I'm going to die, and" . . .

C. Yes, and he couldn't feel his heart beat.

E. What did you do then?

C. Well, we'd tell him, "Walter, you're not going to die, you'll be all right," but he'd say he couldn't see his heart beating and you know he is big, though he's lost a lot. When he left school in June he was a hundred-and-sixty-nine, and he's gone down to one-forty-three.

I was led away from a more thorough discussion of the parents' reaction to Walter's crying behavior here, a topic which would have been worth pursuit.

E. He has lost quite a bit of weight, hasn't he?

C. Yes, he has. Well he could stand to lose it, couldn't he? It's the wrong reason for it, I suppose, but . . . he was too heavy.

The impression gained from Walter and from both parents, however, in regard to the consequences of his crying, seem reasonably consistent. In general, the parents had quite a bit to do with him when he cried and expressed anguished concern over dying. Walter made any other reactions difficult, behaving as he did through the night, and the parents evidently tried to calm him down by the simple procedure of telling him to calm down. Clearly this had not worked.

In an inquiry of the kind being developed here, current behavior and the conditions eliciting and maintaining it have investigative priority over dynamics and history, as the latter are usually studied. Nonetheless, in Walter's own statements and in the report of the father, relationships between Walter and his grandmother had assumed special significance. I inquired into this relationship further, starting from a lead provided by Mr. Lilly.

E. I wonder if you'd give me your reaction to something your husband said when he was here. . . . He thought that part of this was re-

lated to the fact that Walter had been babied by his grandmother
when he was very small.

C. Yes.

E. What . . . what would you think of that?

C. I do think he was, because he's carried on quite a bit about his
grandma here lately.

E. It was one of the things he talked to me about too. He said . . .
she was the only . . .

C. It was kind of a hard . . .

E. She was the only one who . . .

C. Yes it was pretty hard to take. . . .

It may be informative, if personally embarrassing, to comment
on the poor interviewing in evidence here. Mrs. Lilly was trying to
tell me either how hard Grandma's death was for Walter to accept,
or how hard her living in the home was for Mrs. Lilly to take. There
is no way to tell from the interview material I had gotten so far.
In fact, I then compounded my error by moving one interpretative
step farther, to the idea that Walter was saddened so deeply by his
grandmother's death because she was the only person who really
"understood" him. The client fortunately prevented me from extending this too far, and some useful material then began to emerge.

E. She died about two years ago did you say?

C. Yes it was in February.

E. And they were very close. . . .

C. Oh yes, like two peas in a pod (laughs).

E. How did she treat him? How did she deal with him? What . . .
what sort of two-peas-in-a-podness did they have together? What
. . . what kind of relationship was this?

C. Well, how am I going to say this?

E. Go ahead.

C. I know. I'm thinking. . . . Well he'd go over there a lot because
her . . . we have a small house. She didn't live in the same house;
she had her own little house.

E. But right nearby, right on the same lot.

C. Oh yes. Our back door, which is our utility room, faces the small
house. She came over a lot, but she had her own house.

E. But she was there a lot, and she was always there when Walter
needed her. So she was close. So then, how did she and Walter get
along? I mean how did she treat Walter that made her such a special
person to him?

C. I don't know how to tell you this.

E. Well, do the best you can.

C. Well as we know, and as you have said, he was spoiled. We'd correct him, and Grandma, she'd . . . she'd say it wasn't the right think to do, and she'd almost cry, so . . .

E. Would she?

C. Yes. . . . Oh I've seen the time where, well we did, we had to have her in our home after she broke her hip . . . and when I tried to correct Walter, she'd just cry. I'll tell you . . .

E. It must have been a very . . .

C. It was rough, I'll tell you, it's been a rough life. I don't advise anyone to do it.

E. It must have been very difficult for you. You were caught right between weren't you?

C. Well, yes. . . .

E. Suppose Walter should do something that you thought he ought to be corrected about, and you tried to do it, and then, if I understand it, Walter would go running to Grandma. . . .

C. Right, that's right.

E. And she would protect him . . . and cry.

C. Yes. . . .

E. And say "there Walter, everything will be fine."

C. Yes. . . .

E. And don't you touch him. . . .

C. Yes. . . .

E. And would you correct him or wouldn't you? How would that turn out? Who won, Grandma or you?

C. Well, I imagine Grandma did . . . just to keep peace, I think, Grandma did.

E. So Walter really wouldn't get corrected.

C. Right.

In the remainder of the interview, the content of greatest interest concerns Walter's relationships with his neighbors, and then more generally with other people.

E. All right, let's talk about a different topic. Walter had mentioned a feeling about his neighbors looking down at him, feeling he's no good, and so on. What is there to that?

C. Oh no, that isn't true at all. They hire him to mow the lawn and so on.

E. Recognize him as a good worker, and hire him to do the job.

C. Yes, mm hm.

E. So this is in Walter's mind, isn't it?

C. Right.

E. This—this feeling that . . . it's a lot of things, isn't it—it's a feeling that the neighbors are looking down at him and thinking he's no good. It's a feeling that the boys in school are looking down on him. . . .

C. Mm hm.

E. And thinking ill of him, that his teachers don't like him. Some kind of . . . general feeling that nobody likes him. That nobody thinks he's any good. . . .

C. Mm hm.

By this time, the scanning operation was essentially finished. In the interviews with his parents, new information was gained about Walter's problems, the historical origins of some of the problems, the current situational conditions supporting problem behavior, and the parents themselves. Extended inquiry, the next phase of clinical procedure as defined in the preceding chapter, was considerably truncated in this case. Walter led a restricted life. Almost the only places he ever went were school and home, so the varieties of contact which might have been needed to understand action in the case of a more liberated, free-ranging human being were less numerous than usual. The full cast of significant others in Walter's life, of course, was not limited to the parents. His grandmother, his neighbors, his lone friend, the strong arm robber at school, all mattered to him one way or another. But as I have previously suggested, understanding any human being totally, in all situations which matter to him, is impossible in principle, and close approximations to total comprehension are ordinarily very difficult in practice. I did not, for this example, see fit to visit Walter's neighbors though they were important in his life. Permission would have been awkward and maybe impossible to obtain; the difficulty seemed to lie mainly in Walter's beliefs and attitudes regarding his neighbors rather than in any of their objective stimulus properties. In any case I was pessimistic that these people were likely to change much in their treatment of Walter even if change were desirable.

The extended inquiry therefore went only as far as the school situation. That seemed fruitful to examine, since Walter's current problem had arisen in school, since there seemed to be some marked differences between his behavior in school and at home, and since even at this early phase I hoped to enlist the help of some of the school personnel in dealing with Walter's difficulties.

I therefore arranged a meeting with the principal, the dean of boys, and three teachers at Walter's school. Our conference began with a description by the examiner of the behavior which had led to Walter's referral, and the accounts which had previously been given were essentially confirmed. The physical education instructor added some richness of detail, however, by recounting a number of incidents in which Walter had failed socially and had become upset before the other boys. He had never been able to learn to catch a ball—basketball, football, baseball, or any other kind—and the instructor's description of an incident in which Walter had been hit on the head by a basketball while he was alone under the opposing team's board was vivid and poignant. Another time Walter had quailed at the brink of the swimming pool until some of his classmates pushed him in. "They shouldn't have done that, of course," said the instructor, "and I bawled them out about it, but it was kind of funny, the way he flailed around."

I asked specifically whether Walter had ever shown any anger under circumstances like these and was told that he did not. The physical education teacher said "That kid is afraid of everything. I wish he would get mad once in awhile."

The other teachers agreed on this point. His difficulties evidently were not restricted to physical education. He had also become upset in a shop course where the boys "got a little rough." Walter had cried and asked to be allowed to leave the course. This he was permitted to do and was placed in an art course, where he had no trouble with the other students but where he was doing inadequate work. In fact, he was doing marginal work in all his courses and was in some danger of failing to pass his grade. He had been given a group intelligence test recently and performed at a dull normal level. This was consistent with an IQ of 88 obtained on a Binet four years before. Discussion turned to Walter's dubious academic and vocational future, and his English teacher said, "I don't know what he'll be able to do for a living. He isn't bright enough for half the jobs in the world and the other half are too rough."

The difficulties which had arisen in getting the parents to deal with Walter's problems were brought up and discussed and, as an interesting sidelight, the principal mentioned that Mr. Lilly himself had cried during the talk that fateful afternoon. "It seemed incongruous," said the principal, "a big rough man like that in tears," but it began to appear that Walter had at least two major exemplars for his tearful behavior.

Most of the rest of the meeting time was spent discussing plans for the future. We considered the pros and cons of withdrawing Walter from the physical education class, and the principal agreed to do this if conditions seemed to warrant such a move, though a medical excuse would be legally required. I said that I wanted to think some more about Walter's problems and what to do about them, and that I hoped the school staff would help me in two ways —by making some observations and reporting behavior on Walter's part, and quite likely by taking part in the effort to help Walter. It seemed obvious to us all that at least the way in which Walter's crying in school was dealt with might be changed, and I suggested that we work that out further in another meeting a week hence.

Apparently significant data can be summarized at this point. Clinical material is always complex, and multiple and varied interpretations could be cast for each utterance in every interview, but at a fairly simple level and in a rather straightforward way, the behavior which has been reported and observed so far does not appear to be very difficult to comprehend. From Walter's point of view, the major problem is a fear of dying by heart failure. This is keenly experienced and is accompanied by a number of physiological anxiety concomitants; a feeling of dizziness, a tight feeling in the throat, and a loss of appetite which has led to a weight reduction of 25 pounds. The acute disturbance has persisted for about a month, though some analogous problems had appeared before, and Walter has cried in school for quite a long time. The most obviously deviant and disordered feature of Walter's behavior in the interview itself was the amount of weeping he displayed. He cried almost continuously throughout the first third of the interview. It is not evident from the typescript or tape, but it is important to note that very few tears were shed through all the sobbing. Walter was watching me through much of his lamentation and a question arose in my mind, as I talked to him, about the function of the crying, more specifically its status as an instrumental as contrasted with an expressive act, for it seemed at least plausible to guess that in some measure the behavior was designed for effect on the interviewer. I believe all his behavior was consistent with the idea that his salient mode of self-presentation emphasized misery, loneliness, and helplessness. "I am a wretched creature, suffering all alone." And this transactional stimulus seemed designed to encourage "understanding," unbounded sympathy, and succor from me. That is the kind of game he appeared to be playing. The partially witting duplicity in it was tempered by evidently sincere wishes for improvement in his way of feeling. At one point, after talking in anguished tones about the subjective fact that nobody really cared for him at all, Walter began crying with especial vigor and said, "You'll help me, won't you? You've got to help me."

There is also a question concerning the covert emotional states which accompanied Walter's crying. There is no reason to suppose these always covary in just the same way. From the mother's report particularly, and in part from Walter's own comment, there is some basis for believing that helpless rage was as much a part of his outburst at school as any kind of pathetic fear.

Over the long course, there appears to be a sense in which the symptoms served to exempt Walter from unpleasant circumstances. He effectively avoided physical education classes by this means; he got out of a shop class where the boys were too rough, and the earlier incident in which he had felt as if he might be sick at the County Fair had extricated him from that situation too, though neither Walter nor anyone else has yet provided information to show why physical education classes, shop courses, or conditions associated with fairgrounds should have such strongly aversive qualities.

His behavior seemed to be related in still indeterminate ways to the attitudes he believed other people had toward him. Very early in the interview with Walter, he began talking about his elderly neighbors, whom he felt did not like him, did not think he was any good, and whom he evidently tried to placate by keeping his own house and yard as neat and attractive as possible. The reports of the parents were particularly helpful in interpreting these remarks. The mother's opinion converged with that of the father to suggest that Walter was responding at least in part to a pseudo-community—that his feelings and beliefs about the neighbors' negative evaluations of him were based less on their behavior than on

Walter's own beliefs about them, and by no very thinly stretched chain of inferences, on his ambivalent, dominantly negative evaluation of himself.

Indeed the affectional attitudes of others seemed to be of extraordinary importance to Walter. His maternal grandmother, the only person in his life who "really understood" him, died and left him, and he had been "no good" ever since. His grandmother on the father's side did not care for him, in his view, and at the very end of the protocol above, where he talked about "a grandma that cares" as one of the three wishes, he immediately said "little things like that hurt me." He was thinking, I believe, about the live, rejecting grandmother instead of the dead, loving one with whom so painful a contrast occurred in Walter's experience.

Once more the interviews with parents provide especially useful data for clarification of a family pattern that seems to have had much to do with Walter's present behavior. All three, but mother and father especially, agreed as to the frequent and disturbing recurrence of an action sequence in which some corrigible behavior on Walter's part would lead to an attempt at corrective action by the parents; but this would be aborted by a weeping grandmother who managed all at once to model an infantilism, prevent learning of mature behavior, irritate and possibly infuriate the parents, and establish between Walter and herself a stickily dependent association for which Walter had pined ever since her death.

The good grandmother was gone, the surviving grandmother was bad, and except for his own mother, Walter did not think anybody "understood" or cared for him at all. He had only one friend, and his classmates at school served mainly to torment him, extorting money, "screaming" at him, "picking" on him, and never never coming to him with friendship to give. Walter's need for affection was very strong, and his present supply was very weak.

The lack of satisfactory peer relationships evidently constituted a problem in its own right—Walter mentions the need to have some friends as his first wish—and Mrs. Lilly identified his not having friends as the second problem, right after his difficulties about physical education in school. She also gave some useful hints about transactional patterns which might serve to prevent Walter from forming friendships. Friendly advances from other children met only rebuff from Walter, for whatever reason, and it is not surprising that the others turned away from him.

When the behavior of most immediate clinical interest, that is the expressed fear of dying, was displayed at home, Walter's parents evidently tried to talk him out of it. All three clients agree about that. If Walter's comment about the "loud" behavior of his father is interpreted in the most obvious and direct way, it would appear that Mr. Lilly became at least irritated and possibly quite angry over Walter's whining. The mother seemed to be less quickly disposed to irritation, but she was unable to think of anything except reassurance to offer when Walter talked of death.

Walter's own angry behavior received neither mention nor display until late in his own interview, but then, when he told about his "bad mouth," and the way he "screams off" at home, it grew clear that Walter did not always appear as the sad and pitiful person the social worker described and which he seemed to be at first. A situational difference in behavior is obvious. Walter "don't say a word" at school, though he has not directly told us whether his feelings there are those of unmixed anxiety or something more complex.

With this informational base, more definite specification of changeworthy behavior, and the functional relationships associating the behavior to the internal and external conditions which determine it, can provisionally be formed. No pretense of completeness is offered. The depth of possible interpretation is unlimited, and it would not be too difficult to support the hypothesis that Walter's concern over dying represented an unconscious wish to join his departed grandmother. The extent of psychosocial field dependence of behavior is also limitless. As restricted as Walter's life may seem, it would be a fairly easy matter to exhaust several months exploring the stimulus properties and other characteristics of all the people who mattered to this boy. I suspect change to an affectionate reaction from his living grandmother would have a considerable effect on Walter. The behavior of the neighbors, of his lone friend, and of a lot of other people who might become friends would all have to be comprehended in any full account of Walter's interpersonal situation. How far back to go historically is not easy to decide. One cannot confine himself strictly to current circumstances if any general action pattern is to be established at all. Walter and his parents themselves came early and spontaneously to talk of the grandmother, a figure of the past who evidently helped determine some behavior patterns in the present. One could go beyond that if he chose, and the next inquiry might reveal the basic fact, the illuminating clue to which all others are related.

But one has to stop somewhere, and the relatively brief inquiry conducted so far was richly productive of data needed for planning certain forms of treatment and for developing the added observational and experimental operations by which new knowledge might be gained. The tasks of pursuing further inquiries and of planning treatment are not merely related, in part they are identical. These both consist of the designation of a specific problem behavior, or a set of such behaviors, in their situational and dispositional context. In Walter's case the most obvious problem was his fear of dying, as he subjectively experienced it, along with the crying and other lamentation overtly associated with the fear. The reaction was most visibly occasioned by threatening social circumstances, particularly the physical education class, but fairly wide generality is now apparent. According to the father, Walter "howls and moans" at home each night, and he cried through most of the interview with me. So far, no one was able to deliver a social consequence with any effect in reducing the behavior. There is in fact some reason to suppose that the kinds of reaction which Walter's crying most commonly evoked, namely sympathy, reassurance, cajolery, occasional muted irritation, and other forms of attention, served principally to maintain the behavior. Even the anger which his father appeared to show sometimes cannot automatically be regarded as an aversive consequence. Walter gave several indications of anger along with his fear, and later interviews showed how intense the anger toward his father could occasionally be. To an angry boy, reciprocal anger on the part of a hated object may be the most effective positive reinforcer of all.

One hypothesis concerning the origin of the symptom and a possibility for treating it was developed very simply by regarding Walter's expressed fear and crying as an unadorned excuse for getting out of the threats and unpleasantries of physical education. He had a history of avoiding difficulties by tears and fears, and it seemed most parsimonious to construe the symptoms provisionally as a complex instrumental avoidant action.

This hypothesis was put to test the first week of treatment in a way which provided a limited amount of observational baseline data on the symptom itself, and yielded results suggesting that the symptoms indeed appeared to have an instrumental avoidant utility, but that there was more to the behavior than that.

I had arranged to see Walter and his parents for a planning session four days later and had asked them during this time to do two things; first to take Walter to his doctor for a thorough physical examination, and second to keep a rough count of the amount of time Walter spent crying and the number of times he expressed concern about the way his heart was working, about dying, or anything related to his fear of death. I called the principal at school to ask for the same kinds of information, but as it turned out Walter stayed home from school for the next week so the only information available came from the home.

Walter had a particularly bad time in the three days after I saw him. The parents did not keep an hour-by-hour record of his behavior, but for clinical purposes I found their semi-quantitative statement adequate. Walter (and the parents) "hadn't slept hardly at all" the night following his interview with me because Walter was so badly upset. The following night, according to the father, they "had a better time—maybe four-five hours of sleep." The third night, following the afternoon in which I had seen the mother, was a difficult one again. "Walter was up most of the night," and so were the parents.

In the planning session the next day, all three members of the family were seen together. The results of the medical examination were available by that time; the findings were completely negative as far as cardiac disorder was concerned and the first thing we did was discuss this reality in the most direct possible fashion. There was nothing wrong with Walter's heart, he was not going to die, and that was all there was to that.

I acknowledged, however, that this did not lessen Walter's fear and I resonated again to the painful subjective reality of Walter's experience. To Walter I said, "I know what a terrible feeling this has to be for you—I know you still *feel* afraid even if your heart is all right," and to the parents, "Heart trouble or no heart trouble, things are pretty rough with all of you these days, and we have got to do something about the way Walter has been feeling and behaving." I told them that I intended to work directly with Walter in getting rid of the fear by teaching him to relax whenever he felt the fear coming on, and that I would want to see Mr. and Mrs. Lilly too, possibly quite often, to help Walter feel and act in a better, happier way than he had before.

We discussed at greater length the advantages and dangers of taking Walter out of the physical education class. He was enthusiastically in favor of withdrawing and his parents wanted him to get out too. With some clinical ambivalence but with an investigative interest in seeing what this measure alone would do to Walter's behavior, I agreed to arrange for an excuse from the class. Mr. and Mrs. Lilly were asked to keep notes on Walter's crying and fearful behavior and another meeting with them all was set for a week hence.

For two days following announcement to Walter that he would not have to attend the physical education class his crying nearly stopped, though he still worried about dying and spent a good deal of time with his fingers on his pulse or feeling his chest to see if his heart was still going. Mr. Lilly said, "I thought we had it beat there," but his optimism was not long to last. The next day Walter began to cry again and by the time we met once more, five days after that, Walter was crying nearly as much as he had been during the earlier acute disturbance and he was still as afraid of dying as he had been before.

I met with the family together again in the next session and began to tell the parents how they might eliminate the crying behavior which was upsetting them all. I reiterated the clear medical fact that Walter was physically healthy and that he was not going to die. I recognized the equally clear fact that Walter still felt afraid, and assured everyone there with the most potent placebo I could muster that I would be able to help Walter get rid of the fear. And I then said that Walter's crying, though it was related to his fear, was something we ought to deal with in its own right. I remarked that the crying was not helping matters any and in fact was probably making the fear worse. In as kindly as possible a way for a remark so blunt, I told Walter and all assembled that he was too big to be crying like that and that as the fear went away his crying should too.

Walter was excused then and I told the parents to ignore Walter's crying whenever it occurred. ("Don't scold him, don't argue with him, don't do a blooming thing when he cries. Just go on about your business. Pay no attention to him at all. But if he does . . . anything else—nearly anything at all that a fifteen-year-old boy should do or talk about—then you talk to him. Show him you're interested in that.")

The next day I visited the school and made the same suggestion to all of Walter's teachers (one of whom could not attend the meeting and had to be informed indirectly). Of course I planned to employ the same extinction procedure in the meetings Walter and I had together and when we next met I did indeed look out the window and remain silent whenever Walter cried. I offered attention only when his speech was free of the sniffs and sobs which generally characterized it.

In that session I began a desensitization series by establishing an anxiety hierarchy for various objects and situations which brought fears of death to Walter's mind, and introduced some training in relaxation. Following fairly standard procedures as outlined by Paul (1966), relaxation was taught by having Walter alternately tense and relax various muscle groups. Images of feared situations were induced in the following order: watching an accident report on a television news program, seeing a minor automobile accident, seeing an automobile accident in which someone was hurt, seeing an empty hearse standing by the curb, seeing a hearse with a casket inside, seeing an old person in a crowd become sick and collapse, seeing a boy his own age become sick and collapse, hearing his physician say the patient had heart trouble, feeling his own heart begin to beat more slowly, having a heart attack without experience of pain, having a heart attack with pain, difficulty in breathing, and the experience of death itself. As usual in this procedure whenever anxiety was signalled on introduction of a new stimulus the therapist "backed off" and got the patient to relax again. Sometimes this was done by inducing fantasies farther down the hierarchy and in a few extreme cases by having the patient think instead about the most placid scene he could imagine, lying under a tree on a hot summer day.

In addition to desensitization in the office I attempted late in the series to establish generality by giving Walter personal control over the basic procedure. I instructed him to relax as completely as possible whenever he began to think about dying. "Whenever you get the idea that your heart might stop or that you might die, you just relax yourself wherever you happen to be. Find a soft chair someplace or lie down if you can, but the important thing is to relax yourself. Tense and then relax your muscles just the way you do here and keep on doing that until you actually are relaxed. You will find that by then the fear has gone away." According to his own report, Walter attempted this a number of times and was successful in all but one instance. The entire desensitization procedure took eight sessions.

By that time Walter's crying had entirely ceased in the interview situation, and in the brief supportive checking interviews I had with Walter's father, it appeared that his crying had almost stopped at home too. Reappraisal seemed in order and this was done the following week. The first brief interview was with Walter himself.

E. I want to know how your problems look to you right now. Remember when you came here you felt that you had some fairly serious problems. How about your fear of dying, are you still afraid you're going to die?

C. (Laughs) No . . . well not really . . . once in a while I still feel like something's wrong, but it's not like it was. . . . Well once in a while I hear about some boy my age dying and things like that . . . and then I get sort of a feeling something might be wrong. . . .

E. With your heart?

C. Something might be wrong with my heart. But I don't really believe that any more and it don't bother me like it used to. . . . It's better, much better.

The central symptoms—a subjective fear of death and overt displays of crying—thus appeared to have subsided a good deal, though the idea that "something might be wrong" still crossed Walter's mind from time to time. It is interesting to note that other changes had evidently occurred while the major symptom reduction was going on. For one thing, Walter expressed a different attitude toward his neighbors, though I do not believe they were mentioned at all in our conversations after the first interview.

E. I can remember your being concerned about your neighbors . . . and how they felt about you. What about that now?

C. They're more friendlier. They seem to be. They don't care what I do —that's my business.

E. Mm hm.

C. They're different than they were. I don't know. Maybe they're no different than they were before, but it seems like they are. I don't let 'em bother me.

Later in the interview I asked him to think of three wishes again. You may recall that before he had wanted to have some friends, to be "himself" again, the way he was before his acute disturbance, and "to have a grandma that cares." Now he said he wanted "a car, good grades, and to be happier . . . more . . . happier."

There were still difficulties in the way Walter got along with other people. These had never really been dealt with; I believe they had and still have focal importance in Walter's life. He freely mentioned some of the problems he was continuing to have with other boys at school.

E. When we talked last, you said you weren't getting along too well with other people at school. How about this now? How are you getting along with other people your own age?

C. Well I still have a problem there with a colored kid. . . .

E. Do you?

C. Trying to take money again. I don't know why. I hate that. Every time I go in class he's right there, after me, pushing me around, taking money right out of my pocket.

E. How did that go? What did you do then?

C. I was in there, and he come in there, and he threw me against the . . . mm . . . bookcase there, and he said he wanted some gum and I was supposed to buy him some . . . gum.

E. Yes.

C. And I said I didn't have any money, and then he went and took the money out of my pocket.

E. Just strongarmed you?

C. Yes, just reached right in my pocket and got it.

E. He's bigger than you, and he just took it.

C. Yes, he's about my size, but he's . . .

E. Tougher . . .

C. Yes, he's . . . they carry knives and things. . . . I couldn't fight him.

E. So he just took the money and walked off.

C. Yes.

Not only were negative experiences of this kind continuing to occur, the absence of positive friendships was still conspicuous in Walter's life.

E. What about relationships of a better kind? You said before you wanted more friends. . . . Do you have any friends now?

C. Just the same one boy. That's all I seem to get. I don't know, just that boy.

E. Well let's not talk about *getting* friends. Have you done anything to *make* friends with anybody else?

C. No, just that one boy.

E. Are there chances for you to talk to other people?

C. Yes.

E. Well, why . . . why don't you?

C. I don't know. I—I never could talk to other people like that.

E. If somebody says "Hi, there," you can't just start a conversation.

C. Yes—no—I never could do that.

No interview was conducted with Mrs. Lilly at this time. It was somewhat difficult for her to come in, and the material gained by talking with Walter and his father seemed adequate for the kind of reappraisal that was needed. Mr. Lilly's comments tended mainly to confirm what Walter had said about improvement in the problems which had led to referral.

E. I wanted to check on this. I don't think he's cried at all with me for the past three or four times. . . . How is this . . . how about around home, is he still crying there or not?

C. No, no, he hasn't really cried for a month or so. . . . Now he still does fuss. . . . He still fussed a couple of times last week about his heart. . . .

E. Still worried about that.

C. Yes. He—he was outside working and he came in and he said "Oh, is my heart O.K.? . . . Am I going to live to see my birthday?" So I just ignored him like you said, and then he came up and said I should feel his pulse. "Here, feel my pulse." So I did.

E. You went along with it.

C. Yes, but then I said, "It feels fine to me. You know there's nothing wrong with your heart."

E. O.K.

Following these exchanges, I asked Mr. Lilly to tell me what he could about Walter's lack of friends as this appeared to him now.

E. What about friends? You, your wife, Walter, all three of you said that one of his main problems was that he didn't have any friends. What about that?

C. Well, we are getting him out a little more . . . that's something.

E. Well, that's right.

C. Well one of our mistakes was, he was crying and like he was doing when he first come in here, and he just set around home, but now . . . we went over to Rockville last Sunday, and this Sunday we're going over to New Salem, and we're taking Walter and his friend along.

E. This one friend he has.

C. Yes, his buddy . . . and they have a pretty good time actually, but that's the only friend he's got.

Later in the interview Mr. Lilly spoke of an increase in angry behavior on Walter's part. This was directed particularly toward Mr. Lilly himself, but the account of circumstances under which the behavior occurred and the details of the transactional pattern which took place were quite vague. The increase in angry behavior, however, was very definite as Mr. Lilly saw it. "He may be an angel in school, but he's getting to be a hellion around home."

A reappraisal conference was scheduled at the school where once again the facts of a considerable behavior change were confirmed. As far as anyone could report, Walter had not cried at all in any circumstance whatever for the past four weeks. Everyone who had observed him said that he was much better and that the acute disturbance had evidently ceased. There still were problems with Walter's behavior, however. He was no more assertive nor even socially responsive than he had been before, either in the classroom or in his extra-class dealings with other children. "He just sits there," said one teacher, "I guess he hears things but there is no way to tell. He never raises his hand to answer a question and sometimes I'll call on him and he manages to get out some kind of an answer, but usually he says he doesn't know."

Another teacher commented that Walter still behaved in the same timid way with other boys. "You know some of these kids are a little rough. They won't say 'May I please borrow a pencil?' They'll say, 'Give me a pencil, man,' and Walter gets scared out of his boots. They don't really mean to bother anybody, but Walter acts like they're going to beat him up."

There was, then, by the client's description and the reports of others, a substantial change in the behavior which had been selected as a major target for modification. At relatively little therapeutic cost substantial apparent improvement had been brought about in Walter's crying and fear of death, but there were obvious residual problems in interpersonal relationships and in some of the beliefs and attitudes which influenced those relationships. Deciding whether to continue, interrupt, or terminate treatment was therefore not an easy matter to be determined directly by the facts in the case.

I do not believe that such decisions ever are dictated by the facts of a case record. The notion of a total personality reconstruction is a psychiatric will o' the wisp. Whatever problems are resolved, there will always be more in any human life. Whatever changes may be accomplished, other changes can be conceived, may still be desired, and may still be actively sought. A treatment decision of this kind can never be rooted in the idea that the patient is cured or that he is incurable. With sufficiently extreme changes in the stimulus circumstances surrounding behavior, some change could be evoked in some aspect of behavior for any living human being. And any improvement a therapist might accomplish could always be followed by others. The human capacity for disorder has no limit. Beyond every problem lies another. And the human capacity for change, some kind, some measure of change, is equally boundless.

The decision to treat or not is essentially administrative. One must weigh predicted accomplishments against the predicted costs of therapeutic action and together with the client and others importantly affected arrive at the most satisfactory possible decision for all concerned.

In this case we decided to continue. In a talk with Walter and his father I said I could see at least three problems we might do something about, namely the angry behavior Walter was displaying at home, the ineffective way Walter was dealing with intimidation by other boys at school, especially the one who had been taking money from him, and the lack of friends on Walter's part. I suggested that we deal with each of these in turn and Walter and his father agreed to come in for weekly visits to see what might be done to work the problems out.

Over the next four visits we three talked together about Walter's anger outbursts. These had been occurring with greater and greater frequency lately and turned out on somewhat closer inspection to be angry exchanges, fights between father and son, rather than unilateral explosions on Walter's part alone. We were unable to define any very general transactional pattern. Critical conditions seemed to change from one fight to the next. But we were able to locate a limited number of conditions which prevailed in substantial numbers of incidents and proceeded to see what could be done about changing those.

One rather common form of transaction went roughly as follows. Walter would nag his father incessantly to do something that he, Walter, wanted. One time it was to work together repainting their garage, another time Walter wanted to look at used cars with an eye toward possible purchase of an automobile for his own use. Mr. Lilly, for one reason or another, would be unable or unwilling to do what Walter wanted, but his mildly stated refusals did not have much deterrent effect on Walter. So Walter would increase the intensity of his demands until they became provocatively angry. He would shout the demands at these times, cursing the father, "screaming off," as he had described it at the very start of our work. Mr. Lilly would then get angry too, and had sometimes struck his son, but after they both had cooled down a bit Mr. Lilly would feel guilty about his own loss of control, and to "make it up" to Walter they would go ahead and do whatever it was Walter had demanded in the first place. In spite of the fact that there was no prospect whatever of their getting a car for Walter, they had gone to look at some anyway and Walter then began to pester his father to buy him a slightly used Oldsmobile which had caught his eye.

Obviously the reinforcement schedule in effect for Walter delivered intermittent rewards for intensely emotional behavior, and the partial relationship which had evolved between father and son was one of nagging, ultimately angry demands upon a grudging, equally angry giver. Among us we developed a provisional solution to the problem in which the father was to decide as soon as Walter began to make one of his more insistent demands whether compliance would be possible or not. If he could not meet the demand he should ignore Walter's nagging entirely. He was never to give in to angrily emotional demands on Walter's part. Walter, on his side of the transaction, agreed to try to "catch himself" when he was nagging. He said he hadn't known he was doing it. And he agreed, as we talked in the office at least, to accept his father's decisions in good grace.

As they attempted to practice this new pattern at home there naturally were greater difficulties than were anticipated in the warm enthusiasm and noble resolve of office conversation. Mr. Lilly still lost his temper from time to time. Walter still nagged. But during the course of our remaining contacts the frequency of fights over issues of these kinds reportedly diminished. The last time we talked about this there had been no fights in a month, and at the time the problem was first brought up Walter and his father were engaging in some kind of angry exchange at least two or three times each week.

The same sequential problem-solving approach which had been employed in the conjoint interviews with Walter and his father were employed in additional individual interviews with Walter. We considered first his way of dealing with the boy who had been taking money from him at school. Up to this point he had behaved in an entirely passive way when his tormenter accosted him. Money would be demanded, and except for a few whines and complaints, Walter did nothing to prevent the strongarm robbery from taking place. It would have been delightful, of course, to train Walter in *karate* and let him deal with the problem directly, but we agreed that he had neither the muscular apparatus nor the courage to make such a course feasible in the short time available. Anyway it was quite likely that his attacker knew *karate* too and the prospect of failure in an actual showdown seemed rather high no matter what Walter might have done to prepare himself for it.

After considerable talk we agreed it would be a good idea to let the school authorities know what was going on. Robbery was taking place, whatever the amount of the theft, and not only for Walter's sake, but for the sake of others who might be enduring similar attacks, and of general civic responsibility it seemed advisable to tell the principal and the dean of boys about these occurrences. I insisted that Walter himself do it, though he wanted me to, and on the day following the interview in which this decision was reached Walter went to the dean and told his story. The dean was not surprised. The boy in question had been in trouble before, not only with school personnel but with the juvenile court, and Walter was assured the protection of School and Law alike if the robberies continued. The dean suggested that Walter come directly to him the next time he was approached by his assailant, and Walter agreed to do this.

Neither he nor I was satisfied, however, with transforming Walter from a silent victim into an informer. Most of the boys in school were not bothered by the boy who had found Walter as his mark, only Walter and two or three other people. I asked Walter what the other boys did when somebody tried to get money from them and Walter said that they just told him to go away. So we decided to see if Walter could learn some of the skills needed to put off an attacker in this way. If physical means could not be managed, verbal defenses, along with the protection of school and legal authority, might suffice.

We therefore spent some time in a direct effort to model and encourage the kind of behavior which seemed most appropriate to the circumstances.

E. What would you do? Suppose I come up and say, "Hey Lilly, how much money you got?" What would you do?

C. Probably give you a quarter (laughs).

E. Oh come on now, what would you say instead? Suppose I come up and say, "Hey Lilly, how much money you got?"

C. I haven't got any.

E. What would he say then?

C. He'd probably say "You're a liar," and then I have to show him what I've got in my pockets and then he'll go away if I really don't have any, but first I got to show him. If I don't do it one time he ripped my pocket off. He did it once.

E. Did he?

C. Yes, I should have smacked him down, should have hit him real hard (laughs).

E. Yes, or at least do something or say something besides just letting him have the money. Let's try it. "Hey Lilly, how much money you got?"

C. Nothing. I haven't got any money.

E. You're lying. Show me.

C. (Laughs). Yes, I'll show you.

E. That's what you do, isn't it? You just go ahead and show him. Try something else. "Go ahead, show me."

C. (Laughs). Get lost (very weakly, laughs).

E. There you go. Fine. But put some feeling in it this time. GET LOST!

C. Get Lost!

E. That's a little better. What would he do then? What is it you said that . . .

C. He'd probably walk off, like he did with the other kids. Maybe not.

E. But the chances of his walking off are at least as good as if you just let him have the money. Let's try it again. "Listen you're lying, you got some money. Show me. . . ."

C. *Get lost!*

E. That's better. Still not too convincing, but that's better.

In these sessions, efforts were made not only to improve Walter's mode of handling unpleasant interpersonal situations but to increase the amount and quality of positive relationships with others. This was approached mainly by suggesting that he enter a greater number of situations where enjoyable or at least comfortable meetings with others might take place and by analyzing with him the kinds of transactional behavior which tended to isolate him from other people. In the course of treatment Walter got a job, on his own, as stockboy at a grocery store. He was very much concerned at first about his capability to do the work and about the treatment he would receive from others at the store. He found, however, that his superiors were "real nice"; he worked hard, was extremely conscientious in discharging his duties, and was, by his own and his father's report, doing very well in the job itself.

He stayed aloof from the other boys, however, and in our sessions we devoted attention mainly to the way he acted and reacted toward the teen age co-workers with whom he spent his time. As his mother had noted in the first interview, as his teachers had said, and as Walter himself has sometimes acknowledged, some of his ways of dealing with boys his own age tended to drive them away or at least failed to encourage friendship. We talked about this a number of times. Now and then tasks were assigned to foster development of simple social skills and possibly to modify the ambivalent social attitudes on which the behavioral failures were evidently based.

C. There's one guy at work that makes me awful nervous. I don't know. He's kind of quiet . . . something about him.

E. You feel uncomfortable when he's around.

C. Mm hm. Of course maybe I should talk to him. . . . I don't know.

E. Tell me some more about that.

C. Well, he talks to everybody but me, and I figure, well if you're going to be like that I can be snotty. . . . I can stick my head up in the air and not talk. I don't know why he's that way.

E. You feel he's sort of . . .

C. Independent . . .

E. Leaving you out deliberately . . .

C. Yes. And you hate to see that. When he talks to somebody else and there you are and he won't say a word to you. But I do my job. . . . I don't worry about him.

E. What would happen . . . suppose . . . what would happen if you just came in and said Hi! and just started talking about something. . . . I don't know what it would be . . . the way people do when they just meet and start talking. What do you think he'd do?

C. I don't know. . . . Who would talk first, me or him?

E. You.

C. Oh. . . .

E. What would happen?

C. He'd probably talk. I don't know. . . . I don't know if I could do that. . . .

E. Well, I know this would be hard for you, but suppose you talked to him anyway. What's the worst thing that could happen? Of all the things you can imagine, what's the worst thing that could happen?

C. Nothing. I can't really think of anything bad that could happen.

E. There really isn't anything very bad that could happen, is there? Seems to me the worst thing that could happen is that he wouldn't talk to you at all. Maybe he'd just give you a dirty look and turn away, but that wouldn't matter too much, would it? You feel uncomfortable with him anyway. If he just turned away, that would be pretty stupid behavior on his part. But I think chances are about 99 out of 100 that he'll just talk to you, and that's all there will be to it.

C. Yes, I think he'd talk to me.

E. And if he did, then maybe you wouldn't feel so uncomfortable with him any more.

C. Yes, maybe so.

E. Walter, they're your own feelings, and you are the one who has to work on them, but I wish you could try that one time when it feels reasonably natural to you. You take the first step. See if you can make yourself do it. . . . You know, don't feel that you'll disappoint me tragically if you can't, but see if you can talk to him the next time you are working together. That's your homework for next week.

Walter tried this the next time he went to work and of course encountered no interpersonal disaster. The young man at the store did not become a true friend either, but Walter's discomfort no longer rose in his presence, and the other boy learned to treat Walter in a perfectly matter-of-fact way. He later confided to Walter that he had begun to think Walter was "some kind of a queer," since he never talked to anybody, but kept watching others out of the corner of his eye. Walter's friendly overtures evidently defined him as normal after all, and at least the relational basis for a possible friendship had been formed.

As I write this, Walter and I are still meeting on a weekly basis, though I think we will discontinue soon. At that point, another evaluation will be performed. I think I know what it will show. Some changes of a desired kind have occurred in Walter's behavior and these appear to be related to some orderly changes in the conditions which determined the behavior. The functional relationships between crying and social reinforcement were established and experimentally modified and a change in overt behavior came about. If necessary for some research purpose, this change in response frequency could be stated in reasonably precise quantitative terms. Functional relationship between certain internal stimulus events, thoughts of dying, and a subjective, visceral anxiety reaction were postulated, modified by means of a replacement program—reciprocal inhibition in the desensitization series—and again the change in behavior could be quantitatively specified. Changes in interpersonal behavior were also sought and in some instances achieved. A shift from two or three fights a week between father and son to no fights for over a month is reliably visible as well as clinically important. Some other changes were sought but not attained, or effected in only a limited way. Walter still has no real friends, aside from the one young fellow with whom he is reasonably comfortable. There are still, I believe, basic problems in Walter's affectional relationships with others, and in his beliefs about and evaluations of himself. Maybe these should be examined more closely and possibly attacked in treatment, now that some of the acute problems are out of the way. That will be up to Walter, his parents, others who affect and are affected by him, and me.

THE CARLETON BROWNS: THE STUDY OF A FAMILY

The following case, of a group, and the one after that, of a social system, will be considered in less detail than the study of an individual which was just presented. The principles and procedures of functional analysis are not fundamentally different for systems, groups, and individuals and the only real need now is to show that that is true, not to demonstrate minutely what the principles and procedures are. Thus, the purpose of the next two sections is to illustrate the use of interviews, observations, and planned treatment manipulations in the functional analysis of a group and of a social system. As in the individual case, there is a demonstration not only of the utility, but the limitations of the method as one attempts to apply it in some reasonably typical field situations.

In my first contacts with the Carleton Brown family I did not particularly regard their problems from a social psychological viewpoint, except insofar as social influences are involved in all behavior disorders, and initial treatment efforts were oriented individually rather than toward the group. Carleton Brown, Jr., a twelve-year-old colored youngster, was referred to the Psychological Clinic by the Juvenile Court. He had committed a number of legally delinquent acts over the past year, the most recent of which was the theft of fifteen dollars from one of his teachers and running away from home when his misdeed was discovered. He had been apprehended by the police and taken to a detention home and was there at the time I was contacted by a probation officer whom I had known for some time. The probation officer, a colored man named Wilson, believed that the hope for rehabilitation and prevention of more serious criminality was greater in this case than in many others of an outwardly similar kind. He said that the Brown boy was "not really a hood," and that the parents were "good people," genuinely interested in helping their son achieve a better life. A court hearing had been scheduled ten days hence and psychological evaluation was needed before that time.

I saw Carleton Jr. first, a tall slightly built boy who greeted me without smiling, and was somewhat cool in all senses throughout our first interview. I told him what I had learned of his difficulties from Mr. Wilson, and asked him to tell me in detail what had led to his recent trouble with the law. He said he had been working with a teacher who had been helping him with his schoolwork after hours. She had stepped out of the room for a few minutes and during that time he had gone to the closet and taken money from his teacher's purse. The door of the closet had been open and the purse could be seen from where Carleton sat. When the teacher left the room he simply went to the closet, took the money, and returned to his seat by the time the teacher got back.

From Carleton's own account and from the reports of others, I learned that the theft was not discovered until that evening. The next day everyone who had had much of a chance to take the money, including Carleton who had had an especially good chance, was questioned about the matter. Two other boys simply denied any part in it but when his turn came, Carleton made up an elaborate tale about another boy who had allegedly entered the room while he was there and the teacher was out. This fellow, as Carleton told the story to the school authorities, had taken the money and left again before the teacher returned. Carleton's description of the boy was highly detailed—the fictitious thief was said to have blond crewcut hair and to wear jeans and white sneakers—but the description was somewhere near the mode for at least a hundred students in the school Carleton attended. When asked why he hadn't mentioned the incident to his teacher later, the best Carleton could manage was to say that he thought the boy had the teacher's permission to take money from her purse. His story was sufficiently preposterous to encourage direct accusation and Carleton quite soon admitted that he had stolen the money. The teacher and principal told the boy they wanted him to tell his father what had happened and sent him home, but Carleton did not go home then. He just wandered around for a long while, and late that night decided to catch a freight train for Chicago. He was in the freight yard of

an industrial plant on the Chicago side of town when a watchman
at the plant became suspicious and called the local police. After
a brief chase they captured Carleton and took him to the detention
home.

I tried to find out what the boy was thinking about at the time
he took the money and discovered only that he wanted to see if
there was any money in the purse and he "figured he could get by
with it." He didn't really want to steal from the teacher, he said;
she was a "nice lady" and had been especially kind to Carleton.
As near as I could determine, he just wanted the money. I also
asked about his decision to run away rather than go home to tell
his father. Carleton said, "If I'd have gone home, he [Carleton's
father] would have beat me up—hit me in the face and kick me in
the stomach—I didn't think I could take that. . . . I don't mind
when he hits me with a belt. Fathers are supposed to do that. But
I can't stand getting kicked around like he does."

In our further conversation, I learned that Carleton had run
away at least two times before. One other incident also followed
a theft. That time Carleton had stolen a watch from a neighbor
and when this was discovered he had left home before his father
returned. He had gone to a movie, slept in a parked car that night,
and just roamed around town the following day. Circumstances
preceding the other runaway were vague. Carleton said he couldn't
remember just how he happened to leave, but the sequence of his
return was roughly the same in both cases. The police found him
and took him to the detention home. I asked him how he liked
the home and he said, "That's the best place I've been. . . . The
people are real nice, and there's always some other kids to talk
to . . . I like the food. You can put peanut butter on your pan-
cakes."

Mr. Brown, whom I saw next, was a rather tall, dark, muscular
man, a teacher in a local elementary school. From him I determined
a number of facts about the Brown family. There were four other
children all younger than Carleton; two girls immediately following him at yearly intervals in the age sequence, and two younger
boys. The two boys were evidently having some purely academic
troubles in school but aside from that the other children were "no
bother at all." Carleton was the one who was always getting into
trouble, according to the father who expressed some strong feelings

about that. His concern for Carleton had elements of chagrin as well as concern. "My own blood, in trouble with the police."

Carleton's stories about theft and running away were basically confirmed by his father but some important details were added about the third runaway, whose antecedents Carleton said he couldn't remember. "I'll tell you what happened," said Mr. Brown. "Carleton had sexual relations with his sister. My wife caught them. . . . She hit Carleton with a shoe . . . the only thing she could lay her hands on. She hit him in the legs. . . . That's the time he was gone two days." I asked Mr. Brown how he treated Carleton when he did something wrong and he said, "Well, I do raise my voice a little—in fact I've whipped him sometimes . . . but I could count on the fingers of one hand the times I've whipped the others. It's just Carleton." He was saying, of course, "I am a good parent. Carleton blames me but he is the one who is causing all the trouble."

I talked with Mrs. Brown next. My most vivid recollections of that first interview are of her voice which was high in pitch, strident of tone, and which left me with a general sense of undergoing a kind of verbal rifle fire which she had aimed at me for no particular reason and to no special end throughout our meeting. She added considerably to the number of complaints to be registered against Carleton. Not only had he stolen, fornicated with his sister, and run away, but he told lies ("You can't depend on a word he says"), stayed out when he was supposed to be in, never did any kind of work around the house, ran around with a gang of youngsters who called themselves the "Rebels," and wore his pants too tight. Her negative comments about Carleton lasted perhaps twenty minutes and then she shifted to her husband.

"He don't make it any easier. . . . He's never around when I need him." Mr. Brown, she said, was out of the house four nights out of five, either at work in his office or in some kind of organized civic activity. He was quite prominent in the local civil rights movement and served on several committees concerned with housing and employment practices in the community.

Her version of the way Mr. Brown treated Carleton when he was home was somewhat closer to the son's description than that of the father. Evidently Mr. Brown did a good deal more than raise his voice a little. He had reportedly beaten Carleton rather severely for a number of misbehaviors. Once Carleton had stolen a box of sugar cubes from the kitchen and tried to blame the theft on a younger brother. Mr. Brown became "real mad about that" and "whipped Carleton pretty bad and slapped him around some." The mother said she sometimes lost her temper too. "The time I caught him with Diane I was so mad I didn't know what I was doing. . . . I just hit him with my shoe. It was the only thing I could find."

Diane, at eleven, was a mainstay in cooking and keeping up the home. Mrs. Brown said, "If anything happened to her I don't know what I'd do."

At this point there were still many uncertainties about Carleton, his behavior, and the circumstances surrounding its occurrence, but certain behavioral regularities had also become apparent. A sequential pattern in which he would engage in some forbidden act and then run away had recurred a number of times. I saw no need to search for special explanations for the initial misbehavior. Sexual activity feels good and money is nice to have. The fact that most people do not engage in robbery or incest probably has something to do with the history of consequences for such behavior and the internal expectations and evaluations which accrue from those consequences. In Carleton's history the consequences of misbehavior had been dominantly gratifying. Except for the shoe-beating when he was found fornicating with his sister, nothing unpleasant had ever happened following serious misdeeds so long as he ran away. I had asked both Mr. and Mrs. Brown what happened when Carleton could not be found and they both said they got worried and called the police to help find their son. The police had found him in every instance and taken him directly to the detention home. I suppose this kind of action is intended to serve as a punishment, or at least as a warning, but Carleton had said the detention home was the best place he'd ever been. The overwhelming aversiveness of a beating by his father, if he should stay to face the consequences, made his choice fairly obvious. Nothing serious had happened to him when he was sent home from legal detention. Mr. Brown had said "We talk to him and tell him not to do it again," and Mrs. Brown agreed that that was the way things went.

Next I saw Mr. Wilson, the probation officer in charge of Carleton's case. With the outlines of a treatment strategy already roughly in my mind, I spent most of my time with him enlisting the help of the probation office in a change effort rather than trying to collect much new diagnostic information. For the most part, Mr. Wilson and I spent our time together discussing the possibilities of work with Carleton and his parents and the likelihood of a necessary condition to that kind of treatment, namely a favorable decision by the Juvenile Court at the impending hearing. Because of the number of offenses Carleton had committed there was some chance that he would be given a term at the State School for Boys, though the policy of the court was to avoid institutional placement whenever a reasonably promising alternative plan could be offered for rehabilitation.

I also visited the school to talk with the teacher from whom Carleton had stolen the money in his most recent escapade, as well as to get more general information about his behavior in school. Except for this one incident Carleton had gotten along quite well there. He was having some trouble with mathematics and his teacher had offered to help him after hours. She had been surprised and disappointed when he repaid this kindness with outright theft but she said Carleton was "generally a pretty good boy," not as much trouble in class or on the playground as many other youngsters who had so far managed to avoid entanglements with the law.

Parents, teachers, juvenile authorities, and I all agreed that the first and foremost of considerations for Carleton was to call a halt to his delinquent behavior—not to rummage through his dynamics, not to explore his history, but to stop his delinquency. A treatment plan was therefore outlined to consist mainly of improved supervision, some positive incentives for prosocial behavior, relief from the threat of beatings since this seemed to have played a major part in his running away, and replacement of the beating as a mode of punishment with some more effective aversive controls. I also agreed to see Carleton for psychotherapy at least once each week. The treatment plan was part of the material presented at the hearing and Carleton was remanded to the custody of his parents on condition that the measures proposed in the plan be put into effect.

We started without delay. A conjoint session was held with Carleton, his parents, and the probation officer. In this meeting the first and strongest emphasis was placed on the need for Carleton to stop doing the kinds of things which had gotten him into trouble. The Court had made clear that further theft or running away would lead to a term in the State School for Boys and we agreed that the immediate goal of treatment was to prevent recurrence of these behaviors. It was made clear that the basic responsibility for "doing right" was Carleton's own, but we also agreed that everyone involved should help in the effort as much as possible. Mr. Wilson, as a representative of legal authority, played an especially important role in this part of the session. He fortunately happens to be the kind of person who can treat youngsters in a firm but not malevolently punitive way, and the basic message he conveyed during this time was that we all were going to insist on a stop to Carleton's delinquent behavior.

Rather predictably, Carleton's reaction to this was a series of promises to "be good" followed by some statements in which he attempted, probably with some justice, to place the blame for his misbehavior on persons other than himself. Carleton began to talk, mainly to Mr. Wilson and to me, about his father and the way his father had punished him in the past. He said again that he wouldn't have minded a "whipping" but could not take a "beating." His feelings about being "hit in the face and kicked in the stomach" were discussed in some detail. Mr. Brown, with some emotion, finally agreed that he had given Carleton some "pretty rough beatings" in the past and he said he felt "bad" about that but he then began justifying his own behavior. He thought boys needed to be "corrected"; he didn't believe in "all this permissiveness," and so forth.

I redirected our conversation at this point. To Carleton and his father both I said I did not think it mattered much who was to blame for what had happened, but it was clear that things were going wrong as they now ran—conditions were not working out to the satisfaction of anyone concerned—and we should all spend our time trying to find better ways of dealing with the problems they all were having. This led directly to the search for a more effective aversive control than the beatings which had been Mr. Brown's stock in trade before that time. Both parents and the boy himself agreed that talking had never done any good. Carleton himself offered the suggestion we finally adopted. He said he would think it fair and it would "mean something" to him to be kept in the house, "grounded," if he got into any further trouble. His father said, "So you can play around with Diane some more?" and we spent some time talking about the need for close supervision if restriction were used as a means of control. But in this session the most important events were those in which some aspects of the father-son contract were renegotiated and some commitments to changed behavior were made. The son was to stop his seriously delinquent behavior. The father was to stop beating the boy and to begin employing more rational and hopefully more effective controls for any subdelinquent misbehavior Carleton might display.

Positive incentives were relatively easy to identify. Carleton liked money; he had never had any kind of allowance, and Mr. Brown agreed to begin paying Carleton 25 cents each week as long as he stayed out of trouble. A behavior record unblemished for a week by lying, theft, sexual activity, or running away was also to be rewarded by a movie, which Carleton very much enjoyed attending but which he had very rarely been privileged to see in the past. In this session and two others which followed, major clinical attention was focused on stipulating not only the misbehaviors from which Carleton was supposed to desist, but the prosocial behaviors we were trying to shape. His mother and father had complained somewhat vaguely that Carleton "ran around too much" and was "never home." I asked them to spell out what they meant by that and after considerable talk the parents agreed that they wanted Carleton to be home fairly promptly after school—we settled on four o'clock as a reasonable hour—to ask them if he could go out at any time after that, and to take the basic responsibility for letting his parents know where he was at all times.

Mrs. Brown had complained about the clothes Carleton wore. She didn't like the tight, low-hung trousers and the pointed shoes he preferred, and he said he simply would not put on some of the clothes his mother had picked for him. "If I put on some of those things the other kids would laugh me right off the street." Fairly extended negotiations were conducted in regard to clothing matters too, and in the end Mr. and Mrs. Brown agreed to give Carleton a limited amount of money to buy some of his own clothes, but to reserve veto rights for completely unacceptable creations which he might select on his own. As a matter of record, the veto was never exercised. Carleton bought clothes he liked but managed, in the short time this part of the program was in effect, to avoid any of the extremes which might have aroused a prohibitive parental objection.

The psychotherapeutic interchanges between Carleton and me turned out to be rather enjoyable and informative but not remarkably profitable as a means of fostering change. He was perfectly willing to talk about himself once we got to know each other fairly well and among other things he identified his runaway behavior as a game in which he could get his parents "all worried so maybe they wouldn't do nothing." We talked more about his family and I began to get some better knowledge about the part his parents played in his life. He said "I don't stay around there any more than I have to. . . . All my mother ever does is yell at me, and the only time my father sees me is when he's beating on me. He's nicer lately, but I still don't see much of him—he's so busy all the time."

Carleton talked about his sister, the one with whom he had been sexually involved, but would not tell me much about that relationship except to express some bitterness about the way his parents seemed to favor her ("Everybody thinks she's so perfect") and to suggest that Diane's behavior was not entirely beyond reproach ("What we did wasn't all my fault").

We talked for a time about the things Carleton liked to do and the plans he had for the future. He wanted to be a drummer in a rock and roll combo, he said, and in fact occasionally sat in with one of the local high school groups when they played at dances and other affairs. I was just beginning to consider the possibility of using a set of drums as a major incentive for unusually responsible behavior on his part when he made all my conjecture superfluous by getting into trouble again. He was caught, along with some other "Rebels," breaking radio antennas off cars in his neighborhood. On the same day he was accused by a neighbor of stealing a transistor radio. The accusation was later justified and Carleton, in due time and by due process of the Juvenile Court, was sent to the State School for Boys at St. Charles, Illinois by way of the Reception and Diagnostic Center which the Illinois Youth Commission maintains at Joliet.

I do not know much about the details of Carleton's experience at St. Charles. He stayed there eight weeks and the salient data available to me on his discharge were that he had not gotten into any particular trouble at the institution—he had not tried to run away, had never been placed in the detention cottage, had in general done what the cottage parents, teachers, and other school authorities told him to do. Neither had he shown any strongly positive signs of behavior change—he had not earned a place in the Honor Group selected for exemplary behavior and given greater responsibilities and more privileges than the other boys. I am not personally familiar in any real depth with life at St. Charles, but from a number of visits there I have come to believe there is a very active underlife among the inmates, or students as the staff prefer to call them, controlled largely by a rather stable group of recidivists from Chicago. Given the nature of this group and the character of the institution itself, it is very unlikely that Carleton Brown, a first offender from downstate Illinois, was admitted to the power clique and I do not believe they had much influence on him at all. From Carleton's own report later I learned that he had somewhat been afraid of the older, harder boys, that he was also rather afraid of the school authorities, and would not attempt any of the misbehaviors which if undetected could gain a boy acceptance by the leaders among the boys. Like many others on a first trip, he "played it cool" and did not get into real trouble with anybody. He was released in a relatively short time and I do not think the experience had any great effect on him one way or another.

When Carleton was sent away I was naturally disappointed. The treatment had not gone according to plan, and my own sense of professional competence was none the better for the experience. But I resisted the temptation simply to write Carleton off as a therapeutic failure and at the time of the court action I told the judge, the probation officer, Mr. and Mrs. Brown, and Carleton himself that if they were willing I would like to work with them all when Carleton got back from St. Charles. I did not think this was the end of the world for the boy and I tried to tell them that they should not think so either.

When we met again I saw Carleton with both his parents to outline plans for the future. The first need, I said, was for a reexamination of the problem, the part they all might have played in it, and the part they all might have in a better solution. Following that we would have to put a new treatment plan into effect and see if we could do a better job this time than we had before.

I talked with Carleton alone for nearly an hour. I wanted to find out what the State School episode meant to him. To many boys being sent to a reformatory is a damning experience. It means that they are *really* delinquent, totally outcast. But as near as I could tell, little of this held for Carleton. He said he "didn't mind" the place and in one statement he rather pointedly related his acceptance of the institution to rejection by his father. "It didn't make any difference—Daddy always said I was no good anyhow." Carleton seemed to think his father was most immediately to blame for the misbehavior which had placed him in the institution. "He hit me again," Carleton said, "and I really didn't do nothing."

"Come on now," I said, "you must have done something," and it developed that Carleton had begun to come in a little later than the four o'clock deadline set for him. This had gone on for several days; he and his father had argued about it, and in an evidently impulsive flash of anger, Mr. Brown had reached out and slapped his son. Carleton said, "I didn't do nothing right then. I just shut up and took it. . . . But he said he wasn't going to hit me, and he did. . . . I swore right then I wasn't gonna take it any more." The theft and vandalism had occurred the following afternoon.

He also had some interesting comments to make about his mother. "All she ever does is talk at me. . . . I don't think she's said a good word to me all my life. . . . She does the same with him [Mr. Brown]. I don't think she even likes him, the way she talks to him." Among other things, Carleton was delivering to me an implicit message that I had become very much accustomed to hearing from him—that he was not personally responsible for what he had done. His harsh rejecting father and his nagging mother were basically to blame. I was not, of course, about to accept those evaluations as facts but by the time our talk had ended I had at least more questions than I had earlier about a number of relationships in the Brown family, and I had begun to see the family itself as the unit toward which diagnostic and therapeutic effort would have to be directed in the future.

We went to work first on stipulation of the transactional interchanges which led to the beatings Mr. Brown had given his son. By the most detailed inquiry possible, by attempting to get them to recall as vividly as they could, and recollectively to slow down the many transactions in which Mr. Brown had struck his son, a relatively clear pattern emerged. The sequence would begin with some mild misbehavior on Carleton's part, followed typically by a verbal admonishment from the father. This led usually to a "sneering expression" on Carleton's face, at least as the father saw it. Carleton himself said he didn't know he looked that way. He said he usually felt afraid, not quite knowing what his father was going to do. In any case, the look of defiance on Carleton's face infuriated his father and he struck out in ways which had sometimes been very painful to the boy. Afterwards, Carleton said, all he felt was hurt and anger. Nothing he said indicated that the beatings by his father generated any contrition on his part or made him want to "do better." If anything, the outbursts by the father provided a convenient rationalization for Carleton's misdeeds. The pattern had become a game in which the irrational punishment by the father, excited to begin with by the child's misbehavior, became a sustaining stimulus for further misbehavior. What can you expect of a boy whose father beats him?

The discussion led, as discussions of this kind will, to Mr. Brown's feelings toward his son and in the third conjoint interview of this second series the emotional and cognitive bases for the man's behavior toward his son became clearer than before. He talked about his own childhood. He had been the son of a very poor share-cropping farmer in Arkansas and his whole life had been a grinding struggle to come North, to get an education, to "be somebody." Now he saw his son ruining the dream. "That boy says how I've hurt him but I can't tell you how he's hurt me. I've worked all my life to be decent and to give my family things I never had . . . and now he's turning out like this. . . ."

Better knowledge of Carleton's attitudes toward his father was also obtained in this session. He said to his father, "I've always been afraid of you. . . . But it's getting so I ain't afraid anymore. I'm mad more and I ain't going to take things from you like I used to." There was defiance in his sneer but it was the frightened defiance of a small boy, not quite sure if he can get by with it or not.

In my experience, neither verbal revelation of transactional games nor emotionally expressive dialogue in the therapist's office are sufficient to produce a lasting change in interpersonal behavior. So we went back to the behavior itself to see if Carleton and his

father could find new ways of acting toward each other. The transactional sequence we had been dealing with (misbehavior by
Carleton, threat by father, frightened sneer by Carleton, beating
by father, resentment and ultimately further misbehavior by Carleton) could obviously be interrupted at many points. I tried as well
as I could to get both parties to attempt appropriate changes.
Carleton on his side said he would try to be more careful than he
had been about the misbehavior which began the transactional
chains in the first place. We never quite reached the point of defining his misbehavior as a provocative game in which he would
tempt his father into the punitive irrationalities he had used to
justify his own misdeeds but we came close to that. In his reaction to the four o'clock curfew, for example, Carleton had quite
obviously been pressing the limits of his father's tolerance as far
as they would go and he was told that that kind of thing would not
do any more. Mr. Brown changed some attitudes and beliefs as
well as explicit behaviors. In this particular aspect of their relationship he cast a new interpretation on the sneer which had previously enraged him. He really hadn't known his son was afraid
before. All he had seen was defiance and the possible wreckage
of his family ambitions. He agreed to attempt firmer control of his
angry outbursts but as the relationship developed between father
and son, no specific effort of this kind was required.

The restrictive controls, the "grounding" arrangements which
had been attempted before, were reinstated. They were imposed
more regularly and in a more carefully timed way than in the previous effort and this, coupled with the changes just noted, effectively averted the transactional events we were trying to stop.
During the three months the Browns and I worked together there
was not a single instance of the misbehavior-beating-misbehavior
pattern which had occurred so often and so disastrously in the past.

The relationship between Carleton and his father was improved
in positive ways as well as by alleviating some of its more negative
features. Carleton had said long before, and his father now agreed,
that the only times they ever had anything to do with each other
was when Carleton did something wrong. Mr. Brown was incapable
of generating sudden spontaneous desires for friendly occasions
with his son. They had a long history of limited compatibility and
in some ways a fairly strong mutual dislike. Each, furthermore, had

dominant interests of his own which simply excluded the other. But Mr. Brown, who had been a rather good athlete in high school, did begin to work out with his son on a driveway basketball court which he and Carleton set up together. At least there they had some pleasant times together while before they had scarcely had any. A few signs of mutual respect began to appear. Carleton began to make some favorable comparisons between his father and those of some of his friends. Mr. Brown said he really admired Carleton's "spunk."

That is about as far as we went with the father-son relationship, which is not to say that that is all there was to it, or that all the problems in the relationship were resolved. No very penetrating clinical sense is required to recognize that many attitudes and beliefs of each about the other, any one of them potentially capable of causing further difficulty, were left completely untouched. I think Mr. Brown had some very serious anxieties concerning his adequacy as a middle-class professional man and some pervasive resentment about his race and the opportunities he felt he had been denied because of it. Carleton had some very serious identity problems of his own. We did not deal with any of these matters, not because they did not exist but because with groups as with individuals, total cure is a clinical illusion. We had changed a damaging transactional pattern materially and visibly, an important interpersonal relationship appeared to be improving in certain specifiable ways, and we agreed to settle for that for the time being.

At this point Mrs. Brown was invited to rejoin the group and the next session was consigned mainly to a restatement of her difficulties. She was asked to tell how their family situation looked to her now and particularly to note the main problems in the Brown family as she saw them. She said that Carleton and Mr. Brown were getting along much better than before and told a number of anecdotes to show that was true. But then she appeared to run out of things to talk about. After a number of rather long pauses she finally said that some of her main problems had nothing to do with Carleton at all, but revolved around the fact that Mr. Brown spent so little of his time at home. She talked to me as she said this, rather than to her husband. "I know he's busy but he's not home more than one night a week and I don't think that's right." For the time being I took this at face value and asked where Mr.

Brown was spending his evenings. I learned then that he belonged to a rather staggering number of fraternal and civic organizations—exclusively male organizations for the most part. He was not merely a member but held office in several of these and spent his time at one meeting after another.

I surmised that Mr. Brown's evening activities were in part legitimately fulfilling social service works, in part a way of gratifying the strong social status needs he manifested in other ways, and in part a means to keep him away from an unpleasant wife. Whatever else they might have been, I did not know and never really tried to find out. The problems I began to anticipate were more focally marital than familial so Carleton was excused from the next few meetings to facilitate concentrated work on the relationship between Mr. Brown and his wife.

We did not get very far in our next meeting. I was unclear just where we were supposed to be going except that our aims probably had something to do with unpleasantness in the family situation which drove Mr. Brown out of it as much as he could manage. Mr. Brown spent some time talking about the high social importance of the activities he was so involved in and Mrs. Brown kept saying that his family and his home were important too, but that is about all we did. I was of little help to them during this time except possibly by curbing a fairly strong tendency to confuse the situation still further by suggesting sundry irrelevant problems and solutions to them. Early in the following period, however, some meaningful material began to develop. Mrs. Brown had just completed some particularly sharp comments about her husband's shortcomings when he said, "I'll tell you one thing that's wrong—she never has a kind word to say about anybody. I can't remember her saying anything nice about anything. All I ever hear from her is what's wrong with something, isn't that so? You tell me, Dr. Peterson, isn't that so? Have you ever heard her say anything that wasn't some kind of complaint?" I said, "No, as a matter of fact, I really can't remember hearing much but complaints from you." At least I addressed her directly as I said this. She glowered at me and said, "What else do you expect me to do? You keep asking what's wrong. . . . I don't do that at home."

I had to admit that I had only our own conversations to go by and that there could be a real difference in the way she behaved at home. As much to relieve my discomfort by settling the argument as to foster the aims of behaviorally oriented clinical inquiry, I suggested that both she and her husband keep track of the pleasant and unpleasant things she said during the next week. They did this and the results were quite surprising to Mrs. Brown. Despite a considerable apparent effort on her part to increase the frequency of favorable remarks—she greeted her husband with a sarcastically sweet "Hello, honey" and counted that as a pleasant remark—the number of negative comments far outweighed the positive ones, in her own record as well as that of her husband and she said the next time we met, "I really didn't know I sounded like that. . . ." We talked a bit about this and I did everything I could to encourage her resolutions to try to act in less aversive ways in the future.

The next session I saw her alone and buttressed the somewhat altered belief she had begun to have about her own behavior by replaying the tape recording of our first interview. She had spent a good part of that time complaining about many aspects of Carleton's behavior, from thievery to tight pants, and most of the rest of it complaining about her husband. "My God," she said when it was done, "do I sound like that?" "Yes ma'am," I said, "you do."

The complaining behavior on Mrs. Brown's part was part of a transactional pattern which occurred quite often and in a number of situations, but which was most clearly and uniformly evidenced when Mr. Brown came home from work. He would be rather tired, typically, scarcely ready for a fight and not really prepared to bear anybody else's burdens. Except for recent deliberate efforts on her part she had seldom greeted him at the door. When he got home she was usually involved in one distasteful activity or another—cleaning up a mess one of the children had made, trying to calm a crying youngster, or something of the like—and without saying hello, she would launch into a piercing account of the unpleasantries of her day. Mr. Brown had listened to this early in their marriage, even sympathized somewhat, but for several years now all he did was avoid her in preference for the newspaper if he could do that, listen as little as possible if physical avoidance could not be managed, and leave the house as soon after the evening meal as his good manners would allow.

It was obviously essential to bring about some reduction in

Mrs. Brown's complaining behavior but to do only that would have been to ignore the transactional nature of the interchange. Both of these people wanted something from their marriage—more specifically, they wanted certain kinds of behavior from each other—which they were not receiving. Probably Mr. Brown wanted friendly warmth and an occasional ego boost, or at least relief from the nagging he usually got from his wife. Mrs. Brown wanted love and attention from her husband, or at least a greater concern for her problems and those of the family than he was showing by his nightly disappearances. In a nonverbal way, each was complaining to the other about the lack and at the same time gaining whatever personal gratifications he could at the expense of the other. For a more satisfactory relationship it was obvious that each would have to give more, as is usually true in troubled marriages. The clinical problem, also as usual, was to find a way of encouraging them actively to do so.

I have found it helpful in cases of this kind to deal with very specific interbehavioral patterns, which are clearly not providing the outcome both parties would like to have, and then inculcate a quasi-experimental attitude toward changing the patterns. Reinforcement theory and my experience both tell me that if the change measures work, i.e., are mutually gratifying, they will tend to be sustained.

So we dealt in still further detail with the transactions which took place each evening and Mrs. Brown agreed to try an absolute exclusion of nagging, unpleasant behavior at the time her husband returned from work. She correctly noted, however, that this change would have to be met by increased participation in family life on the part of her husband. I asked her if she didn't really mean that she wanted her husband to spend more time with her. She said that was so and after some rather uncomfortable banter, Mr. Brown agreed to try to do that. The next time we met he had withdrawn from two of the organizations which had previously occupied nearly all his evening time and was seeing to it that he and his wife went out some place together at least once a week.

For three more sessions Carleton was brought back into the conjoint family sessions and we spent part of each period talking about his own behavior—the way he was getting along with his father and a variety of problems of a relatively minor nature. The rest of the time each session was spent monitoring the relationship between Mr. and Mrs. Brown and over this span Mrs. Brown had managed to stop nagging entirely during the after-work-before-dinner period. "It's going so well maybe I'll stop it other times too," she said, and they both laughed.

In the final session a general reappraisal was conducted. By now 13 weeks had passed since Carleton returned from the training school and none of the delinquent behavior which had originally brought him to the Clinic had recurred. He had not stolen anything, he had not run away, so far as we could tell he had not committed any heterosexual misbehavior. As just noted, a number of transactional changes had occurred too. None of the provocations and beatings which had gone on between father and son had taken place since the second treatment series began. The angry interchanges had been at least partially replaced by some more friendly dealings between father and son, though Mr. Brown indicated that his ardor for basketball was beginning to cool a bit, and some other possible father-son activities were discussed. With these interbehavioral changes, in and of these changes, the relationship between father and son had improved. So had that between husband and wife, in the way they treated each other, the things they did one to the other in the daily living of their marriage.

How long will the changes last? I do not know. There is no sure way to answer a question like that. I think a number of self-sustaining behavior patterns were set up in the course of treatment, but to say that any client, group or individual, is permanently improved, is arrogant and foolish. Have we dealt with the real problems? I am not sure about that either. There is simply no denying the limitations, in extent as well as depth, of treatment in this case and in others similarly approached. I worked only with the Brown family, but Carleton is also a member of other groups, some of whom may be, or at least may become more important to him than the members of his own family. What about the "Rebels" for instance? Carleton was forbidden by court order to see any known members of the gang during the period of his probation, but they are still lurking out there, and even if we deal with this particular gang there will always be another. That is a sociological problem. The most we can hope is that Carleton's family is now sufficiently important to him and his home situation attractive enough to prevent the progressively stronger gang affiliation which was apparently in progress before. That is a hope, not a certainty. Not only were extra-family influences of many kinds excluded in the case coverage, we did not even deal with all of the Brown family. The conjoint family treatment consisted of manipulation in transactional patterns, hence relationships, dyad by dyad, as these seemed most urgently in need of repair and most vulnerable to change. But Carleton has relationships with other people in his family too—we know about some with his sister—and these were left untouched. The depth of treatment was also limited, not only in an intrapsychic sense but in regard to the interpersonal relationships on which therapeutic attention was mainly focused. I am quite sure that Carleton still harbors some resentment toward his father. The relationship was improved, but there still are undeniable imperfections in the way those two people get along. The same holds true for Mr. Brown and his wife. I think it is extremely likely that their sexual relationship leaves something to be desired, nothing was done directly about that, though this might be absolutely fundamental to the formation of a durably fulfilling relationship between the two of them. And the interpersonal inadequacies of all the people involved have strong roots in the intrapersonal dispositions of every one. It would be possible, for example, to spend a lifetime trying to understand, and to help Mr. Brown understand the tangled intricacies of his own existence—this man born of a sharecropping "nigger," trying to create some middle class comforts and some human dignity for himself and his family in a cruel and messy society which changes as soon as a person begins to think he knows what it is all about.

The clinical study and the treatment reported here, then, have acknowledged shortcomings. But the same should be said of any method of inquiry and any form of treatment—psychoanalytic, existential, or any other kind. Each may have promise but each must have a limit and it is important to realize what the bounds are. The advantages of the present approach appear to lie in the relative predictability of lawful change. There have been some changes in the Brown family in the ways they treat each other. I am reasonably sure I know what these changes have been, and I think I know what caused them. I believe I will be able to do the same kinds of things again as new needs arise, with this family and these people, or with some other families and other people. But one can never be absolutely certain about the effects one has tried to produce; the amount of effect is always limited, and the possibility of creating other desired effects is always there, whatever may be accomplished in any given case at any given time. To know some facts but to tolerate inevitable uncertainty, to change a course of events but to know that the changes may be small and that there always could be others, is all any clinician can reasonably expect.

ELBA STATE HOSPITAL: THE STUDY OF
A SOCIAL SYSTEM

The third case study concerns a state hospital where I have worked as a consultant for several years, and in particular a program for children and adolescents which is under development there.

Elba State Hospital is fairly typical of the "asylums" which were built throughout the country around the turn of the century to house the "insane" of an earlier generation. The hospital is situated on the outskirts of a small city, by the bend of a gentle river. It must have seemed an ideal location to the people who selected the site, a haven where madmen could escape the filth and barbarity which would otherwise have been theirs in the jails and poorhouses of the day.

But as our society expanded and changed, and as conceptions of disordered behavior changed, Elba State Hospital, like the other institutions it resembles, became less and less effective as a treatment center for disturbed and disturbing human beings. The buildings, poorly maintained through several economic depressions and two world wars, gradually deteriorated, and to the medieval character established directly by the stone walls of the buildings, the pillared gate, the iron fence around the grounds, and the high tower of the administrative center, was added the authenticity of decay.

The staff deteriorated too. Once Adolf Meyer worked at Elba. The administrators still trade on his name. But now the wards are run by less distinguished physicians, nearly all of whom are foreign-born, and many of whom scarcely know the language, let alone the cultural traditions of the people they are supposed to be helping. The superintendent is of Eastern European extraction. His English is not bad, by the standards of most physicians there, but nearly every time we meet he asks "Why don't you send me more Ph's?" I have never quite been able to keep from recoiling when I hear that, nor have I ever had the courage or the kindness to tell him that the correct designation, if he cannot say "psychologist," is "Ph.D." For all that, he is very strongly interested in getting Elba State Hospital accredited by the American Medical Association, he is beset with the nearly impossible demands of providing adequate treatment for the patients and responsible protection of society on an operating budget of about $5.25 per patient per day, and I believe he is running the hospital as well as he knows how.

Besides the physicians, the staff at Elba is like that in most hospitals of the kind. For a population of about 3500 patients, there are 18 workers in Social Service, only three of whom have Master's degrees; 34 in the Activities Service, five of them college trained and the rest not; three graduate nurses; 52 registered nurses; and 594 aides, none of whom have more than the most rudimentary training in modern treatment procedures. There are six psychologists on the staff. The Chief Psychologist has a doctoral degree. So does another, a research psychologist whose functions are quite distinct from those of the clinical psychology department itself. The rest of the psychologists have Master's degrees and in some cases many years of clinical experience, but until very recently their numbers have been so few, their training so limited, and their positions so narrowly defined that they have spent most of their working time in routine diagnostics. Functionally, this has meant the administration and interpretation of psychological tests, designation of diseases and dynamics, discussion of test results at case conferences, and entry of the material in the files. The diagnostic work has had no obviously beneficial effect on patients.

Despite many recent efforts toward improvement, the hospital is still organized more for convenience as a custodial center than for effectiveness as a treatment agency. It is divided administratively into two main sections, a so-called Acute Intensive Treatment Service (AITS) and a Continuous Treatment Service (CTS). Titles notwithstanding, little real treatment goes on in either place. Group therapy meetings are held regularly on three of the five AITS wards.

These are conducted by psychologists with varying degrees of training and experience, and of the most diverse ideological persuasions. Drugs are used abundantly and the medical and nursing staffs seem more preoccupied with matters of dosage and kind of drug than with any other aspect of planned treatment. Beyond chemotherapy they mainly cope as well as they can with the emergencies which arise from hour to hour in any mental hospital. The doors are locked on most of the wards and light physical restraints are used as needed.

The patients take part in various aspects of the general intramural program in effect at the hospital. Activities of several kinds are offered; volunteers associated with various programs periodically appear and do what they can. For the most part, however, the 200 to 250 patients who enter the Intensive Treatment Service each month spend their time waiting for the diagnostic work-up to be accomplished. By state and hospital policy, this must be done by team enterprise and signed by the physician in charge. Whatever else may go into the record, the emphasis is on a typological diagnostic label stated in the terms of official American Psychiatric Association nosology. Most of the staff still refer to the AITS as diagnostics and I think this is more than a verbal habit.

If for some undiscernable reason a patient on the diagnostic service improves during his stay there, he may be discharged, and Social Service actively tries to articulate the release with action by the patient's family or by agencies with whom the patient has been associated in the past. This is very difficult, however, since about 90 percent of the patients come from the Chicago area, about 60 miles away, and basic changes in the situations which played a part in causing the disorders to begin with are only very rarely made.

If AITS patients do not improve within three months they are sent to one of the CTS wards for continued treatment. The assignments are made partly on the basis of sex—female patients go to the north wards and males to the south wards—partly by age—male and female geriatric services are in operation and a juvenile unit is being formed—and partly by the characteristics of the disorder a person displays. Except for alcoholism and definite physical illness, this last criterion reduces operationally to the ease with which nursing management can be accomplished and determines whether the patient goes to a maximum security ward or one of the very few open wards on the grounds. The final and in many ways the most decisive factor in assigning any patient to a chronic ward is the availability of bed space. If one ward has more room than another it is likely to get the main flow of new patients until it is full.

The same hospital services which are given to new admissions are also offered to patients on the Continued Treatment Service. Except for the most severely regressed patients and some of the maximum security cases, they have activity programs too; patient government meetings are now held on many of the wards; volunteer programs are in formal effect. But volunteers, like most of the staff, tend to prefer patients who are socially more interesting, who smell better and are esthetically more attractive than the average chronic mental patient at Elba, so most of those people live on year after year with little more to their benefit than drugs and minimal care for purely physical needs.

Except for drugs, the life of a patient on one of the regressed wards at Elba is not much better than it was fifteen years ago, and in many ways not as good as it was a hundred years ago. I visited one of these wards again last month, to talk to some aides and to remind myself again of the nature of my reality. It was the female regressed ward, "3-North" at Elba, and the view I had on entering must not have been very different from the sight which confronted Pinel at Le Bicêtre. The paint on the walls was chipped and peeling, tile had been picked off the floor wherever a piece came loose. Little light came through the screened windows and the air was fetid in the heavy oppression of a hot summer afternoon. Most of the patients were seated on the hard oak chairs and benches lined up in the middle of the dayroom, staring ahead, rocking now and then, obviously under heavy sedation. A few were shuffling around the ward, mumbling to themselves. A scrawny white-haired woman who appeared to be about seventy years old was lying in her own excrement near a water fountain. One of the two aides on duty tried to clean this up while I was there. The smell was overpowering. I have visited wards like this many times since I became a psychologist, but I have never gotten used to the smell of human urine in the back wards of mental hospitals, and I still must fight down a swell of nausea whenever I enter one. Maybe it would be different if I worked there every day. I am as enthusiastic as anyone I know about the ideals of social psychiatry and community psychology. That is where the main hope lies for improving conditions such as these. But the difference between the ideal and present reality is very harsh. Do not sing me any pretty songs about the accomplished wonders of community action. The back wards at Elba smell just as bad as they ever did.

Despite the dreariness of the situation I have just described, some very real progress has recently been made at Elba and in the Illinois mental health system more generally. In 1960, a referendum provided $150,000,000 for capital improvements in the mental health facilities of the state. A favorable political climate at that time encouraged the appointment of a competent and energetic psychiatrist as Director of the Illinois Department of Public Welfare, and shortly thereafter a distinct, professionally oriented Department of Mental Health was created. The Director and the staff he soon collected put into motion the acts required for establishment of a zone system of mental health services in the state. This involved as a major feature the construction of seven new facilities along lines recommended by the Joint Commission on Mental Illness and Health in their 1961 report (*Action for Mental Health*). The zone centers are distinguished from traditional mental hospitals mainly by their location near major population centers, their relatively small size, and the comprehensiveness and the community orientation of the services to be offered there. At this writing, only one of the centers is actively in operation in Illinois. The rest are still under construction, and in the zone where Elba State Hospital is located the effect of the zone system on the operation of the hospital was negligible at the time observations for the present account were being made.

Improvements are underway continuously in the hospital. Many of the older buildings are being extensively remodeled. The daily per capita expenditure for patients has risen from less than $3.25 per day in 1955 to approximately $5.25 in 1965. Some of the wards are open now where once none were. Patient government and group therapy meetings occur with some regularity where a few short years ago scarcely anything of the kind took place. Staff salaries are gradually being increased. A research psychologist has been appointed at Elba, a hospital improvement project for aide training has been approved, and if additional grant funds are awarded a major behavior modification project will soon be set in motion. My appointment as a consultant, and the appointment of others like me from Chicago and the University of Illinois, is evidence of the interest State Department of Mental Health staff have in the constructive criticism and improvement of clinical services.

But there is a paradox in this, for all these efforts at improvement of the state hospital take place in a situation where the smaller urban zone centers are supposed to make the state hospitals obsolete. At one and the same time the hospitals are supposed to be improving and liquidating themselves, and this anomalous identity, this uncertainty of direction, affects all programs which take place within and revolve about the hospital. It is in such a context that the children's program at Elba must be understood.

It is hard to say just when the program began. About two years ago, a psychologist who had been conducting group therapy meetings on one of the AITS wards began to hold special sessions for a number of adolescent patients in his charge. The youngsters seemed to have certain common problems, distinct from those of the older patients, and the meetings, as the saying goes, seemed to be quite profitable. As some patients moved onto the chronic wards, however, their wishes to continue with the group work were administratively difficult to fulfill. Some casual and accidental conversation between the psychologist, the school principal and an activities supervisor led to the discovery that all of them were having similar problems in dealing with the children at Elba. An informal survey conducted at that time revealed approximately 50 patients under 21 years of age scattered over 17 different wards of the hospital, under the care of 12 different ward physicians, two clinical directors, three different chiefs of service, and an indeterminate but very large number of aides and nurses. It did not take an especially penetrating inquiry to show that little was being done for the children by way of treatment at the time, aside from school for those who were able to attend, group meetings for those who happened to have passed through the wards where the meetings went on, and the minimal custodial care a typical state hospital provides. It was equally obvious that no coherent program could be mounted as long as the children were scattered as widely as they were among the wards and services of the institution.

I talked with the psychologist at the time and agreed to work with him and with his colleagues in planning a children's program.

We recognized from the start that the residential location of adolescents within institutions is a somewhat controversial matter. Some people maintain that it is best to keep the younger patients with adults, to approximate the extra-hospital world somewhat and to prepare the children for the adult life they should soon be entering. At Elba, however, this issue was academic. The children there were not being prepared for adult life outside the hospital in any systematic way. They were simply being housed with the adults, and not even the rudiments of an adequate program for them had ever been set in motion. Issues concerning the desirability of institutionalization were also academic. It is of course debatable whether children should ever be sent to a state hospital, but the question became coldly senseless at Elba. The children were there already. Some had been there for several years and there was no sign that the flow of new patients would cease in the foreseeable future. We had to do the best we could for them there, within the walls of Elba, however appealing a more general solution might seem to others and to us in our moments of higher idealism.

A proposal to transfer all patients under 18 years of age to a separate unit, along with a tentative treatment plan for them, was therefore drawn up and presented to the superintendent. After about a week's delay, he approved the general proposal, and appointed a Committee on Juvenile Patients' Affairs to coordinate the program in the months ahead. The committee included the psychologist, the school principal, and the activities supervisor who had started the whole operation, along with three clinical directors— all physicians, three social workers, two other activities workers, a chief nurse, and the Director of Volunteer Services at the hospital. Aides on the various shifts were invited to attend as their work schedules might allow and some of them have in fact attended on an irregular basis ever since. One of the clinical directors who spends almost all his time at the hospital in administrative committee work was appointed Chairman of the group. I introduced myself to this man, offered to work as a consultant with him and with the Committee, and after the matter had been taken under consideration for a short time, was invited to do so.

At first, the main task simply was to get all the youngsters together and to find other placements for those who were unlikely to profit from the program. An early census showed that about 40 percent of the patients were mentally retarded by both legal and psychometric criteria, and the staff, especially the social workers, spent very large amounts of time and effort in the first weeks trying to make other arrangements for these children. Where possible, they were sent to noninstitutional locations. Many were sent to state schools, but some were not relocated at all because other facilities were not available. The population of children at Elba therefore still contains about fifteen children who are mentally retarded in a legal sense, who got into the state hospital for several more or less gratuitous reasons, but who continue to make the establishment of an effective program more difficult than it might be if all the patients were of adequate intellectual competence. For the time being at least, this is one of the conditions we have to live with.

For the next two months, almost the only thing that happened by way of program development was that the committee continued to meet regularly. The problems they considered were many in number, various in kind, and ranged in gravity from questions of carpentry (most of one session was occupied with a discussion of the relative merits of Dutch doors versus single doors for the clothing room) to the basic philosophy of the treatment program. A study of the minutes of the committee meetings suggested that little was being proposed, much less done, by way of improved treatment for the children, so I undertook a more thorough study of the program at that time.

I talked with many people, from the Zone Director to the patients, and I stayed long enough on the wards to gain some reasonably stable and consistent beliefs about the daily lives of patients there. Clearly very little was going on by way of active treatment. One of the girls whom I had asked to describe a typical day on the ward said she got up about six in the morning, had breakfast, and cleaned her room. People with ground passes were let out then but most of the people did not have these, and the restricted patients spent the rest of the morning "just watching TV, when it works—it ain't working now—or just sitting around." At eleven, they "had medicine," and at twelve they had lunch. After noon, those who went to school were let out for that; the rest just sat around the ward again. At four the school pupils returned to the ward, had dinner an hour or so later, and then were confined through the evening until medicine and bedtime came around again. She said,

"It gets pretty bad around here sometimes. We fight because there's nothing else to do. Sometimes we bug the aides. . . . At least there's something going on that way."

The aides were clearly preoccupied with matters of control. One of them showed me a table knife she had taken away from a patient and said "This can be a lethal weapon." She then told me, with a good deal of emotion, that she "loved kids" but didn't know how much longer she could "take it" in this ward.

The other personnel with whom I talked emphatically stressed the great difficulty they were having getting anything done for the children. More child care workers had been promised but none had appeared. A special training program for them had been approved but nothing had been done to get this underway. New space was needed for an activities program but none had been found. It was clear from all my inquiries that fundamental administrative support for the program was less than enthusiastic, so I went to see the Superintendent.

There was, I learned from him, a basic ambivalence about the children's program which he personally experienced and which had roots in higher level administrative indecision about psychiatric care for children. The history of all this was fantastically complex. The outcome was that no one in power had ever really decided whether there were to be children's services in the state hospitals or not, and that the Superintendent wanted to "do something for the kids" but was reluctant to move forward too rapidly until he "got the word from the Central Office." He said if he really got a program going at Elba and everybody knew about it, he would be overwhelmed by a flood of disturbed children from Chicago. The mental health facilities there were woefully inadequate to accommodate the need, but sending the unmanageable horde to Elba did not seem to offer a very helpful solution to the problem either.

Conversation with the Zone Director showed that he was personally opposed to developing a large children's program at Elba. He believed that it would be vastly preferable to "turn off the flow from Chicago," and was working toward that end with the staff in the central office.

This impasse clearly had to be overcome, one way or another, if progress toward an effective program were ever to be made. At about that time, a commission had been established by the State

Director of Mental Health to study the problem of children's psychiatric services. The members had recommended that quantitatively limited but clearly defined children's units be set up in all state hospitals, and the Director had asked for comments from a great many of the people who would be involved in the programs.

I wrote a letter to the Director suggesting that the administrative miracles which would stop the flow of juvenile patients into state hospitals did not seem in prospect of occurring in the immediate future though we all were committed to that as an ultimate goal. It seemed a good idea in the meantime to develop the most effective programs available resources would permit. With all possible emphasis, I said that whatever decisions were reached should be stated with sufficient force to guarantee dependable support for any actions people might begin to undertake in the hospitals themselves. I am sure other people expressed opinions too, and that not all of them were in favor of developing explicit children's programs in the state hospital system, but the ultimate decision of the Director was to encourage programs of this kind.

In a phone conversation with the Zone Director a short time later, I was told that there would be a distinct children's unit at Elba, and indeed that funds for construction of cottage facilities for children had been given a high priority in the capital budget for the next biennium. The Superintendent at Elba then released one floor of a very large building for use as a gymnasium by the juvenile patients, and a number of other program developments very quickly began to transpire.

Within three months' time, regular patient-staff meetings were occurring on all the wards, a rather full activities schedule had been planned for the children, a group of volunteers from a nearby Catholic school had begun to come in one afternoon each week to assist with the activities program, arrangements had been made to take the children swimming at the local YMCA, and an explorer scout troup had been organized.

I was not especially concerned with any elegancies of program evaluation at this time. The first job was to get a program of some kind going, and to initiate action where there had been none before. I did everything I could to encourage development of the program right then, no matter how chaotic it all seemed to the scientist in me. The changes were allowed to consolidate for approximately three more months, and then another informal inquiry was undertaken. The length of hospital stay was determined for the very first group of children who had been assembled in a single location when the program began. There were 14 patients in this sample and the mean length of hospitalization was 10.09 months. This value was compared with that for a sample of 66 patients who had entered the juvenile unit around 18 months later, after the various kinds of program enrichment mentioned above had been put into effect. The average length of hospitalization for this group was 6.27 months and the difference between that and the mean of 10.09 months for the earlier sample is not only statistically reliable but appears to be of some clinical and administrative importance.

The difference itself, of course, says nothing about origin. There is no way of telling whether the effect was created by the volunteers, the milieu therapy meetings, the increased involvement of the children in extra-hospital community life, the mere fact that hospital administrators noticed the children more now that so many of them were all together instead of allowing them to get lost in the hospital bureaucracy, or some indeterminant combination of these and other factors.

From additional observations on the wards and particularly from talking with the staff, it became obvious that while "things were much better now," the program left much to be desired by way of coherence and clarity. The aides were uncertain about their positions in the program. They were not supposed to be the passive-authoritarian custodians they had been before, but no one had really told them what else to be. They spoke of a "lack of communication" and of "working blind" with the children. The three shifts operated quite independently of one another "like three different hospitals," as one aide put it, and neither the staff nor the children knew quite what to expect from one another.

Manifestly the program required a better statement of objectives, a clearer delineation of staff positions, an improved means of communicating useful information among the various agencies and people who were working with the children, a better means of training personnel, and as usual a more orderly way of evaluating the program than had been achieved so far. Progress toward all these ends was considerably furthered by two new developments. One was the appointment of a permanent Unit Director to provide the functional leadership the program had previously lacked. Three different physicians had administered the program over its history. None of them had much training in psychiatry, let alone child psychiatry; none had any experience working with children; and not one of them, despite their good intentions, really knew what to do in shaping the program. The Unit Director now in charge of the unit has had two years of residential training in psychiatry and two additional years of experience working on the children's unit of another state hospital. He shows a strong desire to develop the best program possible for the children at Elba; he is intelligent, willing to acknowledge deficiencies and remedy defects when these appear, and above all he tends to agree with me about the basic features of the program. We work together very well, and I cannot pretend my favorable regard for him is uncolored by that fact.

The second major development, beyond appointment of the Unit Director, was the institution of a behavioral merit system for the children. I encouraged development of the general concept as strongly as I could, and incidentally found the phrase *merit system* much more acceptable to most hospital personnel than such terms as *token economy*, though the basic principles and operations are much the same. The concrete definition of behavior classes and the tactics of administration, however, were left to the Unit Director and his working staff. I think it is far more important to gain the personnel involvement of the people who are going to do the work in an enterprise of this kind than to define the substantive and tactical details of the action in a compulsively careful way. The classes of behavior which emerged from the discussions of the Unit Director and his staff thus seem less than ideal with regard to such desiderata as behavioral specificity and independence among classes, and they reflect the interests of aide management in a predictably unilateral way. The Director and the aides decided to rate the children on good grooming, room care, peer relationships, response to authority, punctuality, cooperation, and courtesy. When I saw the list, I said "Great! That's fine! Let's get it going!" in the knowledge that we could change it later on, and indeed that the need for changes would probably become self-evident as the work progressed.

In additional staff meetings, the details of a six-point scale from extremely good performance (5) to total failure (0) were worked out; it was agreed that grounds passes should be employed as the major incentive for good behavior, or from another viewpoint, the privilege to be earned by demonstrated responsibility on the part of the children.

The privilege contingency itself was deferred one week, however, while the aides familiarized themselves with the ratings and baseline data were obtained. Then the merit system was announced to the children at one of their regular patient government meetings. They were told how many points they would have to accumulate for a grounds pass and what they would have to do behaviorally to earn the ratings.

The procedure has now been in effect for six weeks on the adolescent boys' ward. It has only been in use for a week on the wards for younger boys and for girls, so only the results for the older male patients are reported. The main findings are shown in Figure 6-1. During the first baseline week, ratings averaged only slightly more than 2.00, a poor performance as the scale was de-

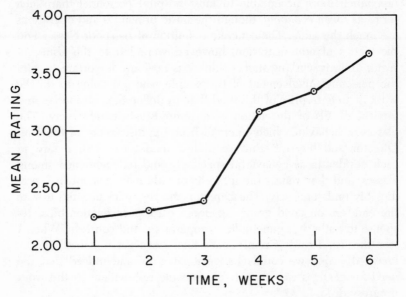

Figure 6.1. Increase in mean rating of ward behavior following institution of a merit system.

fined. During the second and third weeks, after the privilege system was in effect, very little happened to the ratings, and there was no reason to suppose that any changes were actually taking place in the behavior of the children. I talked with some of them at this time, and found that many did not really believe their own behavior would determine what happened to them. One said, "They're going to let me out when they feel like it, just like they always did." A few began "making points" in earnest, however, and the variance in ratings was significantly higher in the second and third weeks than in the first. The major changes took place in the fourth, fifth, and sixth weeks. By then the children had seen for themselves that the Unit Director meant what he said; the children who had visibly shaped up were given freedom and a certain responsible status which others were denied, and more and more of them began to show average to good behavior. The mean rating for the sixth week of the program is significantly different from that for the first week ($P_t < .01$) without even taking the substantial correlation between first- and sixth-week scores into account.

Through interviews with several aides, I learned that they were pleased with the changes which had taken place in the behavior of the children, and hence in the general situation on the ward. In the typical comments of one woman, "It really works great . . . now I know how the kids are doing on the night shift and maybe over at school too. They'll call me if somebody really fouls up. . . . There's better communication than there used to be." She cited a number of examples of children who had changed considerably in the short time the system had been in effect, but added, "Some of these kids are just little con men. They're out to make points, but they aren't really changing." I avoided philosophical argument with her on this point, but tried to find out what she would regard as a real change. We finally agreed that if a child was not just putting us on with his good behavior, but had adopted the goals as his own, and especially if he would continue to show the improved behavior in other places and for a reasonably long time after he left the ward, the change would be about as real as human behavior changes ever get.

The merit system was not evaluated with complete favor by the children, but all of those I talked to agreed that changes had occurred and most of them approved of the way things were going on the ward at the time. One said, "It's a lot stricter around here than it used to be, but I like it better. . . . You know what to expect." Other signs of change were also evident. The aides and children reported far less fighting on the ward than took place before, and property damage had been visibly reduced. Before the merit system went into effect, an average of eight windows per week were broken on the boys' adolescent ward. Only two have been broken in the past three weeks.

Just a week ago, two other organizational changes were made at Elba. Both are aspects of the general shift to unit operation, and they seem likely to have considerable effect on the children's program in the future. After extensive discussion, the Committee on Juvenile Patients' Affairs voted itself out of existence, probably the most decisive action it has ever taken, and the authority for day-to-day operational affairs has been transferred formally and firmly to the unit staff, with the Director in administrative charge. This change was accompanied by general agreement that decisional power should be decentralized as much as possible, with the children themselves ultimately taking as much responsibility for their own lives as their capabilities and the constraints of circumstance would allow.

The second organizational change concerns the input of patients. In the past they have gone just to the diagnostic service, where they have spent an average of three weeks, waiting for the study to be completed. Now they are to be placed directly in the children's unit, and at least the administrative precondition for continuity and immediacy of treatment as well as for improved unity in the assessment and modification of behavior has finally been met.

It is too early to say what the effects of these measures will be, but I am quite certain that they will shorten the hospital stay still further and faster with more effective help for the children than has been available in the past.

That is where we stand now. For all the shortcomings of the program, it is fair to say that some changes have taken place, and in fact the contrast with conditions two years ago is rather marked. There have been some changes in the basic aims of treatment. At the time when the children were scattered throughout the hospital, the real goal of institutional management went very little beyond custodial care and coping with crises. To a very appreciable extent now, the aides, the physicians, the activities workers, and all the others who work with the children have a more definite and higher objective. It is to change the behavior of the children in ways which will help them get along better in their lives within and beyond the hospital. The number of people who regard this as an aim in which they have an important personal part to play has been increased. The aides are involved to a degree they were not before, and the children are coming to realize the part they themselves must take in the attainment of personal responsibility and social competence. The organizational structure of the children's unit has progressed from literally no organization at all, through a long period of formation by a central committee, to a reasonably accurate facsimile of local unit operation today. The procedures used to accomplish collective aims within this structure have changed from the custodial nursing of the early continued treatment service, through a phase of vigorous but chaotic program development, to the somewhat greater coherence provided by the merit system now in effect. And the statements of staff and patients alike offer reason to say that some changes have taken place in the belief systems, in the cultural assumptions, on which the aims, the organizations, and the procedures all are based. I have not once in the past three months heard the aides talk about mental illness. To an increasing extent, they are talking instead about the ways the children are behaving, and are asking what they can do to improve the behavior.

These claims can be made with no denial of remaining faults in the program. Elba is not the dumpheap it once was, but it is not exactly a showplace of psychiatric excellence either. The merit system, for example, can be improved and extended in many ways. The need for individual behavior assessment is still unmet. As the code is now defined, some generally desirable forms of action have been stipulated from the viewpoint of the Unit Director, the aides, and the hospital management generally. But no one yet is trying very hard to identify desired behavior changes for each child, to assure that patients and staff alike know what the target behaviors are, and to establish effective ways to encourage their emission. It will be far easier to do this as a part of the general merit system now in effect than it would have been before. All we need to do is add a column or two for individual changes, and this could be accomplished at no clerical cost by eliminating some of the redundant characteristics which staff now have to evaluate. The intercorrelations among *peer relationships, cooperation,* and *response to authority,* for example, range from .93 to .97, and one rating will obviously do for them all. Inclusion of individually defined target behaviors should help fortify each child's conviction that the people in the hospital are trying to help *him* get better, and would qualify more truly as a therapeutic system in effect at the present time.

It would be a fairly simple matter to bring reinforcing consequences closer to behavior by manipulating grounds privileges on a daily rather than a weekly basis. A week's restriction is a hazy lifetime for some of these children, but they may be able to look a day ahead and pattern their behavior accordingly. A token system might be instituted. Other incentives and deterrents could be employed. Disturbed twelve-year-olds tend to have the utmost contempt for anyone who will work for lollypops, but they really do like candy bars, and properly offered and well delivered, a hundred dollars' worth of incentive material might go a long way in encouraging the children's need to develop in their own self interest. A camping trip has already been held as a privilege to be earned by mature behavior rather than as a necessarily salubrious activity which every child should enjoy as a matter of right. Movies, trips to the swimming pool, and other experiences could be regulated in a similar way. We can also do more than we have to generalize the present merit system, or some revised version to be developed in the future, across and beyond the hospital. The teachers and activities workers can take part in the rating operation. They too can know, encourage, and help define the kinds of behavior to be expected of every child, and a more coherent treatment program can be extended over all situations and through all the hours of the daily lives of the patients. A well defined merit system can also serve as the vehicle for extending treatment into the community. The children who come to Elba are not generally blessed with intact and effective families or they would probably never have gotten to Elba in the first place. But sooner or later every child is released to some kind of famloid group, and a change in social service procedure might readily be made to transfer the information and techniques developed in the hospital to the people in charge outside. A talk with those involved, telling them what had been set as the behavioral goals at Elba, how these were accomplished if indeed they were, and what the parents or others might do to keep the action going and maybe to increase benefits still further, should be feasible even within present limits of time and personnel, and might be the opening wedge of a more generally effective community program in which work in the hospital is related more closely to work outside than it has ever been before.

The need for better training of personnel is woefully evident. We must train a larger sector of the staff with emphasis on aides and nurses, but with proper attention to other personnel, including the physicians, if we can get to them. The aides, nurses, teachers, and others must not only be told that they are to take more active roles in treatment than before, but they must be shown how.

A training program of sorts is in operation now for aides and nurses. About half of those assigned to the children's unit have attended a series of lecture-discussions by University of Illinois psychology consultants, and have learned something about behavioral approaches to hospital treatment. I believe the acceptance and use of the merit system is related to that experience. The training of aides is controlled by the Nursing Service, however, and the content they acquire still stresses medication and custodial care in all too emphatic a way. Several of us have talked to the Director of Nurses' Training at the hospital, and I think that a more thoroughgoing behaviorally oriented training program can now be put into effect if we can get the time and trained manpower to do it. This movement has both political and interpersonal aspects of considerable complexity, but in general I have found that programs will be accepted by hospital staff largely in proportion to the programs' practical effectiveness. There may be delays, and the persuasion requires time, patience, and no small measure of social skill, but the people I have worked with at Elba have most of the same goals I do. If I have a genuine contribution to offer, and present it effectively, they tend to accept and employ it, in their own way, with a caution born mainly of experience. Other "new answers to the mental health problem" have been ardently propounded by previous consultants, tried more or less enthusiastically by the hospital staff, and then absorbed into the system as a whole to its slow but perceptible advantage. As an idea merchant, I have found field personnel understandably wary but not impervious to sensible ideas for useful change, and I believe we will soon be able to improve substantially the training of the staff at Elba.

The procedures for program evaluation need to be extended, systematized, and embedded in the more general operating procedures of the hospital. So far, I have been the only person in the whole operation who has had any basic concern for systems analysis, experimental change, and outcome evaluation. The self-corrective function of program evaluation needs to be meshed with the machinery of the program itself. The Research Psychologist at Elba has agreed to work with me along these lines, and the merit system provides one source of regularly gathered behavioral data for the continuous evaluation we both have in mind. The procedural details still need to be defined, but they surely will include frequencies of behavior of certain designated kinds on the part of patients and staff alike, and regular surveys of both patients and staff, to find out what the major problems are in the operation and to identify possibly useful ways of solving the problems.

I believe these all will be helpful measures to take, though getting them into effect will be no easy affair. A consultant, for that matter any change agent, is only one influence among many and the degree of effect and order he may expect to attain is inherently limited. I think there is no way to order life completely, either by way of comprehension or control. What I have learned from the Elbas and the Carleton Browns and the Walter Lillys of my experience is that I come for a time into the lives of others, learn what I can about them, change something if I can and hope it is for the better, and then move out again while the people and the groups and the organizations I have known go on somehow without me.

7

Scientific, Professional, and
Ethical Issues

The major propositions of this book may be summarized as follows. The central aim of all clinical assessment is to gain change-relevant information about behavior in functional relationship to the conditions under which it occurs. Adequate assessment methodology thus requires far more attention to disordered behavior itself and to the situational determinants of behavior than has traditionally characterized psychodiagnostic practice. Within the general realm of social behavior, three classes of phenomena may be distinguished, namely the action of individuals, the interaction of people in primary groups, and the organization of social systems. Clinically desirable changes may be effected through three parallel modes of treatment, namely individual behavior modification, the modification of transactional patterns in groups, and the modification of organizational characteristics in social systems. In all three cases, the fundamental process of assessment consists of an initial evaluation to determine what changes need to be made, the institution of the changes themselves, and re-evaluation to determine the functional effects the changes have brought about. The process may be re-cycled indefinitely. No special methods are needed to accomplish the task of clinical assessment. The basic methods of behavioral science, observation, elicitation of behavior, and experiment, are appropriate and sufficient to the practical demand. Extension of these methods to clinical problems should help promote the unity between science and service which has been sought for so long and so slowly developed in the social sciences and in those professions concerned with psychological change and social action.

The implications of a view like this are far-reaching, important, and not always easy to grasp. The prospect of an army of behaviorally trained social psychiatrists and community psychologists marching stoutly off to do good for mankind, with only a faintly glimmering awareness of the meaning of their actions, is terrible to conceive. It is important to understand that a viewpoint like the present one has ramifications that are more than merely technological, and some of the implications social-behavioral views of clinical assessment appear to have for research, for the organization of professions, and for social ethics are sketched in the following paragraphs.

ASSESSMENT AND RESEARCH

If the discipline of clinical trial is harsh, the discipline of scientific research is merciless. The history of psychiatry and clinical psychology is fraught with accounts of procedures which felt good to practitioners, impressed clients with a proper sense of mystery, and seemed to work in some crude pragmatic sense, but which were later seen in the glare of scientific investigation to be useless. It is unlikely that this fate will befall such basic methods as observation, interview, and experiment. If that happens, we will have to abandon behavioral science itself. But the particular observational, elicitative, and experimental techniques which are developed to accomplish clinical aims need to be examined very closely to determine the extent to which those aims are in fact fulfilled by the procedures in question. Something akin to traditional reliability and validity research needs to be done, though the conventional psychometric concepts have to be modified considerably for application in a functional behavioral framework.

Assessment of validity by correlation with criterion values, for example, becomes difficult to conceive if not totally meaningless in the present context. The observational and experimental measures employed as diagnostic procedures *are* the criteria against which any other procedures would have to be evaluated. The traditional notion of test-retest reliability no longer is pertinent when attention is focused on changeworthy behavior and deliberate efforts are mounted to bring desired changes about. For some of the parameters of major concern, the best procedures would be those for which test-retest reliabilities were *lowest*. Still concern must be given to the truth of the propositions we assert, and to the effectiveness and dependability of the procedures employed in generating those propositions.

The primary data for behaviorally oriented clinical assessment are classes of events; in the most fundamental sense they consist of stimulus-response frequencies. This does not immediately solve the measurement problem, however, especially in such definitions of a behavioral viewpoint as the present one, where covert behavior and indirect reports of events are admitted in the interest of clinical effectiveness. Given the fact that behavior varies from one situation to another and that clinically important stimulus-response rates change over time, many of the most important measurement problems become questions of situational and temporal generality rather than reliability or validity in any usual sense. If behavior is observed more than once in more than one situational context, then the assessment problem is one of stating dependably what has happened at each time under each set of circumstances, and regarding the resultant indices relating information over situations and occasions as mere descriptive facts rather than as reliability or validity measures. If results are stated in correlational terms, for example, there is no reason to expect values obtained in different situations or at different times to approach unity. They will simply fall wherever they fall, and the meta-procedural questions that matter will be concerned more with the dependability of the correlations than with their size.

Adequate study of dependability, however, requires research that goes beyond the usual clinical assessment operation by way of experimentally redundant replication of data-gathering operations. There is no other way to go about the business of examining the accuracy of assessment methods except to multiply those methods beyond the efficient limit for clinical action, to extend some of the observations, in directness and duration, beyond anything which would ordinarily be feasible in everyday clinical practice, and then to see which procedures yield needed information most effectively and efficiently. The essential data are agreement indices of various kinds and not all of them should be expected to attain the same magnitude. In general, the more specific the classes of behavior involved, the greater the comparability of situations in which behavior is observed, the shorter the time between observations, and the greater the similarity between methods of observation, the higher the agreement indices ought to go. The embarrassing problem in clinical psychology has been that *none* of the required reliability or validity indices have come anywhere near the size required for useful clinical description. It seems likely that some of the observation and interview procedures outlined here will improve assessment performance materially and maybe dramatically, but that remains to be demonstrated. The necessary research is rather difficult to do, and very little of it has been done to date.

If the dependability of assessment procedures can once be indexed, then the way is clear to systematic and continuous improvement of the procedures themselves. This too can be viewed as an experimental procedure—as a self-corrective process in which the appraisal methods themselves are at least periodically appraised, improvements are proposed as rationally as possible, and the effects of the changes are once again assessed at a later time. The notion of a test or a battery of tests which can measure fixed characteristics once and for all should be abandoned. Methods of studying a changing behavioral reality are eternally and inherently capable of experimental improvement.

So far in this chapter and generally throughout the book, the emphasis has been upon the profits to be had from applying the methods of science to clinical practice, but gains should accrue in the other direction as well, and in the long run the second advantage may be the more important. In part the gain in scientific knowledge about social behavior should come about simply because some tolerably effective procedures become available for studying significant human problems in individual psychology, social psychology, and sociology. The definition of procedures in a scientific framework, the application of these to clinical problems, and their improvement by continual research in clinical situations seems likely to generate some procedures whose applicability goes beyond immediate practical problems to more general issues of fact about human behavior.

But more is involved than an exchange or even an identity of procedures. Ultimately, I believe, the general viewpoint of which this book is one expression will foster a change in basic conceptions of social science. To an incredibly large extent, our scientific views of behavior are still directed and constrained by some concepts of classical physics which progressive physicists have long since discarded. The most offensive concepts are those of a true, mathematically specifiable reality which can be given absolute and inviolable statement independent of the conditions under which the reality is observed, and of scientific research as a class of fully objective, entirely controlled investigative operations, preferably laboratory experiments, by which truth can be ascertained once and forever. This view of science has created an artificial but unbridgeable gap between pure science and clinical application in those disciplines concerned with social behavior, so that science has gone on its tight little course, producing nothing of any use to those concerned with individual treatment or social action, and the applications have proceeded loosely as practical demands arose, untrammeled by the rules of science.

Closing the hiatus requires a more scientific definition of clinical procedures, but it also demands a change in the definition of science to include planned changes in individual behavior, programmed changes of social interaction, and deliberately planned forms of social engineering as legitimate forms of behavioral experiment, contributing at one and the same time to clinical improvement of the human condition and to basic knowledge about human nature. Ever since Heisenberg elaborated his principle of indeterminacy, ever since relativity and quantum theory began to undermine classical Galilean and Newtonian concepts of space and matter, physicists have recognized that the hope for immutable law can never be fulfilled, that the results of observation are always influenced by the observation itself and that the principles of which science is built are always conditioned by the circumstances under which the principles have been developed. It is high time social scientists saw the same light.

Hospitals and clinics are not laboratories. The clinical contract limits the extent of control which can be exercised and the direction in which that control can legitimately be applied, but the major differences between research and clinical action are of degree and not of kind. There is no excuse for thoughtless action and planless *laissez faire* in clinical work any more than there is in a well conducted scientific investigation. In effective clinical action as in research, some controls must always be exerted. But in research and clinical action alike the controls are always imperfect. The scientist, like the clinician, is never entirely removed from the investigative enterprise. He too evaluates the phenomena with which he deals. He too influences the observations he makes. The notion of science as a fully precise, totally objective, value-free, extra-human enterprise has long outlived its usefulness.

Laboratory investigation is still obviously important in behavioral science. To support some propositions, variables still need to be isolated and clinically unmanageable controls must be imposed. One controls whatever one must and manipulates whatever one can in order to gain whatever kind of information appears to be needed. But so long as dependable observations and effective inquiries are made to determine facts, so long as formulations of phenomena are stated provisionally and then subjected to planned test, the essential requirements of scientific investigation have been met. And to the extent that scientists recognize the conditional nature of the principles they are trying to define, to the extent that they recognize the essential imperfection of all efforts toward absolute control and objectivity, the difference between pure science and its application may cease to seem so great, and the barriers between research and practice may begin to fall away.

ASSESSMENT AND PRACTICE

This book began with a mildly caricatured description of the "clinical team." It returns at this point to a consideration of professional roles, within teams and without, in light of the conceptual and methodological propositions developed in the intervening chapters.

It seems to me that the traditional organization of the clinical team is very badly confused. As things now stand, the labor of assessment and treatment is divided in part by distinction among operations to be performed by the clinicians and in part by differences among aspects of the problems the clinicians are attempting to deal with. Thus psychologists give tests, while dynamic interviews are often left to psychiatrists. That is an operational basis for dividing work and defining roles. But social workers are assigned to cover the descriptive facts of social history, while psychiatrists and psychologists converge in their efforts to elucidate intrapsychic functions. That kind of role differentiation has more to do with differences in aspects of the problem to be attacked, with "sectors of the life space," as it were, than with the clinical operations performed. In the earliest formal definitions of team position, psychiatrists were assigned major or exclusive responsibility for treatment, though the obvious utility of social workers in dealing with significant others in the lives of patients, the apparent success of psychologists in doing psychotherapy, and the general refusal of qualified psychiatrists to work in the situations of greatest need, such as state hospitals, soon made that assignment practically unfeasible and professionally intolerable. As a result, all the major helping professions came to share in the work of therapy, despite sporadic declarations by the American Psychiatric Association that only physicians should treat the sick.

None of the formal definitions of clinical team structure has ever made much sense. Professional roles in the traditional team are irrationally derived from a hodge-podge of operational and substantive considerations. The delineations of function have not really been planned. They have simply happened by historical accident. Despite elaborate efforts to rationalize on-going activities in the professional literature, roles have never been designed by careful definitions of social problems, of the operations needed to deal with these, and of the professional roles related to those operations. The clinical team has just grown, willy nilly. It is time for us to examine it more reasonably and change it as we need to.

The priests were there first, long ago, and then they were replaced by the physicians. When other professionals offered to help they were greeted with warmth, for the physicians in charge were sincerely dedicated to the welfare of their patients. But the newcomers were also greeted with reserve, for the physicians, in all their dedication, really were in charge and they took very very seriously the responsibility for the welfare of patients, as well as their own socio-economic interest. As social workers and psychologists entered the field of clinical action, they were given a place, but their roles were defined more by the skills they rather fortuitously brought to the clinic and the hospital than by the problems all clinicians faced and the work which needed to be done. Social workers were accustomed to working in the community, so they soon were interviewing spouses and employers. Psychologists could give tests and do research, so that is what they wound up doing.

But the assignment of professional responsibility for alleviating human distress and social malfunction is far too important to leave to chance. The sanction for influence on the lives of others and the right to intervene in social process must not be lightly given. It surely must not be conferred by historical accident. A very careful analysis of the problem is needed and professional roles must rationally stem from that.

As conceived here, the essential problems confronting all mental health professionals are psychosocial in nature. We are concerned with malfunctions of individual action in relation to accompanying environmental conditions; with disorders of group behavior, especially the natural primary groups in which most people live their daily lives; and with ineffective or otherwise faulty organization in social systems, particularly those social systems most directly concerned with the control and alleviation of disordered behavior. We are not, of course, dealing with diseases except by very loose generally inappropriate analogy. Naturally any medical problems presented by mental patients should be medically corrected, but that holds equally for all members of our society. The treatment changes which need to be made are conceived to be psychoeducational measures in the case of individuals and primary groups, and consist of administrative, educational, and political measures where social systems are concerned.

None of the traditional helping professions offers a model of sufficient scope and diversity to match the size and complexity of the problems we face, and all contain vestigial encumbrances of one kind or another which impede fully adequate professional work. The ministerial model is pertinent to the task, for clinicians are moral agents whether they want to be or not; but the model will not do as it now exists, for psychosocial problems are more than spiritual, and they do not readily yield to the rigidly and critically moralistic solutions which come so naturally to people trained in a religious priesthood. Educators provide another pertinent model. They too are engaged in a culturally institutionalized effort to improve individuals in a democratic society, and the parallels between remedial special education and clinical treatment have often been noted. But again the clinical problems go beyond pedagogy, and the restriction of teachers to the school grounds is unacceptably confining. The medical model seems to offer a closer fit, for we are all trying to alleviate human distress, and in the public health enterprise, as in social psychiatry, medicine is trying to reduce collective distress in general and lasting ways. But the concept of illness is badly stretched when it is made to cover problems in living of the kind we all must face. Mentally "sick" people are not responsible, for one thing, and there is something offensively overbearing about the authoritarian doctor-knows-best attitude which probably has to prevail in competent medical training. Clinical psychology appears to come nearer yet, for psychosocial functions as substance and behavioral science as method are emphasized in the training and tradition of psychologists. But the stress on a narrow definition of science in most academic definitions of scholarship and the failure to establish a clear professional identity have loosened the congruence between social problem and professional role in this field too. Of all the major professions currently dealing with the problems of psychosocial disorder as they have been defined in this book, social work offers the closest approximation to the needed ideal. It is outspokenly a service profession and has never pretended to be anything else. Concerned as social work has traditionally been with man-in-society, no basic redefinition of substance is required. Organized as it has been to function in individual case work, in group work, and in community organization, no fundamental realignment of structure is needed. But social work has its problems. It is mainly a female profession in a society dominated by men. It has historically accepted and hence has tended to attract a generally less capable class of trainees than have gone into psychiatry and clinical psychology. In many of its training centers, narrow medical viewpoints and psychoanalytic theories have become so overwhelmingly dominant that little room is left for the traditional, fundamentally more appropriate concerns of the social work profession.

Many contemporary professions are involved in behavioral engineering, and piecemeal, their identities are related to the tasks we face. In one aspect or another—in an attitude here, a technical skill there, in a view of man or a way of helping him improve his state—education, the ministry, medicine, psychology, social work, and undoubtedly other professions as well, all have something to offer. But it is equally true that no profession now in functional operation in our society is clearly, explicitly, directly, and entirely concerned with clinical management of the psychosocial problems of disordered behavior, and such a profession is badly needed.

Professions can change, of course. They can and do change continually as new social needs evolve and as conceptions of function are redefined. A psychiatry curriculum without an offering in community mental health is badly out of date these days, and a training program in clinical psychology which does not pay some heed to behavioral treatment methods is sorely in need of revision. One solution to the problem of matching profession to social need is simply to revise present training systems while retaining most of the semantic labels and traditional viewpoints which prevail today. Future generations of mental health practitioners will thus be better equipped to deal with disordered behavior than their teachers originally were, and presently functioning previously trained practitioners can be retrained in workshops, institutes, and any other systems of retraining which may be developed.

Training for the full range of psychosocial problems as outlined here requires enormous breadth of education and experience, and a very high level of skill by the standards of any present mental health profession. A rather extraordinary grasp of behavior theory and psychoeducational technique is required for competent performance of the clinical task of assessing and changing relevant patterns of action, interaction, and social organization. For the highest levels of professional work, very extensive training is needed, and the cost of training is bound to be very high. All the major helping professions contain anachronistic irrelevancies of one kind or another. We cannot retain these much longer, just because they fell there through the vagaries of professional evolution.

Most of the training psychiatrists receive in physical medicine is completely unrelated to the work they will be doing in psychiatry itself. Most of the training clinical psychologists receive in the narrow disciplines of experimental science are of no use whatever later on. The language study demanded by Ph.D. tradition is completely useless. It is time we did away with waste of this kind, and if academic traditions require abandonment of such labels as the M.D. and the Ph.D. along the way, no serious loss will result. The labels do not matter much, not to the people seeking help. What they need is competent assistance. The exact letters behind the name of the practitioner are really of very little concern to anyone, except possibly the practitioner himself, and if he is actually effective in the performance of an important and challenging job he wants to do, that concern should quickly vanish too. A profession beyond the tradition of the Ph.D. does not mean abandonment of scientific attitudes on the part of professional clinicians; a profession outside the tradition of the M.D. does not mean repudiation of the attitudes of professional responsibility and basic concern for the welfare of patients as it now pervades good medical education. There is no need to cut ourselves off altogether from our history. But there is an urgent need for highly skilled professionals to perform the unified task of assessment and change in the field of psychosocial disorders; it is desirable to train people expressly for those positions without hiding any longer beneath the mantle of medicine or science; present training systems are functioning with less than full effectiveness in producing the personnel we need; and our society is technologically, economically, and culturally ready for such a professional development now.

No new doctoral profession, however carefully designed, will solve the social problem of disordered behavior. The needs for professional assistance are so pressing, the level of required training is so high, and the cost of training is so great that no doctoral training programs imaginable can ever satisfy the demand for direct service. Professional behavior analysts will therefore have to function increasingly as strategists in behavior change and social engineering rather than as active functionaries in the work of assessment and change itself. The highest level professional positions must thus become mainly administrative and consultative in function. It is simply not very efficient for a man with doctoral training to spend much of his own time recording behavioral events, shaping operant action, or desensitizing phobias. Members of other professions, nurses and teachers for example, and various nonprofessionals such as parents and volunteers, must therefore be trained to assume much of the responsibility for the day-to-day work of clinical assessment and psychosocial change. In time a variety of new technician roles may profitably be defined. These should probably be set at a variety of levels in regard to the degree of professional responsibility involved, the amount of training required, and the labels, salaries, status locations, and other less important paraphernalia that go along with function. At the present time it is difficult to predict just how many and what kinds of professional and subprofessional roles should be delineated, but the need for high level doctoral training of an explicitly professional kind is obvious, and we should move toward that goal with all reasonable speed.

In professional training, as in the basic tasks of clinical assessment and treatment, we will have the best chance of moving ahead of social need, instead of merely keeping pace or falling farther and farther behind, if we are able to adopt a genuinely experimental attitude toward deliberate change in training methods. In the professional training system as in any other, we must appraise the organization as it is functioning now, judge as rationally as possible what must be done to improve it, institute the change with every possible care, evaluate the effect as fairly as possible, and then proceed to the further changes future reappraisal will surely suggest.

ASSESSMENT AND ETHICS

A great deal has been said and written recently about the moral implications of clinical action in regard to human behavior. As long as psychotherapists sustained the illusion that they were really letting their clients direct the course of the clinical process, as long as they believed that their own behavior was evaluatively neutral, and especially as long as they were ineffective, there was no moral issue to worry about. But now it is clear that clinicians do influence their clients. The influence is necessarily directional and this inherently presupposes evaluation. Above all it is now apparent that some clinical procedures really work, and this appalling discovery brings the moral problem of behavior modification and the inquiry needed to direct that modification squarely before us.

The Ethics of Assessment

Insofar as psychosocial assessment presents ethical problems distinct from those of behavior change, the paramount questions are those of human privacy and its possible violation. As clinical inquiry extends beyond the therapist's office to the social setting in which disordered behavior occurs, and especially as evaluations begin to comprehend social systems as well as individuals, issues of privacy, the rights, duties, and constraints of investigative inquiry, become more acute and more complex than they once appeared. Simple solutions, however old and honored, will no longer suffice. It is no longer possible to issue such appealing categorical statements as, "Absolute confidentiality is assured," and expect all moral problems to be resolved. Professional clinicians concerned with disordered behavior are acting in the interest of a larger society as well as the individuals who make up the society, and this fact creates a much more complex problem than that confronting a doctor dealing with an individual patient. As psychosocial welfare functions become more and more completely socialized, fundamental contracts bind the professional more closely to organized society than to the individual patient. The money is controlled by the organized agency, and with economic controls go others of a subtler kind. This very fact should insure the cultural survival of private practice in psychotherapy, for some people are bound to have personal problems requiring complete privacy and total confidentiality in any conceivable version of an affluent modern society. Yet there is little doubt about the trend toward increasing socialization of psychosocial assistance functions in the recent past, there is little reason to doubt a continuation of the trend in the future, and this can scarcely help but sharpen the realization that professional clinicians are serving organized society as much as the individual patients with whom they deal.

Recognizing this, it becomes clear that people are not at perfect liberty to be disturbed; they do not always have a right to be "sick." Where personal malfunction begins to cost others in society, either by way of some offensive action on the part of the individual involved or merely because of the burden to others a crippling psychological disability will entail, clinicians may sometimes be obliged to change behavior whether the patient likes it or not. They are also obliged to conduct whatever inquiries are needed, whether or not the patient wants to have them done. This is as much a part of professional responsibility as the protection of the patient.

The issue of personal privacy is further complicated by the fact that failure to inquire, where inquiry would be helpful, is just as serious a professional dereliction as the positive conduct of an inappropriately invasive inquiry. If one is entrusted with the responsibility for making the most accurate predictions possible about a course of events, personal or social, all pertinent information must be gathered, whether all the people involved in the inquiry approve or not.

Where social organizations are concerned, the very identity of the people whose rights are at issue becomes difficult to specify. Sometimes the most significant facts in an evaluative inquiry concern the functions of administrative leaders. Whose permission is the professional to seek? Must we always have a leader's permission to find out what is doing?

There is no easy solution to the moral problems of psychosocial inquiry. Simple formulas, inflexibly applied, simply will not do. When one deals clinically with man-in-society, the ethical problems of investigation and change become greatly more complex than they ever were when we thought we were healing the individual sick. A more adequate set of professional codes is needed, but this is neither the place, nor might it be quite the time, to attempt its formulation. Instead, we might consider some methods by which ethical principles can be evaluated and improved.

The Assessment of Ethics

In a clinical system where diagnosis is related to treatment, where assessment is always directed toward change, the ethical problems of assessment are inseparably tied to those of behavior modification. The latter issues have been discussed so well and at such length in other recent writings (see especially London, 1964 and the references he cites), that little can be added by further discussion here. There may be some advantage, however, in pointing out the extent to which professional ethics governing behavior change are related to more general codes in the society where the professional activity takes place. Wherever the professionals are acculturated in the society where their work is done, and especially when they operate vocationally in a bureaucracy supported financially and otherwise by the larger society, no other relationship can prevail.

As relativism is inevitable for the general codes, so must it be for professional ethics, though the generality of a class of ethical principles may approach moral absolutes as a logical limit. It is even conceivable that some of the principles may be rooted in man's biological make-up or in some cultural condition so firmly implanted and so widespread it might as well be biological. However stable and general some of the principles may be, the only concession needed for the present argument is that any of the codes of a system of ethics, professional or otherwise, are in principle subject to change. This does not mean that anything goes. It does not mean that the rules can be casually violated. This concept of relativism is neutral as to the substance and severity of sanctions. The rules, while in effect, are written into the contract systems which form the basis of any orderly society and so they must be taken seriously. But the moral codes of a general society, and hence the ethical codes of any profession concerned with human behavior, are not absolute, they are not eternally inviolable.

If we can agree on this, the way to a rational, self-corrective ethical system may begin to grow clear. Having repudiated revelation and every other form of irrational authority as a way of arriving at a satisfactory morality, man has nothing left but to shape his own—deliberately, rationally, with an eye both to the historical and the contemporary cultural diversities of other codes, as well as the logically predictable social consequences of any new ones he may propose. These, however, must then be asserted provisionally rather than absolutely, and subjected, like any other system in a planned society, to continual appraisal and revision.

In a somewhat limited sense, that is what social philosophers have always done. Their pronouncements, however, have usually appeared as absolute imperatives rather than as conditional normative statements, and they have been much more disposed to arm-chair cognition as a way of revising codes than to the systematic collection of antecedent-consequent facts. In the tradition of American pragmatic humanism but with an increased emphasis on an experimental approach to social philosophy, the basic viewpoints and methods of behavioral science may be just as pertinent to the generation and self-correction of ethical codes as they are to the planned evaluation of procedures for psychosocial assessment or the detailed collection of data for a single clinical case.

CLINICAL ASSESSMENT IN RETROSPECT AND PROSPECT

A major revolution is now taking place in the professions concerned with disordered behavior. Change from exclusively individual conceptions of personality to radically expanded views of man in society, the emphasis on explicit behavior as well as inner mental function, and the consideration of situational as well as personal determinants of behavior are all aspects of the revolution. This book is primarily concerned with one matter, the assessment of behavior in its situational, interactional and organizational context, but that is an extraordinarily important facet of the general problem now confronting the mental health professions and behavioral science. For the value of all our work depends on gaining valid, useful knowledge about individual, group, and organizational behavior, and present methods for doing this are badly in need of improvement.

The detailed technology successful professions require is only beginning to form. It is not even infantile; it is fetal. The development of the technology is literally interminable in prospect, and it is important to acknowledge, along with the apparently considerable promise of social-behavioral approaches to clinical assessment, how far we have to go in the creation of new procedures and in showing that they are not merely new, but dependable and effective. Revolutions are always exciting, but excitement is not enough for this. Attending conferences and mouthing slogans will not accomplish what has to be done. We need sustained, intelligent effort, a lot of hard and sometimes tedious work.

The work offers its own daily satisfactions, of course, but there are even brighter hopes to pull us through the weary years—not just for better techniques of studying behavior, not just for more effective professions, not just for a more useful science of man—but for a genuinely improved and continually improving society. We need not embrace a doctrine of infinite perfectibility, nor ignore the realities of human weakness and evil. In witness of a humanity patently degraded by ignorance, prejudice, and blind self-interest, and of a world situation marked by poverty and cruelty, by needless famine and endless warfare, the hope is sometimes hard to keep alive. For all this, man has progressed over the centuries toward a more civilized, human existence than he has ever had before, and the strides now being made in that direction are especially large and rapid. Despite obvious flaws in implementation, the problem of production has essentially been solved, and the necessary condition for a rationally planned society has in principle already been attained. As populations grow and technologies improve, human problems become increasingly social rather than material, and the need for social planning becomes a need instead of a luxury.

The concept of a planned society is hardly novel, but the widespread engagement of behavioral scientists and professionals in the planning is relatively new. The question no longer is whether social scientists and professional mental health workers should be involved in social engineering and the control of human behavior, but how much and what kind of engagement is appropriate. Societies do not just run themselves. They are always controlled by somebody, one way or another. It is just a question of who does the controlling and the way controls are effected. The politicians, financiers, and others who now direct our society are not likely to deliver authority and power to professional do-gooders without reservation and sometimes not without a fight. Even if they would, it is undesirable that they should. The design of a democratic society must never be dictated by a single group. But professionals and scientists concerned with disordered behavior have fewer purely selfish interests at stake than nearly anyone else involved, and they know, or at least have a system for learning more than most of the other groups. Their active participation in this enormously difficult but challenging task, the deliberate social planning of a democratic society, is more than an opportunity, it is a positive responsibility.

The history of action in the management of disordered behavior has taught above all a respect for the difficulty of the problem and very cautious reserve in evaluating any new proposal for its resolution. Too many zealots have been wrong too often to allow excesses of enthusiasm to flare unchecked. In this book I have proposed an approach to the clinical study of social behavior. It is designed to replace some other approaches, and I have tried to be decisive about that. But dear as my own views may be to me, I am absolutely sure that they should *not* be adopted uncritically by the professional society as a whole. There is nothing to be gained by replacing one orthodoxy with another. Other conceptions and other procedures must not merely be tolerated but encouraged, for the true test of worth can only be made in the field of empirical trial, not by verbal argument. We need to examine our own activities as squarely as human nature will permit. We must be willing to recognize accomplishment where this is found and to acknowledge failure where failure occurs. Above all we need the vision to see where changes should be made and where traditions should be continued. And then we must have the courage to change, or not, as the problems we face demand.

References

Ackerman, N. W. *The psychodynamics of family life.* New York: Basic Books, 1958.

Allport, G. W. *Personality: A psychological interpretation.* New York: Holt, 1937.

Allport, G. W. Traits revisited. *Amer. Psychologist,* 1966, 21, 1–10.

American Psychiatric Association. *Diagnostic and statistical manual of mental disorders.* Washington, D.C.: Amer. Psychiat. Ass., 1952.

Ayllon, T. Intensive treatment of psychiatric behavior by stimulus saturation and food reinforcement. In L. P. Ullmann & L. Krasner (Eds.), *Case studies in behavior modification.* New York: Holt, 1965.

Bach, G. R. *Intensive group psychotherapy.* New York: Ronald Press, 1954.

Bachrach, A. J. (Ed.) *Experimental foundations of clinical psychology.* New York: Basic Books, 1962.

Bandura, A., & Walters, R. H. *Social learning and personality development.* New York: Holt, Rinehart and Winston, 1963.

Barker, R. G., Schoggen, M. F., & Barker, L. S. Hemerography of Mary Ennis. In A. Burton & R. E. Harris (Eds.), *Clinical studies of personality.* New York: Harper, 1955.

Barker, R. G., & Wright, H. F. *Midwest and its children, the psychological ecology of a midwestern town.* Evanston, Ill.: Row, Peterson, 1955.

Baruch, D. W. *New ways in discipline.* New York: McGraw-Hill, 1949.

Bateson, G., Jackson, D. D., Haley, J., & Weakland, J. Toward a theory of schizophrenia. *Behav. Sci.,* 1956, 1, 251–264.

Becker, W. C. The matching of behavior rating and questionnaire personality factors. *Psychol. Bull.,* 1960, 57, 201–212.

Bell, J. E. Recent advances in family group therapy. *J. child Psychol. Psychiat.,* 1962, 3, 1–15.

Bender, L. Group activities on a children's ward as methods of psychotherapy. *Amer. J. Psychiat.,* 1937, **93,** 151–173.

Berne, E. *Transactional analysis in psychotherapy.* New York: Grove Press, 1961.

Berne, E. *Games people play.* New York: Grove Press, 1964.

Bijou, S. W. Experimental studies of child behavior, normal and deviant. In L. Krasner & L. P. Ullmann (Eds.), *Research in behavior modification.* New York: Holt, Rinehart and Winston, 1965.

Bijou, S. W., & Baer, D. M. *Child development: A systematic and empirical theory.* New York: Appleton-Century-Crofts, 1961.

Blodgett, H. C. The effect of the introduction of reward upon the maze performance of rats. *Univ. Calif. Pub. Psychol.,* 1929, **4,** 113–134.

Bowen, T. W. Typological analysis of conduct disorders. Unpublished Master's thesis, Vanderbilt University, 1960.

Brunswick, E. *Systematic and representative design of psychological experiments.* Berkeley: University of California Press, 1947.

Buber, M. *I and Thou.* (2nd ed.) Trans. by Ronald Gregor Smith. New York: Scribner; Edinburgh: T. & T. Clark, 1958.

Burnham, W. H. *The normal mind.* New York: Appleton, 1924.

Campbell, D. T., & Stanley, J. C. Experimental and quasi-experimental designs for research on teaching. In N. L. Gage (Ed.), *Handbook of research on teaching.* Chicago: Rand McNally, 1963.

Cattell, R. B. Formulating the environmental situation and its perception in behavior theory. In S. B. Sells (Ed.), *Stimulus determinants of behavior.* New York: Ronald Press, 1963.

Cox, H. *The secular city.* New York: Macmillan, 1965.

Cronbach, L. J., & Gleser, G. C. *Psychological tests and personnel decisions.* Urbana, Ill.: University of Illinois Press, 1957.

Cronbach, L. J., & Meehl, P. E. Construct validity in psychological tests. *Psychol. Bull.* 1955, **52,** 281–302.

Cumming, J., & Cumming, E. *Ego and milieu: The theory and practice of environmental therapy.* New York: Atherton Press, 1962.

Dewey, J., & Bentley, A. R. *Knowing and the known.* Boston: Beacon Press, 1949.

Dollard, J., & Miller, N. E. *Personality and psychotherapy.* New York: McGraw-Hill, 1950.

Dulany, D. E. Hypotheses and habits in verbal "operant conditioning." *J. abnorm. soc. Psychol.*, 1961, **63**, 251–263.

Dunlap, K. *Habits: Their making and unmaking.* New York: Liveright, 1932.

Ellis, A. *The theory and practice of rational-emotive psychotherapy.* New York: Lyle Stuart, 1964.

Ellsworth, R. B. The psychiatric aide as rehabilitation therapist. *Rehabilit. counsel. Bull.*, 1964, **7**, 81–86.

Emerson, W. R. P. The hygienic and dietetic treatment of delicate children in groups. *Boston med. surgical J.*, 1910, **163**, 326–328.

Endler, N. S., & Hunt, J. McV. Sources of behavioral variance as measured by the S-R Inventory of Anxiousness. *Psychol. Bull.*, 1966, **65**, 336–346.

Endler, N. S., Hunt, J. McV., & Rosenstein, A. J. An S-R inventory of anxiousness. *Psychol. Monogr.*, 1962, **76** (17, Whole No. 536).

Eriksen, C. W. (Ed.) *Behavior and awareness.* Durham, N. C.: Duke, 1962.

Estes, S. G. Judging personality from expressive behavior. *J. abnorm. soc. Psychol.*, 1938, **33**, 217–236.

Eysenck, H. J. *Behavior therapy and the neuroses.* New York: Pergamon, 1960.

Ezriel, H. A psychoanalytic approach to group treatment. *Brit. J. med. Psychol.*, 1950, **23**, 59–74.

Fairweather, G. W. (Ed.) *Social psychology in treating mental illness: An experimental approach.* New York: Wiley, 1964.

Festinger, L. *A theory of cognitive dissonance.* Evanston, Ill.: Row, Peterson, 1957.

Ferster, C. B. Classification of behavioral pathology. In L. Krasner & L. P. Ullmann (Eds.), *Research in behavior modification.* New York: Holt, Rinehart and Winston, 1965.

Fiedler, F. E., Hutchins, E. B., & Dodge, J. S. Quasi-therapeutic relations in small college and military groups. *Psychol. Monogr.*, 1959, **73** (3, Whole No. 473).

Fiedler, F. E. Engineer the job to fit the manager. *Harvard Bus. Rev.*, 1965, **43**, 115–122. (a)

Fiedler, F. E. Leadership—A new model. *Discovery*, April, 1965. (b)

Fishbein, M. An investigation of the relationship between beliefs about an object and the attitude toward that object. *Human Relat.*, 1963, **16**, 233–240.

242   References

Fishbein, M. (Ed.) *Readings in attitude theory and measurement.* New York: Wiley, 1967.

Freedman, M. B., Leary, T. F., Ossorio, A. G., & Coffey, H. S. The interpersonal dimension of personality. *J. Pers.,* 1951, **20**, 143–161.

Garfield, S. The clinical method in personality assessment. In J. M. Wepman & R. W. Heine, *Concepts of personality.* Chicago: Aldine, 1963.

Gill, M., Newman, R., & Redlich, F. C. *The initial interview in psychiatric practice.* New York: International Universities Press, 1954.

Glueck, S., & Glueck, E. T. *Unravelling juvenile delinquency.* New York: Commonwealth Fund, 1950.

Glueck, S., & Glueck, E. T. *Ventures in criminology.* Cambridge, Mass.: Harvard, 1964.

Goffman, E. *Asylums.* New York: Anchor, 1961.

Greenblatt, M., Levinson, D. J., & Williams, R. H. *The patient and the mental hospital.* Glencoe, Ill.: Free Press, 1957.

Greene, J. S. *I was a stutterer: Stories from life.* New York: Grafton Press, 1932.

Hammond, K. R. Representative vs. systematic design in clinical psychology. *Psychol. Bull.,* 1954, **51**, 150–160.

Hanks, L. M., Jr. Prediction from case material to personality data. *Arch. Psychol.,* N.Y., 1936, **29**, No. 207.

Hathaway, S. R. Increasing clinical efficiency. In B. M. Bass & I. A. Berg (Eds.), *Objective approaches to personality assessment.* Princeton, N.J.: Van Nostrand, 1959.

Heider, F. *The psychology of interpersonal relations.* New York: Wiley, 1958.

Henderson, D. K., & Gillespie, R. D. *A textbook of psychiatry.* New York: Oxford, 1946.

Hobbs, N. Group-centered psychotherapy. In C. R. Rogers, *Client-centered psychotherapy.* Boston: Houghton Mifflin, 1951.

Homans, G. C. *Social behavior: Its elementary forms.* New York: Harcourt, Brace & World, 1961.

Hovland, C. I., Janis, I. L., & Kelly, H. H. *Communication and persuasion.* New Haven: Yale, 1953.

Hunt, J. McV. On the judgment of social workers as a source of information in social work research. In A. W. Shyne (Ed.), *The use of judgments in social work research.* New York: Nat. Assn. of Social Workers, 1959.

Hunt, J. McV. Motivation inherent in information processing and action. In O. J. Harvey (Ed.), *Motivation and social organization: Cognitive determinants.* New York: Ronald Press, 1963.

Hunt, J. McV. Concerning the impact of group psychotherapy on psychology. *Int. J. group psychother.,* 1964, **14**, 3–31.

Jackson, D. D., & Weakland, J. H. Conjoint family therapy. In D. M. Bullard (Ed.), *Chestnut Lodge symposium, 1910–1960,* 1961, 30–46.

Jacobsen, E. *Progressive relaxation.* Chicago: University of Chicago Press, 1938.

Jones, M. C. The elimination of children's fears. *J. exp. Psychol.,* 1924, **7**, 382–390.

Jones, M. *The therapeutic community.* New York: Basic Books, 1953.

Kagan, J. Impulsive and reflective children. In J. Krumboltz (Ed.), *Learning and the educational process.* Chicago: Rand McNally, 1965.

Kahn, A. J. The case of premature claims—public policy and delinquency prediction. *Crime & Delinqu.,* 1965, **11**, 217–228.

Kelly, E. L., & Fiske, D. W. *The prediction of performance in clinical psychology.* Ann Arbor, Mich.: University of Michigan Press, 1951.

Kelly, G. A. *The psychology of personal constructs.* New York: Norton, 1955.

Kilpatrick, F. P. (Ed.) *Explorations in transactional psychology.* New York: New York University Press, 1961.

Kirk, S. A., & McCarthy, J. J. The Illinois test of psycholinguistic abilities—an approach to differential diagnosis. *Amer. J. ment. Defic.,* 1961, **66**, 399–412.

Krasner, L. The therapist as a reinforcement machine. In H. N. Strupp & L. Luborsky (Eds.), *Research in psychotherapy.* Vol. 2. Washington, D.C.: American Psychological Association, 1962.

Krasner, L., & Ullmann, L. P. *Research in behavior modification.* New York: Holt, Rinehart and Winston, 1965.

Leary, T. *Interpersonal diagnosis of personality.* New York: Ronald Press, 1957.

Lecky, P. *Self-consistency.* New York: Island Press, 1945.

Little, K. B., & Schneidman, E. S. Congruencies among interpretations of psychological test and anamnestic data. *Psychol. Monogr.*, 1959, 73 (6, Whole No. 476).

London, P. *The modes and morals of psychotherapy.* New York: Holt, Rinehart and Winston, 1964.

Lord, E. Experimentally induced variation in Rorschach performance. *Psychol. Monogr.*, 1950, 64 (Whole No. 316).

Lorr, M., Klett, C. J., & McNair, D. M. *Syndromes of psychosis.* New York: Macmillan, 1963.

Luft, J. Implicit hypotheses and clinical predictions. *J. abnorm. soc. Psychol.*, 1950, 45, 756–760.

Luft, J. Interaction and projection. *J. proj. Tech.*, 1953, 17, 489–492.

Mandler, G., & Sarason, S. B. A study of anxiety and learning. *J. abnorm. soc. Psychol.*, 1952, 47, 166–173.

Masling, J. The influence of situational and interpersonal variables in projective testing. *Psychol. Bull.*, 1960, 57, 65–88.

Matarazzo, J. D. The interview. In B. B. Wolman (Ed.), *Handbook of clinical psychology.* New York: McGraw-Hill, 1965.

McCulley, R. S. Current attitudes about projective techniques in APA approved internship training centers. *J. proj. Tech. pers. Assessment*, 1965, 29, 271–280.

McDonald, W. F. Relations among rating, self-support and projective test measures of certain personality traits. Unpublished Master's thesis, University of Illinois, 1964.

McGill, W. J. Multivariate information transmission. *Psychometrika*, 1954, 19, 97–116.

Meehl, P. E. The cognitive activity of the clinician. *Amer. Psychologist*, 1960, 15, 19–27.

Meeland, T. An investigation of hypotheses for distinguishing personality factors A, F, and H. Unpublished doctoral dissertation, University of Illinois, 1952.

Menninger, K. A. *A manual for psychiatric case study.* New York: Grune & Stratton, 1952.

Mischel, T. Personal constructs, rules, and the logic of clinical activity. *Psychol. Rev.*, 1964, 71, 180–192.

Mowrer, O. H. *The new group therapy.* Princeton, N.J.: Van Nostrand, 1964.

Mowrer, O. H. The behavior therapies, with special reference to modeling and imitation. *J. Ass. Advancement Psychother.*, 1966.

Mowrer, O. H., & Mowrer, W. M. Enuresis: A method for its study and treatment. *Amer. J. Orthopsychiat.*, 1938, 8, 436–459.

Noyes, A. P., & Haydon, E. *A textbook of psychiatry.* New York: Macmillan, 1940.

Orne, M. T. On the social psychology of the psychology experiment: With particular reference to demand characteristics and their implications. *Amer. Psychologist*, 1962, 17, 776–783.

Osgood, C. E., Suci, G. J., & Tannenbaum, P. H. *The measurement of meaning.* Urbana, Ill.: University of Illinois Press, 1957.

Patterson, G. R. A learning theory approach to the treatment of the school phobic child. In L. P. Ullmann & L. Krasner (Eds.), *Case studies in behavior modification.* New York: Holt, Rinehart and Winston, 1965.

Paul, G. L. *Insight vs. desensitization in psychotherapy.* Stanford, Calif.: Stanford, 1966.

Peterson, D. R. The age generality of personality factors derived from ratings. *Educ. psychol. Meas.*, 1960, 20, 461–474.

Peterson, D. R. Behavior problems of middle childhood. *J. consult. psychol.*, 1961, 25, 205–209.

Peterson, D. R. Scope and generality of verbally defined personality factors. *Psychol. Rev.*, 1965, 72, 48–59.

Peterson, D. R., Becker, W. C., Shoemaker, D. J., Luria, Z., & Hellmer, L. A. Child behavior problems and parental attitudes. *Child Develpm.*, 1961, 32, 151–162.

Peterson, D. R., & London, P. Neobehavioristic psychotherapy: Quasi-hypnotic suggestion and multiple reinforcement in the treatment of a case of postinfantile dyscopresis. *Psychol. Rec.*, 1964, 14, 469–474.

Peterson, D. R., Quay, H. C., & Tiffany, T. L. Personality factors related to juvenile delinquency. *Child Develpm.*, 1961, 32, 355–372.

Piaget, J. *The construction of reality in the child.* New York: Basic Books, 1954.

Pratt, J. H. The class method of treating consumption in the homes of the poor. *J. Amer. med. Ass.*, 1907, 49, 755–759.

Pratt, S., & Tooley, J. Contract psychology and the actualizing transactional field. *Int. J. soc. Psychiat.*, 1964, 1, 51–69.

Preu, P. W. *Outline of psychiatric case study*. (2nd ed.) New York: Hoeber-Harper, 1943.

Raush, H. L., Dittman, A. T., & Taylor, T. J. Person, setting, and change in social interaction. *Human Relat.*, 1959, **12**, 361–378.

Redl, F., & Wineman, D. *The aggressive child*. Glencoe, Ill.: Free Press, 1957.

Reik, T. *Listening with the third ear*. New York: Farrar, Strauss, 1949.

Renner, K. E. The idiographic-experimental study of personality. Urbana, Ill.: University of Illinois, 1965. (mimeo)

Rhodes, W. C. Delinquency and community action. In H. C. Quay (Ed.), *Juvenile delinquency: Research and theory*. Princeton, N.J.: Van Nostrand, 1965

Rogers, C. R. *Client-centered therapy: Its current practice, implications and theory*. Boston: Houghton Mifflin, 1951.

Rogers, C. R. Persons or science? A philosophical question. *Amer. Psychologist*, 1955, **10**, 267–278.

Rogers, C. R. & Dymond, R. *Psychotherapy and personality change*. Chicago: University of Chicago Press, 1954.

Rosenthal, R. On the social psychology of the psychological experiment: The experimenter's hypothesis as unintended determinant of experimental results. *Amer. Scientist*, 1963, **51**, 268–283.

Rosenthal, R., & Fode, K. L. The effect of experimenter bias on the performance of the albino rat. *Behav. Sci.*, 1963, **8**, 183–189.

Salter, A. *Conditioned reflex therapy*. New York: Putnam, 1961.

Sells, S. B. *Stimulus determinant of behavior*. New York: Ronald Press, 1963.

Schilder, P. The analysis of ideologies as a psychotherapeutic method especially in group treatment. *Amer. J. Psychiat.*, 1936, **93**, 601–617.

Shoben, E. J. Psychotherapy as a problem in learning theory. *Psychol. Bull.*, 1949, **46**, 366–392.

Skinner, B. F. *The behavior of organisms*. New York: Appleton-Century-Crofts, 1938.

Skinner, B. F. *Science and human behavior*. New York: Macmillan, 1953.

Skinner, B. F. *Cumulative record*. New York: Appleton-Century-Crofts, 1959.

Slavson, S. R. *An introduction to group therapy.* New York: Commonwealth Fund, 1943.

Spielberger, C. D. The role of awareness in verbal conditioning. In C. W. Eriksen (Ed.), *Behavior and awareness.* Durham, N.C.: Duke, 1962.

Staats, A. W. A case in and a strategy for the extension of learning principles to problems of human behavior. In L. Krasner & L. P. Ullmann (Eds.), *Research in behavior modification.* New York: Holt, Rinehart and Winston, 1965.

Staats, A. W., & Staats, C. K. *Complex human behavior.* New York: Holt, Rinehart and Winston, 1963.

Stanton, A. H., & Schwartz, M. S. *The mental hospital.* New York: Basic Books, 1954.

Sullivan, H. S. *The psychiatric interview.* New York: Norton, 1954.

Sullivan, H. S. *Schizophrenia as a human process.* New York: Norton, 1962.

Sundberg, N. D. Psychological testing in clinical services. *Amer. Psychologist*, 1961, **16**, 79–83.

Sundberg, N. D., & Tyler, L. E. *Clinical psychology.* New York: Appleton-Century-Crofts, 1962.

Szasz, R. S. *The myth of mental illness.* New York: Hoeber-Harper, 1961.

Taft, R. The ability to judge people. *Psychol. Bull.*, 1955, **52**, 1–23.

Thorne, F. C. *Principles of personality counseling.* Brandon, Vt.: *Journal of Clinical Psychology*, 1950.

Tiffany, T. L., Peterson, D. R., & Quay, H. C. Types and traits in the study of juvenile delinquency. *J. clin. Psychol.*, 1961, **17**, 19–24.

Tolman, E. C., & Honzik, C. H. Introduction and removal of reward, and maze performance in rats. *Univer. Calif. Publ. Psychol.*, 1930, **4**, 257–275.

Tucker, L. R. The extension of factor analysis to three-dimensional matrices. In N. Frederiksen (Ed.), *Contributions to mathematical psychology.* New York: Holt, Rinehart and Winston, 1964.

Tyler, L. Toward a workable psychology of individuality. *Amer. Psychologist*, 1959, **14**, 75–81.

Ullmann, L. P. *Institution and outcome: A comparative study of psychiatric hospitals.* New York: Pergamon Press, 1967.

Ullmann, L. P., & Krasner, K. *Case studies in behavior modification.* New York: Holt, Rinehart and Winston, 1965.

Voss, H. L. The predictive efficiency of the Glueck Social Prediction Table. *J. crim. Law, Criminol., police Sci.,* 1963, **54**, 421–430.

Wallace, J. An abilities conception of personality: Some implications for personality measurement. *Amer. Psychologist,* 1966, **21**, 132–138.

Wetzel, L. C. The convergent and discriminant validity of verbal personality measures. Unpublished Master's thesis, University of Illinois, 1965.

Wittenborn, J. R. *Psychiatric rating scales.* New York: Psychol. Corp., 1955.

Wolpe, J. *Psychotherapy by reciprocal inhibition.* Stanford, Calif.: Stanford, 1958.

Index

Ability tests, 139
Ackerman, N. W., 44
Action, 68–82
Allport, G. W., 30, 108
Anxiety, concept, 27–29, 36
  S-R Inventory, 139
Aretaeus, 35
Asessment, clinical method, 102–109
  ethical issues, 233–234
  experimental method, 13–14, 129–
    138
  procedures, 12–14, 102–141
  professional training, 226–232
  research, 222–226
  tests, 1–3, 138–141
  and theory, 9–11, 59–101
  and treatment, 8–9, 32–58
Attitude, 39–40
Authority, 52, 94
Awareness, 40
Ayllon, T., 77, 114

Bachrach, A. J., 62
Baer, D. M., 62
Bandura, A., 60, 77
Barker, L. S., 110
Barker, R. G., 110
Baruch, D. W., 60
Base rate problem, 26
Becker, W. C., 21, 22
Behavior, theory, 9–11, 59–101
  behaviorism, 62–67
  therapy, 9, 35–38, 56
Behavioral hypotheses, 75
Behavioral intentions, 72
Belief, 39–40, 80–81
  See also Cognition
Bell, J. E., 44
Bender, L., 43
Bentley, A. R., 85
Bernard, C., 29

Berne, E., 43, 85, 86, 87, 88
Bijou, S. W., 62, 112, 131, 133
Blodgett, H. C., 40
Bowen, T. W., 5
Brave New World, 54
Brunswick, E., 29
Buber, M., 125, 126, 127
Burnham, W. H., 35
Buros, O. K., 2

Campbell, D. T., 132
Cattell, R. B., 16, 22
Causality, 63–64
Circularity, 59–61
Classification, psychiatric, 2, 5–6
Clinical interview, see Interview
Clinical method, procedures, 12–14,
    102–141
  traditional, 102–109
  See also Assessment
Clinical psychologist, 1, 3, 226–228
  sensitivity, 102–105
Clinical team, 1–2, 226–227
Coffey, H. S., 18
Cognition, and behavior change, 39–
    41
  in behavior theory, 74–82
  and emotion, 40
Cognitive dissonance, 40, 81
Communication, 11, 39, 44–45, 52, 94
Community mental health, see Com-
    munity psychology
Community psychology, 48–55
Conduct problems, 22
Conjoint family therapy, 44
Constructs, hypothetical, 60–61, 64
  personal, 6, 39
Contracts, 89
Counter-conditioning, 36–37
Covert behavior, 78
Cox, H., 126
Cronbach, L. J., 32, 65

Cultural assumptions, 96–99
Culture, 91, 95
Cumming, E., 49
Cumming, J., 49
Custodial treatment, 96–97

Decisions, clinical, 32–33, 176
Decoding, 75
Delinquency, 21, 22, 25–27
Desensitization, 36–37
Determinism, 63–64
Deterrent, 70
Dewey, J., 85
Diagnosis, 2–7, 33
    See also Assessment
Dimensions, personality, 2, 5–6
    See also Personality
Directive therapy, 41
Discrimination, 76
Dispositional states, 85–87
Dittman, A. T., 17
Dodge, J. S., 44
Dollard, J., 36
Dulany, D. E., 40
Dunlap, K., 35
Dynamic viewpoint, see Personality,
    dynamic views

Ebbinghaus, H., 108
Eclecticism, 54–55
Ecology, 30, 110
Ego psychology, 50, 81
Ego states, see Dispositional states
Ellis, A., 39, 41
Ellsworth, R. B., 50
Emerson, W. R. P., 42
Emotion, anxiety, 27–29, 36
    and cognition, 40
    and motivation, 69–74
Encoding, 75
Endler, N. S., 27, 28, 29, 139
Epistemology, 62
Eriksen, C. W., 40
Ethics, 232–234
    and assessment, 233–234
    and behavior modification, 234–235
    modification, 235–236
    relativism, 235
Examination, psychiatric, 1, 3
    psychological, 1

Examination—Continued
    See also Clinical procedures and As-
        sessment
Examiner influence, 19–20
Existential viewpoint, 116, 124–126
Experimental analysis of behavior, see
    Functional analysis
Eysenck, H. J., 38
Ezriel, H., 43

Factor analysis, 5–6
Fairweather, G. W., 50
Family group therapy, 44–46
Fatalism, 63
Ferster, C. B., 114, 131
Festinger, L., 40, 65, 80, 81
Fiedler, F. E., 23, 24, 25, 44
Fishbein, M., 40
Fiske, D. W., 2, 104
Fixed-role therapy, 130
Fode, K. L., 20
Freedman, M. B., 18
Freud, S., 55, 81
Fromm, E., 64
Functional analysis, 9, 13, 65, 111,
    129–138
    definition, 111
    of individual behavior, 129–133
    of social systems, 135–136
    of social transactions, 133–134

Games, social, 87–90
Garfield, S., 102, 106, 108
Generalization, 76
Gill, M., 128
Gillespie, R. D., 115
Gleser, G. C., 32
Glueck, E. T., 25, 26, 27
Glueck, S., 25, 26, 27
Goffman, E., 50
Greenblatt, M., 49
Greene, J. S., 42
Group therapy, 8–9, 35, 42–48
    See also Treatment
Guided interview, see Interview
Guthrie, E. R., 68

Hammond, K. R., 29
Hanks, L. M., 103

Hathaway, S. R., 33
Haydon, E., 116
Heider, F., 81
Heisenberg, W., 12, 225
Hellmer, L. A., 21
Henderson, D. K., 15
Herbart, J. F., 81
Hobbs, N., 43
Holistic viewpoint, 103, 108–109
Honzick, C. H., 40
Hovland, C. I., 40
Hunt, J. McV., 27, 28, 29, 40, 42, 81, 139
Hutchins, E. B., 44

I-It relationship, 126
I-Thou relationship, 125–126
I-You relationship, 126–128
Ideals, 74
Idiographic viewpoint, 103, 106–108
Illinois test of Psycholinguistic Ability (ITPA), 139
Incentives, 70–71
Incongruity, see Cognitive dissonance
Indeterminancy, 12, 114, 225
Information, and cognition, 74–82
  processing, 75, 76
  and treatment, 40
Insight, 39, 43, 79–80
Instructions, verbal, 77
Interaction, of situation and person, 19
  social, 68, 82–90
Internship, 4
Interpenetration, 53
Interpersonal relationships, 9, 42–48, 82, 89–90, 123–128
Interview, clinical, 115–129
  content, 117–123
  form, 115–117
  guided, 117
  interpersonal relationships, 123–128
  techniques, 120–123, 146–147
  intake, 1
  psychiatric, 1

Jackson, D. D., 44
Jacobsen, E., 37
Janis, I. L., 40

Jones, M., 49
Jones, M. C., 35

Kagan, J., 78
Kahn, A. J., 26
Kantor, J. R., 62
Kelly, E. L., 2, 104
Kelly, G. A., 39, 80, 108, 130, 139
Kelly, H. H., 40
Kilpatrick, F. P., 85
Kirk, S. A., 139
Klett, C. J., 111
Krasner, L., 38, 60, 62, 112, 131

Laws, and theory, 66
Leadership, 23–25
Learning, and awareness, 40
  in behavior modification, 35–42
  in behavior theory, 68–82
  definition, 68
Leary, T., 17, 139
Lecky, P., 80
Levinson, D. J., 49
Little, K. B., 2
London, P., 40, 234
Lord, E., 19
Lorr, M., 111
Luft, J., 19, 104
Luria, Z., 21

Maintenance group, 45
Mandler, G., 28
Masling, J., 19–20
Matarazzo, J. D., 129
Maxwell, C., 85
McCarthy, J. J., 139
McCulley, R. S., 4
McDonald, W. F., 23
McGill, W. J., 18
McNair, D. M., 111
Mead, G. H., 29
Meehl, P. E., 2, 7, 102
Meeland, T., 22
Menninger, K. A., 116, 127
Mental health, community, 48–55
  systems, 91–93, 96–99
Metaphysics, 63
Method, clinical, 12–14, 102–141
  scientific, 103, 109

Meyer, A., 48
Milieu therapy, 51–52
Miller, N. E., 36
Mind, 63
Minnesota Multiphasic Personality In-
    ventory (MMPI), 2, 141
Mischel, T., 39, 108
Modeling, in behavior theory, 77
    as interview technique, 147
Models, professional, 28–229
Morality, see Ethics
Motivation, and reinforcement, 69–74
    unconscious, 79
Mowrer, O. H., 35, 43, 128
Mowrer, W. M., 35

Neuroticism, 22
Newman, R., 128
Nosology, 4–6
Noyes, A. P., 116

Observation, 12, 110–115
Open door policy, 53
Organization, of social systems, 51–
    54, 90–99
Orne, M. T., 20
Osgood, C. E., 81
Ossorio, A. G., 18

Pastimes, 88
Patterson, G. R., 114
Paul, G. L., 38
Personality, of clinician, 103, 105–106
    constructs, 6, 39
    dimensions, 2, 5–6
    dynamic views, 2, 7, 103, 109
    factors, 20–23
    problems, 22
    tests, 1–3, 6, 138–141, 222–226
    traits, 2, 5–7, 20–23
    types, 2, 4–5
Peterson, D. R., 5, 6, 21, 23, 40, 111
Piaget, J., 65
Planned society, 237
Plans and behavior, 78
Pratt, J. H., 42
Pratt, S., 85, 89
Preu, P. W., 116
Preventive psychiatry, 52–54, 93

Probing, 146
Procedures, clinical, 12–14, 102–141
    and games, 88
    in social systems, 96–98
Professional training, 230–232
Projective techniques, 2–4, 7, 19–20
Provisional restatement, 146–147
Psychiatric aides, role of, 48–49
Psychiatric classification, 2, 5–6
Psychiatric examination, 1, 3
    See also Clinical procedures
Psychiatrist, role of, 1, 3, 226–228
Psychoanalytic theory, 7
    See also Personality, dynamic views
Psychologic examination, 1
    See also Clinical procedures
Psychologist, see Clinical psychologist
Psychopathy, 22
Psychotherapy, 33, 38–42
    See also Treatment
Public health, 52–54
Punishment, 70

Q-factor, see Factor analysis
Quasi-therapeutic groups, 8, 44
Quay, H. C., 5, 6, 21
Questioning, 146

Ratings, personality, 7, 20–23
    generality, 20–23
    reliability, 21
Rational-emotive therapy, 41
Raush, H. L., 17
Reciprocal inhibition, 36
Redl, F., 17
Redlich, F. C., 128
Reductionism, 99
Reflection, 146
Reification, 59–61
Reik, T., 102
Reinforcement, as interview technique,
    147
    and learning, 69–74
    social, 73
    verbal, 73
Relations, among sciences, 99–101
Relationship, existential viewpoint,
    124–126
    interpersonal, 9, 42–48, 82, 89–90
    in interview, 123–128

Relaxation, 37
Reliability, of ratings, 21
  of tests, 222
Renner, K. E., 108
Representative design, 29
Reward, 70
  See also Reinforcement
Rhodes, W. C., 91
Rituals, 88
Rogers, C. R., 55, 80, 124, 125
Role, professional, of clinical psychologist, 1, 3, 226–229, 231
  of mental health personnel, 226–232
  of psychiatric aide, 48–49
  of psychiatrist, 1, 3, 226–229, 231
  of social worker, 3, 226–229
  social, 51, 94
Role Repertory (Rep) test, 139
Rorschach test, 2, 4, 141
  See also Projective techniques
Rosenstein, A. J., 27, 28, 139
Rosenthal, R., 20

Salter, A., 36
Sanctions, 94
Sane Society, 64
Sarason, S. B., 29
Scanning, 120
Schilder, P., 43
Schneidman, E. S., 2
Schoggen, M. F., 110
Schopenhauer, A., 81
Schwartz, M. S., 49
Science, method, in assessment, 103, 109
  and behavior theory, 59–68
  relations among disciplines, 99–101
Self-fulfilling prophecies, 26
Sells, S. B., 30
Sensitivity, clinical, 102–105
  training, 104
Shoben, E. J., 36
Shoemaker, D. J., 21
Situational determinants, anxiety, 27–29
  delinquency, 25–27
  leadership, 23–25
  personality traits, 20–23
  social interactions, 17–19
  test behavior, 19–20

Skinner, B. F., 61, 64, 108, 111, 131
Slavson, S. R., 43
Social engineering, 51, 54, 91–97
Social history, 1
Social organization, 51–54, 68, 90–99
Social position, 51, 94
Social prediction table, 25–27
Social psychiatry, 8, 35, 48–55
Social psychology, 11, 68, 82
Social system, characteristics, 11, 48–54
  cultural assumptions, 93, 98–99
  procedures, 93, 96–98
  purposes, 93, 96–97
Social transaction, *see* Transaction
Social worker, role of, 1, 3, 226–229
Sociology, clinical pertinence, 11, 51, 68
  functional and experimental aspects, 90–99, 135–138
Spielberger, C. D., 40
S-R Inventory of Anxiousness, 139
Staats, A. W., 62, 114
Staats, C. K., 62
Stanley, J. C., 132
Stanton, A. H., 49
Stochastic process, 106
Structure, of organizations, 96, 98
  of interviews, 115–117
Suci, G. J., 81
Sullivan, H. S., 48, 49, 120, 127
Sundberg, N. D., 4, 115
Szasz, T. S., 98

Taft, R., 104
Tannenbaum, P. H., 81
Task group, 45
Tautology, 62
Taylor, T. J., 17
Team, clinical, 1–2, 226–227
Tests, ability, 139
  generality, 1–3, 20–23, 223
  personality, 1–3, 6, 138–141, 222–226
  projective, 2–4, 7, 19–20
Thematic Apperception test (TAT), 2, 4
  See also Projective techniques
Theory and assessment, 9–11, 59–101
Therapeutic community, 49
Therapy, *see* Treatment

Thorne, F. C., 42
Thought processes, 39–41, 74–82
Tiffany, T. L., 5, 21
Tillich, P., 34
Tolman, E. C., 40
Tooley, J., 85, 89
Training, professional, 230–232
Transaction, social, 9, 42–48, 84–87
    complementary, 86
    crossed, 86
    patterns of, 42–48
    ulterior, 87
Treatment, and assessment, 8–9, 32–35
  behavioral, 9, 35–38, 56
  concept, 34
  individual, 35–42
  group, 35, 42–48
  organizational, 48–54
  in social control, 96–97
Tucker, L. R., 16
Tyler, L., 108, 110, 115
Typology, personality, 2, 4–5

Ullmann, L. P., 38, 60, 62, 112, 131
Unconscious motivation, 79

Validity, of ratings, 21–23
  of tests, 21–23, 138, 222
Verbal instruction, 77
Verbal reinforcement, 73
Voss, H. L., 26

Walden Pond, 54
Walden Two, 54, 64
Wallace, J., 140
Walters, R. H., 60, 77
Watson, J. B., 62
Weakland, J. H., 44
Wetzel, L. C., 23
Williams, R. H., 49
Wineman, D., 17
Wittenborn, J. R., 111
Wolpe, J., 35, 36, 37
Wright, H. F., 110